THE ARCHITECTURE OF MARKETS

THE ARCHITECTURE OF MARKETS

AN ECONOMIC SOCIOLOGY OF TWENTY-FIRST-CENTURY CAPITALIST SOCIETIES

Neil Fligstein

PRINCETON UNIVERSITY PRESS PRINCETON AND OXFORD

Library of Congress Cataloging-in-Publication Data

Fligstein, Neil
The architecture of markets : an economic sociology of twenty-first-
century capitalist societies / Neil Fligstein
p. cm.
Includes bibliographical references and index.
ISBN 0-691-00522-2
1. Capitalism—Social aspects. 2. Economics—Sociological aspects. 3.
Capitalism—Social aspects—United States. 4. United States—Economic conditions—1981- I. Title
HB501.F58 2001
330.12′2—dc21   2001021975

British Library Cataloging-in-Publication Data is available.

This book has been composed in Sabon

Printed on acid-free paper.∞

www.pup.princeton.edu

Printed in the United States of America

10 9 8 7 6 5 4 3 2 1

For Kylie

Contents

List of Tables

Preface

OVER THE PAST 20 YEARS, a large number of important books and papers have defined the terrain of a sociological approach to market processes. As it stands, however, the field lacks a coherent intellectual structure. It remains a set of insights into the difficulties that economic analysis runs into when confronted by the real world of firms, states, and courts. Put simply, the problem is that institutions (formal law, rules, and informal practices), governments, firms, and the network of relationships among collective actors within markets operate to produce more social structure than makes sense for most economic theorizing. The various strands of "new institutional" thought in economics have recognized this shortcoming for at least 25 years. These approaches have tried to account for the ubiquity of social structures by producing stylized views showing that the various social structures must be the result of efficient market processes.

I think the real frontier here, however, is to create an alternative sociological view of markets in capitalist society. But to do so requires that one look at these social relations from a sociological point of view. Sociologists have traditionally seen social relations as fundamentally about power (who gets what and why?) and shared meanings (i.e., the production of institutions, rules, and shared understandings) to support systems of power. A coherent sociological view must begin by developing a distinctly sociological view of markets, market participants, and what actors around markets are doing that takes social relations, power, and meaning as its core elements.

I had not intended to write this book. But I found myself frustrated by the contemporary sociological literature, which lacked coherent theorizing about social structures, social relations, and institutions and how they operate to produce stable markets. Sociologists have not done a very good job of thinking about first principles in this context. For instance, what is a market from a sociological point of view? What are actors doing in markets that differs from what economics says they do? What social relations are necessary to provide the "noncontractual basis of contract" that makes markets possible? How do state building and market building interconnect and why? What are the relations between political and economic elites, and how are they pivotal to making sense of market construction?

Thinking about these questions, I realized that in published papers I had tried to tackle the issues in a piecemeal fashion. It is clear that the paper format is a poor way to outline a general sociological view of markets.

Incorporating those pieces of work into a broader framework that claims to provide general answers to the questions just posed will, I hope, enrich and situate those papers. While I do not expect readers to accept all that I say, I hope they find some of the argument coherent and compelling. This book is not the only way to do a more theoretically coherent sociology of markets, but it certainly is one way.

There are a number of people whom I would like to acknowledge in this effort. I had lots of help writing some of these chapters. For their contributions I would like to thank Peter Brantley (chap. 6), Haldor Byrjkeflot (chap. 5), Robert Freeland (chap. 8), and Linda Markowitz (chap. 7). The chapters that appear here are revisions of the original versions but many of the core ideas remain. Loic Wacquant read through these papers and others and urged me to write this book. Peter Evans, Michael Burawoy, Woody Powell, Michael Hout, and Doug McAdam all in some way, shape, or form stimulated me to commit thoughts to paper. I have received wonderful comments from Chris Ansell, John Campbell, Frank Dobbin, Richard Swedberg, Harrison White, and Nick Ziegler. I hope I have incorporated the most important of their suggestions. I would also like to thank Frederic Merand, who helped prepare this book for publication. Resources were provided to me by the Survey Research Center, the Institute for Industrial Relations, and the Center for Culture, Organization, and Politics at the University of California. I would like to thank Henry Brady, Michael Hout, and Jim Lincoln (directors of those centers) for that support. I am also grateful to the University of California, which has provided research support in the form of the Class of 1939 Chancellor's Professorship.

Finally, my wife, Christine, has patiently watched me hatch this project. This book is dedicated to my daughter, Kylie. I have the odd habit of measuring the passage of time by how long it takes to do such projects. Kylie's life has been going on since I began this one. My life has been richer because of her. I hope some of that richness has spilled over to these ideas.

THE ARCHITECTURE OF MARKETS

1

Bringing Sociology Back In

MARKET SOCIETY has produced more income, wealth, goods, and services than any other form of human social organization. It has done so by creating the conditions for social exchange between large groups of human beings, often separated across large geographic spaces. For most observers, the driving forces of this wealth creation have been technology and competition. Opportunistic entrepreneurs find a new market for some good or service. This new market often results from a technological breakthrough. Then, others see the opportunity to enter the same market. This creates competition that forces producers to make products more efficiently and at lower cost. The winners of this battle are those who figure out how to deliver the best goods at the cheapest cost.

But even the winners eventually face obsolescence. Someone comes along with a different way to do things and produces new products that simply transform the market. Occasionally, these new products unintentionally reconfigure large parts of the economy by creating entirely new opportunities to produce wealth. So railroads, electricity, telephones, automobiles, pharmaceuticals, and computers have changed the economy by opening up possibilities for people to make new markets.

There is much that is admirable about this story. It explains in a simple way something important about the dynamism of modern market society. The main problem with the story is that it is partial at best. As soon as one observes the formation and operation of real markets, it becomes obvious that none of this dynamism is possible without deep involvement by entrepreneurs, managers, workers, firms, and governments. The people who run firms have to conceptualize opportunities, figure out ways to exploit them, and motivate others to help attain those ends. They have to obtain funding, secure raw materials, and build an organization. They have to figure out ways to stabilize their interactions vis-à-vis their principal competitors. Finally, the conflict between owners and those who work for them is under constant negotiation.

Moreover, firms operate against an extensive backdrop of common understandings, rules, and laws. These are most often supplied by governments. One cannot overestimate the importance of governments to modern markets. Without stable, more or less non-rent-seeking states, modern production markets would not exist. War, plunder, and mercantilism would dominate and swamp entrepreneurs. So, for example, patents granted by governments and enforced by courts allow firms to have a legal monopoly to exploit a particular product and gain returns from it. Other laws limit firms' ability to behave opportunistically and exploit others. Rules and laws exist in all of the advanced industrial societies to protect not just producers, but also consumers from shoddy goods and services, and workers from unsafe working conditions.

These social structures, social relations, and institutions have not been created automatically in market society. They have been long-run historical projects ongoing in all of the industrial societies that have worked through waves of crisis (sometimes violent). Solutions that have been crafted required social experimentation during specific market crises and more general economic depressions (not to mention during upheavals produced by war and conquest). These events have pushed people to think about the ways that they needed to organize in order to make and take advantage of market opportunities.

The purpose of this book is to begin to systematically understand how the dynamism of technology and competition is situated in, defined by, and structured through the production of firms, their social relations with each other, and their relations to government. Put simply, the dynamism of market society is made possible by this extensive social organization. Competition and technological change are themselves defined by market actors and governments over time. These forces are not exogenous to market society, but endogenous to these social relations.

Technological change certainly can have independent effects on social structures. But technological change can have these effects only where the social organization exists that makes technology relevant. So, for example, a hunter-gatherer society has little use for highways and telecommunications. But a society in which lowering the costs of transportation and communications makes it easier for firms to move goods and services to where there are opportunities to sell them gives huge incentives to firms that can figure out how to lower those costs.

The creation of new technology is often viewed as resulting from the scientific manipulation of reality. The discovery of new technologies is often led by the perception that a solution to a particular problem would yield large monetary gains. But this is only part of what technology is. Technologies involve figuring out how to make goods and services that can be delivered, that are reliable, and that someone can be convinced to buy at prices at which they can be produced. In order to make products to make new markets, extensive social organization has to come into existence.

Many technologies require entrepreneurs to figure out what the technology is good for. At the turn of the century, few observers believed that the automobile with an internal combustion engine could find a mass market.

This was because autos were expensive and difficult to make and maintain. Moreover, there was a lack of roads and no system of distribution for gasoline. But by 1915, Henry Ford was convinced that creating such a market was possible. The social technologies involved in producing the supporting structures for that market were as fundamental as the "narrow" technical aspect of building the internal combustion engine.

Similarly, competition produces social-organizational responses as well. Firms try to find ways to control the worst aspects of competition in order to continue to exist. Much of the market-making project is to find ways to stabilize and routinize competition. Much of the history of the largest corporations can be read as attempts to stabilize markets for these firms in the face of ruinous competition and economic downturns. They have searched for nonpredatory ways to compete. Firms can avoid direct competition by pursuing different market segments (i.e., high or low quality) and by diversifying product lines into related products. They can also use social relations, that is networks, to co-opt suppliers and competitors and attain legitimacy with governments and the financial sector.

In the nineteenth century, the frequent booms and busts of the most advanced market societies resulted in part from forms of predatory competition. Firms overbuilt capacity, sold goods and services under cost, and eventually drove one another into bankruptcy. This caused the economy society-wide to lurch from boom to bust. Finding ways to compete that do not revolve around price competition alone has proved pivotal to producing stability for firms in all advanced industrial societies.

In order to take advantage of new technology, firms need to establish stable relationships to their suppliers, workers, and principal competitors. The ability to establish these relationships is itself dependent on the production of stable societal institutions such as governments and law. In every advanced industrial society, governments, firms, and workers have solved their collective problems by producing rules to help stabilize their interactions. These solutions have varied historically and across societies. They depend greatly on the relative power of different groups to produce the modern state. Modern states have produced social welfare systems, money, and the rule of law and have worked to find solutions to the conflict between labor and capital. They have promoted competition, protected workers, and provided opportunities for basic research, thus developing new technologies. Stable, non-rent-seeking governments make the difference between societies where markets are possible and those where they are not.

This dependence of technology and competition on social factors implies that making sense of economic growth requires we think more systematically about these factors. Economic growth depends on governments, institutions, and the social technologies by which firms are created, class struggle is routinized, and competition between firms is mediated. The purpose of this book is to provide some tools to analyze how and why social factors matter.

I want to use those tools to consider some of the most important political-economic questions of our time. In this book, I provide analyses of contemporary American capitalism to understand the evolution of the "shareholder value conception of the firm." I also provide some conceptual tools to unpack the phenomenon called "globalization." I suggest how to study globalization and consider the degree to which what we know about "globalization" fits our stylized accounts. In particular, I am interested in showing that globalization does not explain the fiscal crises of contemporary welfare states, particularly in Europe. In the last chapter, I consider how the approach developed in this book might analyze the current transformation in industry due to information technology.

My overall goal is to provide scholars and other persons interested in policy with analytic tools to make sense of such phenomena as globalization. Ultimately, my analyses suggest that governments and citizens are part and parcel of market processes. The evidence shows that very different systems of relations among workers, firms, and governments have produced economic growth. The frequently invoked opposition between governments and market actors, in which governments are viewed as intrusive and inefficient, and firms as efficient wealth producers, is simply wrong. Firms rely on governments and citizens for making markets. Their ability to produce stable worlds depends greatly on these relationships. The analytic frame proposed here explores when these relationships produce positive and less positive outcomes for all members of society.

A Critique of the Existing Literature in the Sociology of Markets

Economic sociology is the study of how the material production and consumption of human populations depend on social processes for their structure and dynamics. The past 15 years have witnessed a huge expansion of empirical work in the field.[1] This book limits itself to considering the structuring of production, that is, the sociology of markets. In this area two related literatures have emerged. One version has focused on macroprocesses, for example, comparing the organization of national capitalisms, trying to understand the development of Third World societies, examining the processes of globalization, or studying the market transitions from socialism (this can be called a "political economy" approach). Another body of work focuses more narrowly on microprocesses, the formation of a particular market or industry and the emergence of social structures that affect firms' strategy, structure, or labor market practices (a "firm- or industry-level, approach).

Common to both literatures is a critical analysis of neoclassical views of perfectly competitive markets.[2] The literature in economic sociology has demonstrated repeatedly that different aspects of the social relations between market actors are significant for the survival of those actors' firms and the output and functioning of the market (Baker 1984, 1990; Burt 1983; Fligstein 1990; Abolafia 1996). The relative economic performance of different markets across societies and the differing organization of those markets have led scholars to consider why multiple social structures exist and how they can produce successful economic outputs for societies (Hamilton and Biggart 1988; Lincoln, Gerlach, and Takahashi 1992; Whitley 1992; Aoki 1988). This body of research shows that market structures include a wide variety of elaborated social structures. These relations are shaped by how and when markets were founded, who dominates them, and the social relations among producers and their suppliers, customers, and governments. In contradiction to theories of competitive markets, many markets have complex and stable social structures based on repeated interactions of buyers and sellers and on the status and reputation of market participants. It is also clear that firms have very different internal configurations that reflect these social processes.

Large firms (the focus of many of our studies) participate in many markets and have extensive relations to suppliers, competitors, and customers. We now have a rudimentary understanding of how large American firms have been transformed in the past 125 years (Fligstein 1990; Roy 1997). We have also accumulated evidence on comparative market organization, and we have excellent studies of large firms in Europe, Asia, and to a lesser degree Latin America (Whitley 1990; Hamilton and Biggart 1988; Evans 1979; Lincoln and Kalleberg 1990; Gerlach 1992; for a review, see Fligstein and Freeland 1995). We are also beginning to get good studies of the societies moving from socialism to markets (Stark 1996; Nee 1996; Guthrie 1997, 1999; Szelenyi 1994; Burawoy and Krotov 1992; Eyal, Szelenyi, and Townsley 1998; Wank 1999). These studies have not been done by sociologists alone, but by anthropologists, business historians, institutional economists, and scholars in business schools who study macro-organizational behavior.[3]

Modern economic theory claims to be a general theory about how people interact in order to materially reproduce themselves (i.e., how they allocate scarce resources to different ends), and, therefore, it is assumed to be applicable to all societies at all times. The sociology of markets has a long and distinguished history of questioning this assumption. Three of the most important sociological classics, Karl Marx's *Capital*, Max Weber's *Economy and Society*, and Emile Durkheim's *The Division of Labor in Society*, view the modern market economy as an outcome of the deeper social processes that generated modernity. Karl Polanyi, an anthropologist, built on these understandings to consider how markets became the dominant form of social organization to structure material reproduction. These scholars distinguished between the material reproduction of human beings and the organization of that material reproduction.[4] All societies had to solve the problem of material reproduction, but the exact form of economic organization varied from society to society.[5]

One can recognize the influence of classical sociological theories, particularly Marx's and Weber's, in much of the new work in the sociology of markets.[6] However, in general, the work borrows unsystematically from their ideas. Unlike the sociological classics, the modern sociology of markets rarely connects its theoretical ideas to a broader vision of society or societal change. Instead, most studies focus on their empirical object and the literature in which it is embedded. The element that holds the field together is its opposition to the neoclassical model of perfect competition.

Most economists ignore, or are unaware of, how noneconomists think about economic processes. One reason is the clear disciplinary boundaries. Economists have claimed modern markets as their intellectual terrain, and their prestige in the academy and their overwhelming influence on social policymaking, particularly in the United States, make it unnecessary for them to recognize outsiders.

But there is an even more important reason why economists ignore the body of noneconomic work. Put simply, it is because the work has failed to provide alternative theoretical tools to make sense of economic processes. Scholars have demonstrated that market processes are shaped by social structures. Yet we have done little to generate systematic theory about what we mean by structure and how, why, and which structures are consequential for market organization. This is because sociological approaches lack a broader, organizing frame to understand economic processes as generic social processes operating in a particular institutional situation, that is, the construction of markets. In essence, the sociology of markets lacks a theory of social institutions.

Moreover, noneconomists have been fixated on a stylized reading of the neoclassical view of perfect competition. Current economic thinking about the structure of firms and markets contains some sophisticated notions about the role of social relations in markets. Economists have come a long way in their views about rational action and perfect information. They use ideas of incomplete contracts, agency theory, asset specificity, strategic use of information, and repeated games to characterize the structures and interactions of firms in markets. These ideas are used by economists to account for many of the features of markets that noneconomists think are out of the purview of economics, such as the structuring of ownership relations, the role of financial markets in firms structure and strategy, contracting relations, networks, status systems and the role of reputation, and internal organizational arrangements.

A key focus of economic theory is the efficiency of current arrangements.[7] This concern links the social organization we observe in markets to the broader question of whether resources are being efficiently utilized. For economists, social-structural mechanisms help produce efficient outcomes under varying kinds and conditions of uncertainty. One important implication of a lack of theory in the sociology of markets is that the empirical literature has little to say about whether complex market arrangements utilize resources efficiently. Some sociologists seem inclined to the view that social relations are efficient (Granovetter 1985; Uzzi 1996, 1999; Gulati and Gargiulo 1999), while others are prepared to see efficiency as a social construction (Meyer and Rowan 1977; Fligstein 1996).

Economic theories start with the premise that social institutions would not persist if they were not efficient. In the "new" institutional economics this assumption is not meant to be tested. Instead, the general research tactic is to examine situations where different amounts or sources of uncertainty exist and then predict whether or not one will observe a certain social relation. A relation between uncertainty and social structure is confirmation that these institutions in fact enhance efficiency.

Sociological theories are more descriptive and usually agnostic or skeptical as to the ultimate effect of social structures on efficiency. I, too, doubt that all social structures are efficient. However, without a perspective on the question of efficiency, the sociology of markets finds it difficult to make normative arguments about whether current arrangements should be allowed to persist. Economic analyses of social structures' effect on the efficient allocation of resources have obvious policy relevance. Most sociological analyses of social structures have none.

My criticisms lead me to the following conclusion. To have more impact, the sociology of markets needs to be clarified theoretically. The rest of this chapter gives the reader an overview of how I think this should be done. I begin by considering what questions a sociology of markets should consider in its purview. A subfield should contain a small number of common questions that focus research and get scholars to pay attention to one another's work. This does not mean that scholars must agree on what theories answer these questions. But the questions that organize the field point to what social factors are relevant to making sense of different market situations.

The questions relevant to a sociology of markets also help define its relation to various versions of economic theory. I argue that by focusing on a set of key questions, the sociology of markets can make contributions beyond pointing to the presence of social structures in most markets. It may turn out that, for some scholars, the economic and sociological perspectives are more complementary than contradictory.[8] My version of the sociology of markets suggests that there are real differences in theoretical assumptions and that these differences make the perspectives more adversarial, particularly in their implications for policy.

Theoretical Questions for a Sociology of Markets

Defining the boundaries of a field is, perhaps, a foolish objective. A narrow definition risks excluding issues that should be included. Too broad a definition, on the other hand, risks absorbing research problems that are just too tangential. In either case, of course, scholars can choose to ignore your definition. There are several ways one can proceed. One tactic is to focus on which scholars define themselves in the field. The problem with this approach is that the field of the sociology of markets is sufficiently diffuse that there may be multiple communities of scholars with differing concerns contained within it. Even if one could draw a circle around the field, one would still not understand what its focus or questions were. The opposite strategy is to impose a theoretical definition of the field. This approach has the advantage of focusing on a theoretical perspective, presumably of interest to a wide number of scholars. But one is likely to leave out scholars and issues that are of relevance to the field. You may quickly reduce your audience to those who agree with you.

This brings me to the third strategy, which is to pose a set of core questions of interest to scholars in the field with varying theoretical perspectives. A common set of conceptual concerns may unite scholars who can view themselves as part of a community answering related theoretical questions. This approach may also narrow the field by excluding relevant fields of endeavor. But it has the advantage of getting scholars with different theoretical approaches to orient themselves to each other because they are trying to make progress on the same set of theoretical questions. This is the approach I choose to follow.

I propose the following five theoretical questions to define the terrain of a sociology of markets in modern societies. Here I justify these questions for their theoretical importance and their empirical relevance.

1. What social rules must exist for markets to function, and what types of social structures are necessary to produce stable markets?

There are two types of social relations scholars use to understand how markets work. First, there are the actual relationships among producers, consumers, suppliers, and governments in a given market. In the current literature, these are often discussed as *networks*. Most empirical studies that

use the term networks specify the ways in which the content of these relations is pivotal for what goes on in a particular market. Networks usually
are a stand-in for other sociological variables such as resource dependence
(Burt 1983), power, often ownership (Mizruchi, Stearns, and Brewster
1988; Lincoln, Gerlach, and Takahashi, 1992; Palmer et al. 1995), information (Davis and Stout 1992), trust (Uzzi 1996), or status (Podolony 1993).
Scholars who use networks as an independent variable view themselves as
working within a tradition. They have not tried to present a theoretical
focus uniting their ideas.

Second, societies have general rules, both formal and informal, about
organizing economic activities. These rules provide the social conditions
for economic exchange and allow for the production of new markets. Markets need definitions of property rights, governance structures, and rules
of exchange (Fligstein 1996; Campbell and Lindberg 1990; North 1990).
In all advanced industrial societies formal laws regulate incorporation and
patents to protect and define property rights. Laws also define legal ways
to control competition and require that in economic exchange the parties
receive the goods and are properly compensated. Informal rules define
what organizations "should" look like and how interactions should be
structured. Formal and informal rules affect an organization's chances of
survival (DiMaggio and Powell 1983; Meyer and Rowan 1977). Work that
focuses on formal and informal rules is often identified with the "new institutionalism in organizational theory" (DiMaggio and Powell 1991).

Both approaches suggest that the purpose of social structures in the creation of markets is to produce stable outcomes (i.e., survival) for the firms
that use them. This idea is termed *effectiveness* and has its roots in organizational theory (Thompson 1967; Scott 1995). A set of arrangements is
thought to be effective if a given organization survives from period to period (Hannan and Freeman 1977, 1984). The approach is agnostic about
the optimal allocation of resources in a market, instead focusing on organizational survival.

2. What is the relation between states and firms in the production of
markets?

The model for perfectly competitive markets is a bazaar, a place where
individual buyers and sellers meet to trade (White 1981). The reality is, of
course, more complex. Modern production markets require, at the very
least, investment in physical plant; the building of organizations; legal, social, and physical infrastructures (i.e., forms of transportation, finance, and
communication); complex chains of supply; labor markets and the training
of skilled personnel; regulation of fair and unfair competition; and methods
to enforce contracts. Neoconservative theorists can do a thought experi-
ment in which private agencies provide all of these services. Historically,

however, governments have been involved in providing for these market-building services and structures.

Most discussion of modern governments has focused on either war-making or social welfare functions (Skocpol 1992; Tilly 1975). But governments have also been intimately involved in their economies. I argue that one neglected part of modern state building has been modern economy building. This is not to say that everything that goes on in markets requires or revolves around governments. One can examine already existing markets and their dynamics without reference to governments. New markets can emerge from the production of new opportunities.

But much of what we are most interested in—market formation, stability, and change—can be connected to the intentional or unintentional relations among firms, markets, and governments. For instance, the phenomenon of the Internet is thought to demonstrate the independence of firms and technologies from government control. But it is well known that the government set the Internet up to ensure communications in the event of a nuclear war. Moreover, government agencies have provided extensive support for its development and even now are providing funds to produce versions of the web that will be faster.

Even where changes in a market appear to be caused by invader firms, or firms within the market reorganizing themselves, governments often are in the background. Governments underwrite technology, regulate competition, and adjudicate between competing firms. Because of existing government-firm understandings about firms' behavior, certain courses of action are unavailable. In any context, we need to be aware of what governments are doing in different societies and at different times.

Marxist approaches to markets focus on the organization of economic elites and usually see them as controlling a given market or capturing Congress or regulatory agencies (for instance, Useem 1984; Mizruchi 1989; Mintz and Schwartz 1985). The organization of elites and their ability to co-opt political actors should not be underestimated. But one of the biggest problems of this approach is explaining disunity or conflict within elites. As markets come into existence and are transformed, economic elites frequently come into conflict with one another. One elite with a very different conception of doing business can overthrow other elites. A good example of this was the merger movement in the United States in the 1980s. Managers of many firms were thrown over by hostile management teams who bought the firm. In such circumstances the antagonists often ask the government to negotiate their conflict. The government has to decide whether to choose sides or to let the economic chips fall where they may. These conflicts can profoundly change the nature of business (Fligstein 1996).

Governments develop a great number of rules or institutions oriented toward governing markets. Policies define state regulatory styles (Dobbin

1994), methods of intervention in market crises, and modes of organizing for firms. In this way, rules are path dependent and binding (Pierson 1994). They also can give government officials power that is autonomous from economic elites, particularly when those elites disagree. Governments support these rules by direct intervention in markets, by owning firms, and by the use of courts and regulatory agencies.

Finally, governments can take actions that intentionally or unintentionally force the reorganization of markets. I have shown, for example, how antitrust laws pushed American managers to diversify the number of products their firms produced (1990, chap. 7). The intention of these laws was to prevent the concentration of production in a few firms within an industry. But their unintended effect was to close off that option and encourage firms to merge with firms in related markets. There is a great deal of agreement across the empirical literature that government-firm relations are pivotal to market stability.[9]

3. What is a "social" view of what actors seek to do in markets, as opposed to an "economic" one?

Economic theory begins with the idea that individuals are profit maximizers. Neoclassical theory adds the notion of actors who possess perfect information and uses these two ideas to derive why perfectly competitive markets produce the most efficient allocation of societal resources. Economics and managerial economics (i.e., theories of teams and incomplete contracting, agency theory and transaction costs analysis) have made theoretical gains by relaxing the assumption that actors have perfect information (see for instance, Jensen and Meckling 1976; Kreps and Wilson 1982; Milgrom and Roberts 1982). Social structures in markets are viewed as methods actors use to protect themselves from incomplete information, as it would affect their ability to maximize profit.

For noneconomic models to have similar power, they must have some model of action. Without a model of action, one cannot make an argument about the conditions under which a particular social structure is or is not important to firms. Actors' goals need to be theorized and their cognitive and social constraints made more explicit.[10] Doing so will explain some of the variation we observe in the social structuring of markets. The sociology of markets has accepted the idea that actors are rational (i.e., use means to attain their ends) and that they are trying to produce profits (Granovetter 1985; White 1981). From this perspective, a social structure in a given situation is organized to attain profits.

The problem with this view is that it moves sociologists much closer to institutional economics. If social actors are profit maximizers, then their social relationships are, by definition, efficiency enhancing (Uzzi 1996). Some sociologists disagree with the idea that social structures in markets produce efficient outcomes. If they are right, then an implicit model of action can be developed for the field. Very little work has explicitly considered this issue, one that must be clarified for the field to have an existence independent from economics.[11]

4. What are the dynamics by which markets are created, attain stability, and are transformed, and how can we characterize the relations among markets?

Most of the empirical work done in the sociology of markets attempts to provide examples of actual market processes (for example, the exemplary work of Baker, Faulkner, and Fisher 1998; Uzzi 1997, 1999; Thornton and Ocasio 1999; Haveman and Rao 1997). So far, little progress has been made in abstracting away from specific markets to a more general view of these dynamics. There has been little systematic attempt to characterize the social relations within markets generally (for a preliminary attempt, see Granovetter 1994). The main observation we have that characterizes one market's effect on another is to note that one market depends on resources from other markets (Pfeffer and Salancik 1978; DiMaggio and Powell 1983). Even less consideration has been made of where new markets come from and how existing markets affect the origins, stability, and transformation of other markets.[12]

The most sustained analysis of competition in the sociological literature is available from population ecology (Hannan and Freeman 1989). But so far this view has not been well integrated into the literature that examines social relationships in markets. Scholars have done some empirical work on this issue (Stuart 1998; Stuart, Hoang, and Hybels 1999), but without much theoretical integration. The theoretical answer to this fourth question certainly depends on how one answers the first three questions.

5. What are the implications of market dynamics for the internal structuring of firms and labor markets more generally?

A great deal of empirical work looks closely at the link between the external conditions surrounding organizations and their internal structuring. There are two perspectives at work in the sociology of markets. First, some research suggests that the internal structure is often institutionalized at the founding of the organization. This view implies that an industry converges around a small set of practices because those firms that survive are selected by characteristics of the environment (Hannan and Freeman 1977, 1984). The opposite point of view agrees that local environments affect the practices of firms. But, this point of view suggests that adaptation is possible and that organizations make constant internal adjustments to environmental conditions (see Donaldson 1995 for a spirited defense of contingency theory).

Much work in organizational theory takes the perspective of management in generating its theory of firms' structuring of labor markets (Williamson 1975; Hannan and Freeman 1984). But these labor markets are affected by other factors, such as unions, the professions, and government rules. Some have described firms' internal labor markets as "truces" (Nelson and Winter 1982) or as political coalitions (March 1962; Fligstein and Fernandez 1988). Part of the effort here will be to make some of these distinctions more theoretically explicit.

This universe of substantive questions unites many of the literatures in the sociology of markets. I think these questions bring together scholars who study organizations, firms, organizational change, economic and political elites, political sociology, economic development, labor markets, comparative capitalisms, and the law. If these questions do define the field, then scholars who start out narrowly focused on one of them may gain insights from other scholars' work that at first glance seems far afield.

A Political-Cultural Approach

I want to develop a particular answer to these five orienting questions by using a general approach to understand institutions in modern society, what can be called the political-cultural approach. The key insight of the approach is to consider that social action takes place in arenas, what may be called *fields, domains, sectors,* or *organized social spaces* (Bourdieu 1977; Bourdieu and Wacquant 1992; Weber 1978; Scott 1995; DiMaggio 1985; Fligstein 1996, 1997a; Fligstein and McAdam 1993). Fields contain collective actors who try to produce a system of domination in that space. To do so requires the production of a local culture that defines local social relations between actors.

These local cultures contain cognitive elements (i.e., they are interpretive frameworks for actors), define social relationships, and help people interpret their own position in a set of social relationships. Interpretive frameworks allow actors to render meaningful the actions of others with whom they have a social relationship on a period-to-period basis. Collective actors who benefit the most from current arrangements can be called incumbents and those who benefit less, challengers. Once in place, the interactions in fields become "games" where groups in the field who have more power use the acceptable cultural rules to reproduce their power. This process makes action in fields continuously conflictual and inherently political.

The theory of fields focuses on the opening of new social space, how it becomes and remains stable (i.e., becomes a field), and the forces that transform fields. States and markets are types of social orders that contain fields (Weber 1978, 42). The social order of the state is a set of fields or policy domains where actors claim the power to make and enforce rules for all of the other actors in society (Krasner 1988). In modern societies, these orders are governed by formal (constitutions and laws) and informal (practices) rules that create and limit which arenas can be collectively dominated, who gets to be a player, and how rules are made in the domain.

State building can be viewed as the historical process by which groups outside of the state are able to get domains organized by the state to make rules for some set of societal fields. These rules reflect the interests of the most powerful groups in various fields. Politically oriented social movements, are, by definition, outside of some established field of a given state. They are oriented toward either creating a new domain where they will have power, or taking over and transforming an existing domain or even the entire state. At any given moment, there are political projects in the fields that make up states (i.e., "normal politics") and social movements oriented toward altering incumbents' ability to set rules (Gamson 1975).

By applying the theory of fields to markets, one produces an account that provides an alternative to economic views of how actors behave and why markets have social structures. Local market orders refer to a set of firms that take one another into account in their actions and, in so doing, are able to reproduce themselves on a period-to-period basis. All markets, whether organized in a city, a region, or across societies, can be analyzed from this perspective.

Market orders are governed by a general set of rules. These rules are the common understandings and laws that allow capitalist firms to exist. General ideas of market orders are embedded within a particular society and a government and reflect the society's peculiar history. The dominance of different groups in society means that those rules tend to reflect one set of interests over another. Increasingly, these rules are being established on a transnational basis, as in the European Union, the World Trade Organization, or NAFTA (North American Free Trade Agreement). But there are still national styles of ownership and regulation. Unique labor market institutions within societies reflect the power of various groups to control and define that market. Work and occupations are themselves the outcome of different traditions of development.

Economic theory assumes that the main mechanism that regulates this exchange is price competition. The theory of fields helps us observe these same social structures but interprets them quite differently. The main problem actors face is uncertainty caused by difficulties in finding suppliers and customers and in controlling their own firm. This uncertainty is manifested most acutely between competitors (i.e., firms who define themselves as sellers in the market) since all are trying to figure out how to reduce those uncertainties simultaneously. Competitors naturally come to watch one another and undertake actions to reduce their own uncertainty. They often do this by directly attacking their competitors and undermining their attempts to do the same.

Using the idea of markets as fields requires one to specify what a market is, who the players are, what it means to be an incumbent and a challenger, and how the social relationships and cultural understandings that come into play create stable fields by solving the main problems of competition and controlling uncertainty. I accept the view that a market is a "self-reproducing role structure of producers" (White 1981, 517). A stable "market as field" means that the main players in a given market are able to reproduce their firms. In the literature, this has often caused scholars to focus on the producers in the market who watch one another's actions and use their observations to plot out their reactions. Incumbent firms are those that dominate a particular market by creating stable relations with other producers, important suppliers, customers, and the government. They exploit their position of domination by reacting to what other dominant firms are doing. Challenger firms fit into the dominant logic of a stable market, either by finding a spot in the market (i.e., a niche) or imitating dominant firms.

The sociology of markets that I am developing replaces profit-maximizing actors with people who are trying to promote the survival of their firm. There are four threats to a firm's survival. First, suppliers can control inputs, raise prices, and make firms who require their inputs unprofitable. Second, competitors can engage in price competition, take over market share, and eventually drive the firm out of business. Third, gaining cooperation from managers and workers in the firm presents problems of interpersonal conflict and politics that can jeopardize the ability to produce goods and services as well. Finally, products may become obsolete.

These problems are most acute under conditions of economic turbulence that occur most frequently at the beginning of a market, but that also can reflect a sudden downturn in the market. A firm's product mix and marketing strategies, organizational forms, and relationships with competitors, suppliers, customers, and the government are structured by its attempts to mitigate the possible negative effects of competition and internal political conflict. Social structures in markets and within firms emerge to help firms cope with competition and stabilize their various relationships.

It is important to be clear here about what I am arguing. I am not arguing that firms always find solutions to the problems presented to them by competition. One of the distinguishing features of market society is that new entrants into a market can appear and new technologies can be produced to make a given product obsolete. Moreover, just because actors look for ways to stabilize their environments does not mean that the methods they choose are successful. So, for example, patents may control competition in a particular market under certain circumstances and fail under others. What I am arguing is that many of the actions taken by the owners and managers of firms make more sense if we understand the goal of those actions. Manager and owners are trying to enhance the survival of the firm by utilizing tactics oriented toward reducing the uncertainties they face due to the competition between firms.

I do not want to underestimate the creativity that market society has produced nor the creativity involved in producing a stable set of firms and markets. The opportunity to make money has motivated people to produce an enormous array of products and services. Sociology enters the equation in the problem of how actors produce a social world stable enough that they can sell those goods and services at a price at which their organization will survive. Managing people and uncertain environments to produce stability is a sizable task. Those who do it every day often demonstrate great skill and creativity as they lurch from crisis to crisis.

The theory of fields implies that the search for stable interactions with competitors, suppliers, and workers is the main cause of social structures in markets. The tactics we observe in business are oriented toward producing stable social relations, particularly between competitors. These relationships define fields. Once in place, firms signal one another about their price and product tactics. The relationships define how the market works, what a given firm's place is, and how actors should interpret one another's actions. Incumbent firms use the power of their position to undertake strategies that reinforce that position. To survive, challenger firms must find a place in the existing set of social relationships. I will discuss at length the types of tactics and social structures these interactions produce.

When successful, actors produce social relationships that have the effect of creating stable markets, that is, situations where incumbent firms who take one another into account in their behavior are able to reproduce themselves on a period-to-period basis. Markets produce local cultures that define who is an incumbent and who is a challenger and why (i.e., they define the social structure). They prescribe how competition will work in a given market. They also provide actors with cognitive frames to interpret the actions of other organizations. I have called these local understandings *conceptions of control* (Fligstein 1990).

Another form of creativity in markets is how actors in firms operating in other markets quickly become aware of prevalent conceptions of control. If conceptions of control are perceived as successful solutions to the problems of competition, actors in nearby markets copy them. The industry of management consultants, which has been growing at a fast rate in the past 30 years, is one of the important agents of the spread of successful solutions to problems presented by competition. Organizational learning oriented toward reducing uncertainty for firms is an important process within and across markets.

The theory of fields also suggests how it is that governments as a set of fields interact with markets as a set of fields. Fields of the state contain organizations, some public and others private, that make, interpret, and enforce the rules of a given society. Competitive markets produce instability for both consumers and producers. As unregulated economic exchange increases and prices begin to be set by those exchanges, social relationships are up for grabs, and the firms with the most resources may be able to dictate terms to all others. Indeed, the theory of fields predicts that in order to stabilize the existence of a given firm, its owners and managers will do anything to control others.

This generic problem of attaining stable relationships for organizations that are both buyers and sellers pushes firms toward states. This explains why the economic transition to market society has been so socially disruptive and has usually ended with government regulation of economic activities. In these situations, unstable market relations threaten the survival of all firms. Governments intervene to produce rules to promote stability.

As the forms of fields created by states to intervene in markets respond to and reshape the fields that are markets, state building and market building go hand in hand. Once institutionalized, these rules both enable and constrain subsequent behavior. They constrain behavior by defining how competition and conflict can be legally regulated. They enable incumbent firms to survive and produce stable markets. They also enable firms to create new markets. New market crises bring forth new forms of state regulation. But the new forms usually follow the path of the old (Dobbin 1994). When stable markets become destabilized, it is natural for firms to appeal to governments for help.

One of the key strengths of the political-cultural approach is that it helps to unify micro- and macromarket phenomena. The theory of fields explicitly links the formation of markets and firms to the problem of stability and, in doing so, considers how markets become stable. This model has implications for the organization of market society in a wider way. If producing stability in multiple markets requires rules, then governments are deeply implicated in defining the various social structures that stabilize markets. At the very least, governments have to ratify firms' abilities to use various structures that mediate competition and conflict. At the very most, they directly intervene in market practices to produce stability. Which way and how far governments go depends greatly on the politics of a particular society and the crises that brought that society to modern markets.

Theories are useful to the degree that they provide novel insights into empirical facts. The political-cultural approach and the theory of fields do this in a number of important ways. First, studies show that the historical transition to capitalism is an important moment in societal market formation. The political-cultural approach implies that the historical problems of the instability of markets for market participants, the formation of institutions to deal with those problems, and the configuration of economic and political elites are pivotal to setting up stable markets. Once established, they tend to reproduce entrenched interests and structure the emergence of new markets in that society.

The political-cultural approach explains why governments remain important in market society in general and why there appear to be so many national capitalisms. Later in this book, I provide evidence that national capitalisms do persist in the face of the so-called globalization of world markets. I show that markets are less globalized than some authors imply. I also show that national political and economic elites have a lot at stake in controlling "globalization."

Finally, since World War II, the developed world has managed to avoid economic depression. This 60-year period is unique in the history of modern capitalism. The political-cultural approach, with its focus on stability, presents some provocative hypotheses about why this might be. Firms have diversified their product lines since the depression of the 1930s in order to avoid markets that were declining. Economies have become diversified, and the relative size of developed economies has increased. The political-cultural approach implies that the connections between markets in large diversified economies may be weak. Thus, crises in particular markets do not spread very far. Taken together, these forces imply that we are likely to get recessions or rolling downturns caused by particular market interactions. But the overall diversity and size of large economies makes them stable.

Structure of the Book

The rest of this book is oriented toward convincing the reader that the political-cultural approach is a unified framework with which to understand the key dynamics of the sociology of markets in industrialized societies. The first part explicates the political-cultural approach in more detail. Chapter 2 takes up two issues: (1) important definitions for the political-cultural approach, and (2) the development of the social technology we call markets as a product of modernity. Chapter 3 considers the relation between state building and market building generally in modernity. I consider the role of history in producing unique state-market structures that define the relationship among owners and managers of firms, workers, and governments. I identify ideal typical arrangements that characterize some of the advanced industrial societies and suggest how they enable and constrain patterns of market and state building. Chapter 4 presents a microanalysis of the dynamics of markets. I consider how markets are formed, remain stable, and are transformed. I provide several examples of these processes. I consider the relations between markets and suggest how to think about market crises and globalization.

The second part of the book takes up case studies and literature reviews that show the usefulness of the political-cultural perspective for analyzing important phenomena in contemporary economic sociology. I first apply the political-cultural approach to national employment systems. The next two chapters consider the political-cultural approach as an alternative to "power elite" theories of American corporations. I argue that the political-cultural approach accounts better for the historically specific ways in which firms make money and why these change. I demonstrate that during the 1980s a new conception of control came to dominate large American corporations, the shareholder value conception of the firm. I compare the unique history of the United States to some of its principal rivals. I demonstrate that national capitalisms still exist and suggest why they persist. I consider the implications of the political-cultural approach for study of the "globalization" of the world economy. I offer some data on the extent of globalization and its effects on governments. Finally, I consider the new information technology industries in light of the political-cultural approach.

Normative Implications of the Political-Cultural Approach to the Sociology of Markets

A sociology of markets should not just produce a conceptual framework to describe particular market situations or state-firm relations. It should have some predictive and explanatory power. It should also have a normative edge that has policy implications for policy communities and for political groups who are struggling with the stark anti-state prescriptions of neoliberal theory. What is the normative implication of the search for stability in markets, between markets, and among markets and governments? The ability to buy and sell freely creates a kind of social chaos as the supply and demand for a given good swings widely and produces pressure on suppliers, producers, and competitors. In the face of this chaos, self-interested actors propose to stabilize interactions by creating cultural understandings for themselves and others, and social links to one another. To the degree that these links buffer the core firms in a market, those firms prosper. To the degree that methods to protect firms exist, they spread to other markets. These complex organizing technologies, to the degree they succeed, are creative uses of the individual's right to make money. These methods depend on government enforcement or ratification.

But stability for the incumbent firms in a market is not just a local affair. It requires other institutions to support it. Firms depend on local labor markets for workers, who mostly have invested in their own skills. Firms need roads, telecommunications, financing, property rights, and the enforcement of contracts to do business. They also need stable suppliers and customers who can pay and reliably play their part in market relations.

This stability is not just a local product, but a result of all of the people in society, the other firms and markets, and the government, which enforces some set of rules. Economics gets its normative edge from the idea that market forces are the principal way to efficiently allocate a society's resources. But if I am right, it is within a very wide set of social relationships that firms get their chance to become efficient producers. Without this wider web or nexus, and without legally accepted tactics to stabilize competition, the allocation of resources to efficient uses would be impossible.

This gives social structures an independent role in the process of market formation. General cultural understandings, the ability to mobilize financial and organizational resources, provide the conditions for the private accumulation of wealth. If one takes this perspective, one can consider normative arguments about the social structures within markets, among them, and among the people who live in the society. If market stabilization is about discovering ways to control competition, then the ability to do so is a privilege that a society allows. It helps privately constituted actors to gain advantage. It also reliably provides other people in society with goods and services that they presumably are willing to pay for. Now the customers ultimately pay for the narrowly defined costs of stability. But the ability to create a stable world is a cost borne by the more general society. Moreover, the society also bears the cost of providing infrastructure, public safety, and economic institutions that allow actors in firms to pursue stabilized markets.

A number of normative outcomes are implied by this analysis. First, if firms are effective and not efficient, then the claim that one form of market organization is always superior to other forms is probably false. If firms survive by stabilizing their relationships with their competition, then the social relations that are the outcome of this process are not maximizing the efficient allocation of resources for society. Society is prepared to allow individuals to reap profits by finding legal ways to stabilize social relations in markets because there is a general good being served (i.e., the reliable production of goods and services and the offer of employment). But the ability to engage in this form of control should have a price.

To the degree that costs of providing actors in firms with the right to stabilize markets are borne by others in the society, a given society should have the right to expect that firms obey certain rules and pay taxes as well.

Thus, a whole range of social expenditures and regulation is justified in principle. Economists often discuss how too much regulation and a focus on social justice can cause inefficiency in an economy. My point is that economic actors are totally dependent on social arrangements to make profits. It is clear that certain forms of extreme intervention in economic relations can cause inefficiency. But it is also clear that without laws, states, and the ability to find nonpredatory legal methods of competition, firms cannot exist.

The empirical literature on comparative capitalisms provides us with remarkable evidence that there is a wide range of social relations among workers, managers, firms, and states as regards the organization of firms and markets and the degree to which states are redistributive. Once we move away from the extremes (either confiscatory or predatory states), these various societal arrangements are compatible with sustained economic growth.

A sociological approach to market institutions makes us understand that there is not a single set of social and political institutions that produces the most efficient allocation of societal resources. The real issue for making markets is to create political and social conditions that produce enough stability so as to allow investment. Once these institutions are created, there are a great many ways to organize firms and markets that are compatible with making profits. Since the whole of society is enmeshed in market making, it is logical to argue that many possible interventions to produce a just and equitable society are in fact compatible with profit making. Indeed, one outcome of these interventions is to strengthen the legitimacy of market institutions.

PART I

2

Markets as Institutions

THE MODERN NATION-STATE is linked to the development of market society in myriad ways. The historical problem of producing stable capital, labor, and product markets eventually required governments and the representatives of capital and labor to produce general institutional arrangements (both laws and informal rules) around property rights, governance structures, and rules of exchange for all markets in capitalist societies. Within markets, cultural and historically specific rules and practices came to govern the relations among suppliers, customers, and workers (what I call conceptions of control).

Why do rules matter? Complex patterns of interaction that are stable require actors who share cognitive assumptions and expectations. To get such stability, people need either long experiences with one another, such that they settle into habitual patterns, or more formal rules to govern novel interactions. Rules based on experience or tradition or formally agreed to through negotiation then frequently become habitual in interaction (what in "institutional theory" is called "taken for grantedness" [DiMaggio and Powell 1991, chap. 1]). It is the instability produced by interactions in which actors do not share meanings that pushes actors to seek out more stable social conditions under which to interact (for example, see Haveman and Rao 1997; Dobbin and Sutton 1998).

There are two kinds of situations in which to study rules. In normal times rules are well known and taken for granted, and interactions are predictable as a result. There is conflict and contention between actors, but those conflicts are fought out under established rules, meanings, and practices. Analysts can identify who the players are, whether they are dominant or challengers, what their interests are, and what their actions mean.

In moments of the formation or transformation of political or market fields, actors become self-aware and engage in new forms of interaction to produce new arrangements. Because they try to forge new understandings, their interests and identities are in flux. They try to figure out what they want, how to get it, and how to get along with others who might want other things. The source of rules for new fields is often understandings brought from other fields. Actors modify these understandings in the practice of interacting with other groups and create new practices. But these new practices are often laid down along lines set by existing understandings.

Why the state? As the possibility for complex patterns of interaction in the sphere of economic exchange has expanded, actors have proven incapable of providing rules for themselves. Actors have two sorts of problems. First, in the case of markets, actors have to worry about keeping their firms alive. It is difficult to devote resources to making rules and simultaneously to do business. Second, in the face of uncertainty and difficult competition, firms find it impossible to solve their collective problems of competition. Sometimes firms find a way to eliminate or co-opt their principal competitors. But often this does not happen. These conditions cause firms to seek out help by approaching the government to legislate to promote "fair" competition.[1]

What about power? Rules are not created innocently or without taking into account "interests." If the largest firms are able to work under a set of rules that allows them to dominate the main markets of a society and keep workers disorganized, those rules enforce a system of power. In order to get analytic leverage on real systems of rules and power, it is necessary to think systematically about how government capacity and the relative power of government officials, capitalists, and workers figure into the construction of new market rules to define the forms of economic activity that exist in a given society.

The political-cultural perspective can provide generic analytic tools to understand what a particular set of market arrangements implies about the power structure of a society. Once these arrangements are understood, it is possible to predict how existing institutions will be used by powerful actors to frame subsequent crises. This gives leverage on understanding many of the most important political-economic dynamics within societies.

There are three parts to my exposition. First, it is necessary to define markets and the institutions necessary for them to function. The key insight is that markets are a kind of field, one that depends not just on the power of incumbents, but on more general rules in society in order to stabilize the power of incumbents. Then, it is important to consider how governments in modern capitalist societies have been constructed to deal with problems of market regulation. I argue that governments develop different kinds of capacities to intervene in their economies that are characterized by three dimensions: their ability to intervene, the form of intervention, and whose interests dominate the intervention. I then generate some general propositions about how rules produced by firms and governments produce stability in market economies.

Market Institutions: Basic Definitions

One of the core ideas that differentiates modern society from the societies that preceded it is the idea that social organization is a human product.

This implies that people can make choices and attempt to construct social-organizational vehicles to attain their ends. This does not mean that people are all successful or have the same opportunities to be actors. It does mean that the entire apparatus of modern economies is, at least partially, an outcome of these social technologies of organization. These have been invented and, upon reflection by the actors who use them, intentionally refined.

The organizations and institutions that existed before modernity were obviously social constructions as well. But they were not generally conceived that way. They established who was an actor and what actors could do. As people have become more self-aware in the past 350 years, they have examined existing social organizations, learned what seems to be successful, and used this knowledge to create new social arrangements. Over time, people have found ways to systematically produce new social technologies to attain ends (for example, legal incorporation to organize firms).

Modern governments, social movements, democratic politics, firms, and markets were invented by people collectively attempting to find ways to attain their ends (Fligstein 1997a). Often these "inventions" were accidental or reflected compromises between groups. The relations between the people who produced these social-organizational vehicles was, and continues to be, murky. But once these inventions were in place, other persons became aware of the various ways to organize and self-consciously built on them. The theory of fields is a generic theory of social organization in modernity. Our ability to recover that theory is itself an act of historical self-awareness. By abstracting away from the common experiences of social actors vying for control over their social arenas, social analysts have begun to appreciate that generic social processes underlie the construction of fields across states, markets, and the private nonprofit sector.

The theory of fields assumes that actors try to produce a "local" stable world where the dominant actors produce meanings that allow them to reproduce their advantage. These actors create status hierarchies that define the positions of incumbents and challengers. Actors face two related problems when constructing these fields: attaining a stable system of power and, once it is in place, maintaining it. The social organization of fields broadly refers to three features: the set of principles that organize thought and are used by actors to make sense of their situations (what might be called cognitive frames or worldviews), the routines or practices that actors perform in their day-to-day social relations, and the social relations that constitute fields that may or may not be consciously understood by actors (Bourdieu 1977).

The cognitive maps individuals possess offer them conceptual tools to understand or interpret the moves of others (White 1992; Emirbayer and Goodwin 1994). They also provide actors with tools to create new fields.

Typically, the cognitive models that actors use are not included in conceptualizations of social organization. This is because human agency is typically undertheorized. Sociologists usually think that a person's position in a social structure dictates what the person does, while rational choice theories use interests as the main explanatory variable. Actors' common understandings are not assumed to be consequential to explaining their actions. But in the theory of fields, the skill of actors in interpreting their situations, constructing courses of action, and innovating on existing routines helps construct fields and maintain them once in place (Bourdieu and Wacquant 1992). While one can separate cognitive elements from social relations, social organization depends on both (Giddens 1981).

Social organization is the totality of what produces stable conditions for the privileged and not-so-privileged groups in society. It constitutes them as groups, defines their relations to one another, and maintains a certain order in existing fields. This discussion of the basic building blocks of fields is necessarily abstract. These building blocks contain no substance or, more precisely, "culture" (i.e., practices and local knowledge) (Geertz 1983). They do not tell us much about how a given field is going to be constructed and reproduced in reality because they do not specify what kind of field is being built (state, market, organization) nor the precise principles that structure the relations between the "players."

To apply the theory of fields to market society, it is necessary to define what kind of fields markets are, and what types of social organization are necessary for stable "markets as fields" to exist. Economic exchange ranges from infrequent and unstructured to frequent and structured. Markets are social arenas that exist for the production and sale of some good or service, and they are characterized by structured exchange. Structured exchange implies that actors expect repeated exchanges for their products and that, therefore, they need rules and social structures to guide and organize exchange. While the identities of their customers and suppliers may change over time, producers expect that they will continue to seek out customers and will need suppliers.

Actors in unstructured or haphazard exchange have little invested in the exchange, and participants may or may not interact again (either as buyers or sellers). While they may benefit from the exchange, the sellers' organizational survival does not depend on haphazard exchange. It is when the agents in exchange begin to view their own stability (i.e., reproduction) as contingent on stabilizing trade, that they turn to social-organizational vehicles. Exchange throughout human history has often been unstructured, but markets in the sense I use the term here preexisted modern capitalism. Markets (and this includes almost all modern production markets) are mainly structured by sellers looking for buyers.[2] A given market becomes a "stable market" (i.e., a field) when the product being exchanged has legitimacy with customers, and the suppliers of the good or service are able to produce a status hierarchy in which the largest suppliers dominate the market and are able to reproduce themselves on a period-to-period basis.

These actors produce organizations to make the good and create social relations between competitors to govern competition. Stable markets can be described as "self reproducing role structures" in which incumbent and challenger firms reproduce their positions on a period-of-period basis (White 1981).[3] The sellers generally produce the social structure in the market because their firms' existence is at stake if a stable market does not appear.[4] The particular problems of finding a stable market are the same for all sellers: they are looking to secure suppliers and customers and thereby find a way to reproduce themselves. The social relations between sellers in a stable market are such that one set of firms produces the dominant cultural meanings for the market and the other firms fall in line. This does not imply that the partners to any given exchange between buyers and sellers have to be the same actors. Sellers vie for customers, and customers may switch suppliers. The stability of the sellers, in the sense of their organizational survival, is what is important to the stability of the market. My operational definition of a market is the situation in which the status hierarchy and, by implication, the existence of the leading sellers are reproduced on a period-by-period basis.

For example, the steel industry in the United States, for much of the twentieth century, was a stable market in which firms had persistent identities and defined products. The largest firms reproduced themselves by being vertically integrated and focused on stabilizing prices even as demand shifted radically (Fligstein 1990). Since the mid-1960s, the identities of the suppliers of steel products have been transformed. Many of the largest producers disappeared, and new firms began to dominate the market. The market itself became differentiated between products that were basic commodities and higher-end, higher-value-added products. The newer firms were able to take advantage of these changes to form a new market. The field that once existed has disappeared, and two new market fields have taken its place (Hogan 1984).

I do not mean to obliterate the distinction between a market and an industry. A market is a social arena where sellers and buyers meet. But for sellers and buyers to exist, a product has to exist and someone has to produce it. A market depends on the buyers continuing to "show up" in a particular social space to purchase the product. But the sellers' firms and their status relations define what stability means in the market. They define what the market is about, and their relations define the local culture by which money is to be made and stability produced. While there is obviously an interdependency between buyers and sellers, the sellers' stake in the arena is one of survival.

In spite of elaborate social mechanisms and rules to guide market interaction, markets are inherently unstable from the point of view of sellers. One of the deep insights of economics is that market society makes it very profitable to create new markets. At the beginning of markets, first movers can often reap huge rewards. But as other economic actors realize the opportunity, they enter into the market and prices drop. Moreover, as markets slow down in growth (as they inevitably do), firms have incentives to go after more market share and to cut prices. These forces intensify competition. Products can be delegitimated, most often by being superseded by other products. It is these opportunities and problems that create unstable conditions for producers.

Even where seller relations have been stabilized, they can be upset. The "game" for the incumbent firms is to find a way to produce a market as a stable field. These stable markets contain social structures that characterize the relations between dominant and challenger seller firms. The social relations are oriented toward maintaining the advantaged positions of the largest seller firms in the face of their challengers. They define how the market works and how competition is structured. For example, two main firms dominate the soft drink industry in the United States: Pepsi-Cola and Coca-Cola. These firms compete over market share and use advertising, diversification of products, and price discounts to do so. Although the firms compete, they have produced an equilibrium whereby both survive by following the accepted tactics of competition.

As forms of social organization, market structures involve both cognitive understandings and concrete social relations. The cognitive understandings are of two sorts: general societal understandings about how to organize firms and markets and find stable ways to compete, and specific understandings about the way a particular market works. These specific understandings structure the interactions between competitors but also allow actors to make sense of their competitors' actions. The concrete social relations in a given market reflect its unique history and its dependency on other markets. The links to suppliers and customers play a role in creating stable markets. The constitution of these relations determines which firms are dominant and why, and their relations to challenger firms. The ultimate success of firms in producing stable fields (i.e., social structures to stabilize their relationships with one another) is dependent on the general principles of making markets in their society, and the ability to find a way to do this within a particular market.

The first problem for a sociology of markets is to propose theoretically what kinds of rules and understandings are necessary to make structured exchange (i.e., markets as fields) possible in the first place. There are four types of rules relevant to producing social structures in markets—what can be called property rights, governance structures, rules of exchange, and conceptions of control. These categories are necessarily abstract. They refer to general types of rules that can appear as laws, understandings, or practices. They define issues about which actors who want to generate markets must create general understandings in order for stable markets to emerge. They need these rules whether they are aware of them or not. Failure, for example, to have property rights makes it difficult to have markets. If we do not know who owns what and who has the right to dispose of it, we are in the world of illegal trade and not the world of stable markets.

These four types of social structures have emerged historically as firms and governments have recognized certain generic problems in making markets work and then reflected on general solutions. Through understandings around these institutions actors produce social structures to organize themselves, to compete and cooperate, and to exchange with one another in a regular and reproducible fashion. Each of these types of social structure is directed at different problems of instability. Some are related to the general problem of creating a market in the first place, and others have to do with ensuring the stability of firms in a particular market.

Property rights are rules that define who has claims on the profits of firms (akin to what agency theorists call "residual claims" on the free cash flow of firms (Jensen and Meckling 1976; Fama 1980). This general statement leaves open the issues of the different legal forms of property rights (e.g., corporations vs. partnerships); the relationship between shareholders and employees, local communities, suppliers, and customers; and the role of the state in directing investment, owning firms, and preventing owners from harming workers. The holders of property rights are entitled to dispose of property or earn income from it. Patents and credentials are forms of property rights that entitle their holder to earn profits. The constitution of property rights is a continuous and contestable political process, not the outcome of an efficient process (for a similar argument, see Roe 1994). Organized groups from business, labor, government agencies, and political parties try to affect the constitution of property rights.

The division of property rights is at the core of market society. Property rights define who is in control of the capitalist enterprise and who has rights to claim the surplus. Property rights do not always favor the privileged groups in society. If, for instance, governments own firms and control investment decisions, their decisions can take into account different divisions of profits. Cooperative businesses or partnerships can allow for equal distribution of profits. Workers can receive part of their pay in profit-sharing schemes.

Property rights are necessary to markets because they define the social relationships between owners and everyone else in society. This stabilizes markets by making it clear who is risking what and who gets the reward in a particular market situation. A given firm's suppliers know who is the responsible entity. Property rights thus function to produce two forms of stability: defining the power relationships between constituencies in and around firms, and signaling to other firms who firms are.[5]

Governance structures refer to the general rules in a society that define relations of competition and cooperation and define how firms should be organized.[6] These rules define the legal and illegal forms of controlling competition. They take two forms: (1) laws and (2) informal institutional practices. Laws, called antitrust, competition, or anticartel laws, exist in most advanced industrial societies. The passage, enforcement, and judicial interpretation of these laws is contested (Fligstein 1990), and the content of such laws varies widely across societies. Some societies allow extensive cooperation between competitors, particularly when foreign trade is involved, while others try to reduce the effects of barriers to entry and promote competition. Competition is not just regulated within societies, but across societies. Countries have tariffs and trade barriers to help national industry to compete with foreign competitors. These laws often benefit particular sectors of the economy.

Firms' internal organization is also a response to legal and illegal forms of competition. Firms that vertically integrate often do so to ensure themselves supplies and deny those supplies to competitors. Firms also may horizontally integrate by buying up market share in order to produce stable order in a market. Firms may diversify products in order to protect themselves from the vagaries of particular products. They may also form long-term relationships with suppliers, customers, or financial organizations in order to respond to competition.

Market societies develop more informal institutional practices that are embedded in existing organizations as routines and are available to actors in other organizations. Mechanisms of transmission include professional associations, management consultants, and the exchange of professional managers (DiMaggio and Powell 1983; Meyer and Rowan 1977). Among these informal practices are how to arrange a work organization (such as the multidivisional form), how to write labor and management contracts, and where to draw the boundaries of the firm. So, for instance, firms can compete on price, but if they infringe on one another's patents or trade secrets, they are likely to run afoul of the law. They also include current views of what behavior of firms is legal or illegal. Governance structures help define the legal and normative rules by which firms structure themselves and their relations to competitors. In this way, they generally function to stabilize those relations.

Rules of exchange define who can transact with whom and the conditions under which transactions are carried out. Rules must be established regarding weights, common standards, shipping, billing, insurance, the exchange of money (i.e., banks), and the enforcement of contracts. Rules of exchange regulate health and safety standards of products and the standardization of products more generally. For example, many pharmaceutical products undergo extensive testing procedures. Health and safety standards help both buyers and sellers and facilitate exchange between parties who may have only fleeting interactions.

Product standardization has become increasingly important in the context of rules of exchange, particularly in the telecommunications and computer industries. National and international bodies meet to agree on standards for products across many industries. Standard setting produces shared rules that guarantee that products will be compatible. This process facilitates exchange by making it more certain that products will work the way they are intended.

Rules of exchange help stabilize markets by ensuring that exchanges occur under conditions that apply to everyone. If firms that ship their goods across a particular society do not have rules of exchange, such exchanges will be haphazard at best. Making these rules has become even more important for trade across societies. Many of the newest international trade agreements, including the European Union's Single Market Program and the last round of GATT (General Agreement on Tariffs and Trade), focus on producing and harmonizing practices around rules of exchange.

Conceptions of control reflect market-specific agreements between actors in firms on principles of internal organization (i.e., forms of hierarchy), tactics for competition or cooperation (i.e., strategies), and the hierarchy or status ordering of firms in a given market. A conception of control is a form of "local knowledge" (Geertz 1983).[7] Conceptions of control are historical and cultural products. They are historically specific to a certain industry in a certain society. They are cultural in that they form a set of understandings and practices about how things work in a particular market setting. A stable market is a social field in which a conception of control defines the social relations between incumbent and challenger seller firms such that the incumbent firms reproduce those relations on a period-to-period basis.

The purpose of action in a given market is to create and maintain stable worlds within and across firms that allow dominant seller firms to survive. Conceptions of control are social-organizational vehicles for particular markets that refer to the cognitive understandings that structure perceptions of how a particular market works, as well as a description of the real social relations of domination that exist in a particular market. A conception of control is simultaneously a worldview that allows actors to interpret the actions of others and a reflection of how the market is structured.

State Building and Market Building

Creating a general set of rules whereby stable markets can be produced helps to structure exchange in particular product fields in a particular society. To move from unstructured to structured exchange in a market implies that actors became aware of systematic problems they had in stabilizing exchange. Their awareness stimulated them to search for social-organizational solutions to their problems. But this awareness did not come quickly or all at once. The emergence of the general social technologies that help actors to produce and maintain modern markets depended on discovering the problems presented by property rights (i.e., who owned what), governance structures (i.e., ways to organize, including fair and unfair forms of competition), rules of exchange (i.e., making exchanges), and conceptions of control (i.e., producing local status hierarchies within markets to stabilize the situation of dominant players).

Proposition 2.1. The entry of countries into capitalism pushes states to develop rules about property rights, governance structures, rules of exchange, and conceptions of control in order to stabilize markets.

The timing of entry of countries into capitalism has had huge effects on societal trajectories (Westney 1987; Chandler 1990; Fligstein 1990; Dobbin 1994). The alliances made at this historical moment between workers, state officials, and capitalists structure the way in which states build policy domains and the policy styles that develop in those domains. Once such styles are established, subsequent political and economic crises are interpreted from these perspectives.

This does not mean that societies are forever locked into a set of institutions. But it does mean that any new crisis is interpreted from the current dominant perspective. This works in two ways. First, a system of rules is also a system of power. Incumbent actors try to use the current rules for their benefit. But the current set of institutions also provides actors with a way to figure out how to apply the old rules to new situations. For these reasons, we tend to observe incremental change, barring massive societal failure due to war or depression. Then, crisis open up the possibility for new political alliances and new rules.

For countries just establishing modern capitalist markets, creating stable conceptions of control is more difficult precisely because property rights, governance structures, and rules of exchange are not well specified. Firms are exposed to cutthroat competition and often demand that the state establish rules about property rights, governance structures, and rules of exchange. Creating these new institutions requires the interaction of firms, political parties, states, and newly invented (or borrowed) conceptions of regulation.[8]

People did not realize historically that they had to resolve these issues to make structured exchange possible (see North 1990, chap. 1, on this point). Indeed, many practices evolved in informal ways and stayed informal. Actors in markets found ways of making themselves stable for relatively long periods of time in the absence of formal institutions. But, as time went on, social technologies to solve problems emerged in industrial societies. Large-scale social disruptions such as wars, depressions, or social movements caused political actors to craft general tools with which to respond.

Once actors became aware of more general solutions, the solutions were used in new circumstances. But novel situations often forced the modification of organizing technology. So, for example, the modern American conception of the corporation (a limited-liability joint stock corporation) started out as a state-directed conception that emphasized limits on the exercise of property rights. This gave state legislators a tool to use in development projects whereby they could delegate transportation and communications projects to private firms and still maintain control over the firm. People began to recognize two advantages to the corporate form: it allowed the bringing together of more capital, and it restricted the liability of parties to the agreement to the assets they had invested in the corporation. These advantages pushed entrepreneurs to demand more and more acts of incorporation. Finally, this led to a broad conception of incorporation that made the form widely available (Friedman 1973; Roy 1997).

One way to partially understand governments is to view them as organized entities that produce and enforce market (and other) rules. However, this rule is not a historical necessity. It is theoretically possible for firms to routinize exchange with one another without the benefit of rules or governments. After all, most trade before the eighteenth century was done in the absence of strong states and legal systems (Greif 1989; Spruyt 1994). Before modernity, the problems posed by unstable exchange were solved by private parties to those exchanges.

There was a very practical reason for developing more general rules for markets. North and Thomas (1973) noted long ago that social institutions have made entrepreneurs richer, their firms bigger and more stable. For that reason, they argued, self-interested actors had an interest in producing rules. However, though we know rules encouraged markets as fields, entrepreneurs, managers, and governments did not comprehend that creating governmental capacity to make rules would help create wealth. So, for example, Carruthers (1996) shows that the first modern capital market in England was very much organized along political party lines. People would only trade with those with whom they agreed on politics. One of the purposes of the markets was to reward people in the party, by giving them access to friendly pools of capital.

North, in his later work (1990), realized that modern economic history cannot be read as the gradual reduction of transaction costs for markets by the production of rules that facilitate trade. He saw that entrepreneurs and government officials were unaware that their actions produced positive consequences. Their actions were not framed in these terms; indeed, their actions were often framed to benefit the friends of the rulers and cut out their enemies. Moreover, the rulers of premodern European states had time horizons far too short to understand what produced long-term economic growth. Most market institutions were the outcome of political struggles whereby one group of capitalists captured government and created rules to favor themselves over their political opponents. North's central insight is at the basis of the theory of market governance theory presented here.

The general rules that did eventually emerge reflected years of interactions with various forms of structured exchange and increasing awareness of the difficulty of managing large, complex production without rules. As one problem was solved and one set of markets stabilized, another set of problems emerged. The increasing scale of production, the growth of markets, and the growing awareness of entrepreneurs and managers of their common problems pushed the search for new common understandings.

It is still possible, of course, for structured exchange to occur without shared market institutions. But we now exist in a world where those institutions are ubiquitous and social actors are aware of them. It is this increasing self-awareness that leads modern actors in governments and firms to seek out general rules and forms of enforcement from the outset. As social-organizational vehicles become more sophisticated and ways of managing sources of instability become better known, entrepreneurs and managers realize that common understandings over property rights, governance structures, rules of exchange, and conceptions of control are useful for dominant firms.

There were two historical problems that militated against entrepreneurs and managers producing common rules to stabilize exchanges. If governments were formed by a small number of capitalists to intervene in market processes, the group was likely to make rules to favor themselves and cut out others, thereby capturing the state for their narrow interests. This, of course, frequently happened. But such rent seeking was met by open political conflict.

Capitalists often faced collective action problems when it came to making market rules. How could entrepreneurs who focused on existing conceptions of control in a given market simultaneously develop more general rules about competition, cooperation, property rights, and rules of exchange with actors in other markets? The basic problem is that owners have to worry about organizational survival in the context of scarce organizational resources. Why would they want to produce general rules for all firms in a society?

Systemic economic crises produced economic depressions as a result of unstable systems of exchange. These became more severe and involved more and more people in societies across Europe and North America in the nineteenth century. Those with the largest investments in plants and other facilities found themselves in difficult situations. Managers and entrepreneurs responded to these crises caused by overcompetition by trying to control their main competitors. They used cartels or attempted to form monopolies. Firms also faced workers' organizations that resisted their attempt to lower wages and control labor markets. Class struggle led to bitter disputes between the large groups of workers who were located in the largest factories and the owners and managers (Edwards 1979). But frequently, firms and workers could not construct stable solutions, and they certainly could not construct "general" solutions. This conflict led both sides to go to governments to get them to produce stable outcomes (Fligstein 1990; Chandler 1990).

The organizations, groups, and institutions that comprise the fields of the state in modern capitalist society claim sovereignty, that is, the right to make and enforce the rules governing all interactions in a given geographic area (Krasner 1988).[9] Firms and workers' organizations came into conflict and turmoil, and they both tried to use governments to solve their problems of instability (Fligstein 1990). While most modern discussions of state building have focused on welfare and warfare, modern capitalist states have been constructed in interaction with the development of their economies, and the governance of their economies is part of the core of state building (Fligstein 1990; Hooks 1990; Campbell, Hollingsworth, and Lindberg 1991; Dobbin 1994; Evans 1995).[10]

As was stated in chapter 1, I conceive of the modern state as a set of fields that can be defined as policy domains. Policy domains are arenas of political action where bureaucratic agencies and representatives of firms and workers meet to form and implement policy.[11] The purpose of this policymaking is to make rules and governance mechanisms to produce stable patterns of interaction in nonstate fields. Modern states also typically develop legal systems with courts that adjudicate and interpret current laws and understandings. These legal fields are domains as well that contain judges, courts, lawyers, and law schools. One way to understand the legal system is to realize that legal systems are alternative ways for challenger groups to engage in political action. By using laws against incumbents, challengers can contest the rights and privileges of dominant groups (Shapiro 1980; Stone Sweet 2000).

The building of these domains, what others have called "state capacity" (Evans, Skocpol, and Rueschmeyer 1985), occurs under a set of interactions governed by rules that were usually put into place by a revolutionary social movement or a series of such movements or were imposed by outside invaders (or a succession of such forces). Once a government is formed in capitalist societies, the political processes in a society are about dominant groups building government capacity to ensure their dominant position and challenger groups trying to reorient existing domains or creating new ones to include them. The purpose of this confrontation within domains is to provide stabilizing rules that tend to benefit the most powerful groups.

State building can be defined as the development of domains set up by and for state officials, firms, and workers. The domains, once constructed, reflect the relative power of workers, capitalists, politicians, and state bureaucrats, inscribed in the law and the forms of regulation or intervention at the time they are formed. Domains are often focused on particular industries (for example, bank regulation) but can also be concerned with more general issues that apply across industries (for example, antitrust law or patents that define property rights). The way in which states are capable of intervening in their economies is inscribed by the power relations as constituted in particular domains when they are founded.

Proposition 2.2. Initial formation of policy domains and the rules they create affecting property rights, governance structures, and rules of exchange shape the development of new markets because they produce cultural templates that determine how to organize in a given society. The initial configuration of institutions and the balance of power between government officials, capitalists, and workers at that moment account for the persistence of, and differences between, national capitalisms.

The shape of initial regulatory institutions has a profound effect on subsequent capitalist development. They define the current state of rules and what is permissible. They also provide guidelines for how states can be subsequently organized to intervene in economies as new issues arise. Indeed, any new markets that come into existence do so under a given set of institutions. This is one of the most remarkable features of institutions: they enable newly organized actors to act. They do not just support the status quo, but allow entrepreneurs to come into existence without having to invent new ways to organize.

One can observe that, as countries industrialize, the demand for laws or enforceable understandings is high, and that once such understandings are produced, demand decreases. As new industries emerge or old ones are transformed, new rules are made in the context of the old rules. Dobbin (1994) has argued that societies create "regulatory styles." These styles are embedded in regulatory organizations and in the statutes that support them. States are often the focus of market crises, but actors continue to use an existing set of laws and practices to resolve crises. These general tactics are used to construct arguments about why and how governments should directly intervene in or mediate disputes between firms and workers and intervene in or regulate markets. Property rights, governance structures, conceptions of control, and rules of exchange are institutional issues about which modern states establish rules for economic actors. There can be specific state agencies oriented toward producing and enforcing institutions, such as patent offices for the registration of property rights. More common, however, are multiple domains where institutional issues enter in different ways.

A good example is modern states' extensive policy domains organized around the problems of agriculture. Most advanced industrial societies have programs oriented toward solving problems of competition (for instance, price support programs and subsidized foreign trade) and rules of exchange (for instance, health and safety standards and standard weights and measures). In many advanced industrial societies, these policies are buttressed with concerns for the property rights of "family" farmers. In the United States, special tax laws make it easier for family farmers to pass on their farms to their children.

Proposition 2.3. State actors are constantly attending to one market crisis or another. This is so because markets are always being organized or destabilized, and firms and workers are lobbying for state intervention.

In normal times, change in markets is incremental and dependent upon the construction of interests of actors in and around the state.[12] Having stable rules is often more important than the content of the rules. However, rules do embody the interests of dominant groups, and state actors do not intentionally transform rules unless dominant groups are in crisis. Because of their central place in the creation and enforcement of market institutions, states become the focus of crisis in any important market. Given the turmoil inherent in markets, the state is constantly attending to some form of market crisis.

Pressure on states can from come two sources: other states (and by implication, their firms) and existing markets that can be constructed either locally (within the geography of the state) or globally (across states). As economic interdependence across societies has increased, there has been an explosion of cross-state agreements, particularly about rules of exchange. States provide stable and reliable conditions under which firms organize, compete, cooperate, and exchange. They also privilege some firms over others and often national large firms over small firms and firms from foreign countries. The enforcement of these rules affects what conceptions of control can produce stable markets. There are political contests over the content of laws, their applicability to given firms and markets, and the extent and direction of state intervention in the economy.

Power in Policy Domains and Market Institutions

States are important to the formation and ongoing stability of markets. How they are important and to what degree is a matter of historical process (Evans 1995; Ziegler 1997). Some states have greater capacities for intervention than others, and the likelihood of intervention depends on the nature of the crisis and the institutional history of the state (Dobbin 1994; Evans, Skocpol, and Rueschmeyer 1985; Ziegler 1997; Laumann and Knoke 1987).[13] Current organized interests use current rules to try to reproduce their positions. This explains why there appear to be so many forms of market arrangements across and within developed and developing societies (Evans 1995; Fligstein and Freeland 1995).

Proposition 2.4. Policy domains contain governmental organizations and representatives of firms, workers, and other organized groups. They are structured in two ways: (1) around the state's capacity to intervene, regulate, and mediate, and (2) around the relative power of societal groups to dictate the terms of intervention.

There are two important ways in which to characterize the political structure of policy domains of the state that focus on the relations between government officials, their organizations, capitalist firms, and workers. One important dimension is captured by the distinctions among direct intervention, regulation, and mediation. Domains are interventionist to the degree that government officials can directly make substantive decisions for markets. Governments may own firms, control the financial sector, direct investment, and heavily regulate firms' entries, exits, and competition in markets. Government officials have strong control over firms and workers in these domains. An example of an interventionist state is France, where historically officials in ministries were able to direct investment and control firms by virtue of government ownership.

In contrast, states dominated by regulatory regimes create agencies to enforce general rules in markets but do not decide who can own what or make what investment. Regulatory states put organizations in place in policy domains to play "traffic cop." Theoretically, regulatory bodies do not reflect the interest of any one group but use rules impartially to police the interactions of firms and workers who are represented in the domain. Often, regulatory bodies become captured by the dominant firms in an industry. Examples of regulatory agencies are the Securities and Exchange Commission in the United States and the Monopolies Board in the United Kingdom.

Both regulatory and interventionist states occasionally use mediation in policy arenas to help make policy or settle disputes. Interactions between industry representatives and state officials around an issue of common concern may result in the formation of a policy for a sector of the economy. If there is conflict between the organizations of firms or between firms and workers, state officials can act as mediators. It is clear that the Ministry of International Trade and Industry (MITI) played this role in Japanese development (Johnson 1982; Evans 1995).[14]

The second dimension that structures domains concerns whether or not they have undergone "capture." Economists argue that one problem of government intervention in markets is the temptation by government officials to "rent-seek" (Buchanan, Tellison, and Tulloch 1980). Rent seeking implies that government officials seek out payments from either firms or workers in a sector that involve bribes or taxes. In this case, the sector can be captured by the state. Evans (1995) has described as predatory states in some parts of the Third World that have this capacity.

Capture can occur as well if either a set of firms or an organized group of workers gets control over a policy domain (this is in fact the point of Buchanan, Tellison, and Tulloch's book [1980]). Regulatory agencies or even interventionist parts of ministries often rely on industry guidance for information and personnel. If workers or firms capture domains, they can attempt to use the domain to narrowly defend their privilege against other claims. To the degree that the industry is organized, it is possible for a set of firms to capture the regulatory agency and get government officials to accept their view of the industry and what should be done.

Workers can capture domains as well. Groups of workers may, for example, win the right to certify new workers, which, in essence, gives them the right to decide who has a "property right," that is, who owns a certificate that entitles them to make a profit from their skill. The government may directly intervene in this process or allow certification boards to be selected from members of workers' communities. Professions, such as physicians in the United States, have used this tactic successfully for long periods of time to control the supply of doctors (Starr 1982).

I would like to reconceptualize the language of rent seeking to capture in a more neutral way who, among government officials or representatives of capitalist or worker interests, has the upper hand in making policy in a given domain. Rent seeking occurs in the sense that all groups are oriented toward using their power in policy domains for their own ends. But rent seeking can be more or less venal. When individual firms or government officials use their positions to advantage themselves and disadvantage of others in their fields, extreme predatory behavior can result.

Usually, rent seeking only occurs where there is little countervailing power. If a set of capitalist firms is not opposed by government officials or workers, the firms are more likely to set in place governance structures that allow collusion and rules of exchange that prevent other firms from competing. But it is also the case that the interests of a small set of firms and organized workers may produce the same effect. By such means textile manufacturers in the United States have been able to protect their markets by allying themselves with workers under the guise of saving jobs. These issues are explored more thoroughly in the next chapter.

3

The Politics of the Creation of Market Institutions

My discussion has so far focused on making conceptual distinctions. It is possible to get more theoretical and empirical leverage by considering how ideal-typical domination by one group, or alliances between workers, capitalists, and state officials, affects in the formation of market institutions. These ideal types are useful because they suggest how national governments come to intervene in markets as a function of the historical coalitions between government officials, capitalists, and workers. To apply the ideal types, one can examine the historic balance of power at the formation of market institutions in a given society, discern how actors are currently arrayed, and make predictions about how state organizational capacity will get built and how it will affect the rules of market organization. If one knows that a given set of arrangements dominates a certain society and one understands the roles played by various groups, then one can predict how new crises will be mediated and what kind of domains and rules are likely to be constructed.

Of course the links between general market institutions in a society and the formation of particular markets is a historical process. So, for example, as software firms have emerged, intellectual property rights have become a more salient issue. New kinds of patent laws have emerged that define what can be patented about a particular piece of software. Thus, the particular market problem can have a distinct "cultural solution" that reflects the context in which it emerges. In societies with existing patent laws, new laws were built on existing law. But, of course, new innovations in law were required because of the nature of the industry covered. This give-and-take between existing institutions and new situations for firms and industries characterizes a great deal of the empirical work on development of market institutions. (See, for example, Fligstein and Mara-Drita 1996; Haveman and Rao 1997; Baron, Dobbin, and Jennings 1986; Dobbin 1994.)

It is useful to begin with an abstract and static analysis in order to characterize ideal types. The pure cases (i.e., domination by capitalists; workers, or state officials) of the formation of governmental capacity often exist when one group dominates in the executive or legislative branches of governments and creates rules favorable to itself. Once institutions are pro-

TABLE 3.1
Dominant Groups and Their Effects on Policy Domains and Forms of Economic
Intervention

Dominant Group	Policy Domains	Economic Intervention
State as rent seeker	Predatory	Haphazard; open to corruption
Capitalists	Regulatory	Capture by capitalist interests
Workers	Impossible in capitalism?	
Capitalist-state coalition	Regulatory; state could be directing or brokering development	State controls finance, utilities, infrastructure; represses workers
Worker-state coalition	Welfare state; direct ntervention in product and labor markets	State ownership of firms; extension worker protections
Capitalist-worker stand-off	Policies respond to who is dominant; state acts as broker	Strongest groups get favorable policies; compromise

duced and organizational capacity to organize domains comes into existence, domains that produce and enforce rules take on lives of their own.
Firms and workers who participate in those domains learn to live with a
certain set of rules, even if it disadvantages them. Changing those rules
requires a serious crisis that makes reforms possible. These often occur
only with a regime shift in which new political players remake the rules in
their constituents' interests.

Table 3.1 presents these ideal types. Table 3.2 shows the implications
of these arrangements for property rights, governance structures, rules of
exchange, and conceptions of control in product markets. It is useful to
consider how the pure cases structure the ability of governments to intervene in markets generally and the implications for market institutions.

Government officials in rent-seeking states organize markets by directly
owning firms and using them to support favored groups (such as relatives
and friends) or establishing clientelistic, but stable, relations with a particular group of capitalists. They use their power to extract rents from these
"favored" groups. Organized military regimes often have this character,
as do regimes in many developing countries. Rent-seeking government
officials' ability to dominate economies is often a matter of degree, even

TABLE 3.2
Implications for Market Institutions of Domination by Different Groups

Dominant Group	Property Rights	Governance Structure	Rules of Exchange	Dominant Model of State/ Market Intervention
State as rent seeker	Sold via bribes and payoffs	Bribes and payoffs	Bribes and payoffs	Firms and workers disorganized; markets unstable
Capitalists	No state ownership; shareholders have all the rights	Cartels and control; clear organization of competitors	Capture of regulatory control; enforcement for incumbents	State intervention for incumbents' crises but otherwise stays out of markets
Workers	No private ownership	Competition mediated to protect jobs	Regulations extensive; worker-consumer safety paramount, used to keep out competitors	State intervention to save jobs
Capitalist-state coalition	State control of finance and ownership of public utilities; clear distinctions between public and private	Some product markets protected; others open depending on firms' competitive positions	Rule of law applied to all	State intervention to aid incumbents
Worker-state coalition	State ownership; some stakeholder rights	Oriented to job protection; firms allowed to cooperate; markets protected	Rules extensive and enforced for all	State intervention to save jobs
Capitalist-worker standoff; state autonomy	Go for intervention when both sides agree or if powerful demands from organized groups	Alternatively help sides protect jobs and markets; allow cooperation save jobs	Used for intervention for both sides	State intervention for firms or workers

where workers and firms are sufficiently disorganized that they are unable to produce political movements to counter officials. This is because these regimes often lack personnel who are able to create effective government bureaucracy to systematically rent-seek. Extensive black markets for basic commodities often develop in these conditions, and the ability of government officials to support their styles of life is constantly threatened.

In one extreme version of this situation, governments lack the ability to even collect taxes, and public officials routinely use their positions to obtain bribes and kick backs. Evans (1995) has described this condition as a "predatory state." He identifies Zaire during the late 1980s as an example. One way to characterize this lack of organizational capacity is that policy domains essentially do not exist. Governments require resources and skilled personnel; and, if they are lacking, governments do not have the organizational capacity to enforce rules. With little or no representation of the interests of workers or capitalists, this circumstance translates into difficult and potentially life-threatening situations for owners, managers, and workers.

States that are organized rent-seekers have staggering implications for the production of institutions. Table 3.2 shows that in governments with capacity to police, officials sell property rights to the highest bidder. Those rights remain with those bidders at the whim of officials. Where government officials are not able to enforce deals that are made, bribery can buy property rights. Similarly, rules surrounding competition and cooperation, which permit firms to be organized, either are applied in a clientelistic fashion, in the best case, or simply do not exist. Conditions are determined at the whim of officials on the scene. Finally, simple exchange (shipping, the transfer of funds, buying products brought from outside the country) is fraught with difficulty. Favored groups have more access to channels of exchange. If government officials cannot police such arrangements, then other government officials can upset whatever arrangement is in place.

This is a negative view of the state's role in economic development. Is it possible for state-led development to be more positive for workers or firms even where those groups are disorganized? Evans (1995) posits that this possibility relies on a well-paid, professionally trained administrative staff. This gives administrators an autonomy that allows them to try to produce market institutions that may benefit less organized social groups. Evans and Rauch (1999) provide empirical evidence that educated bureaucracies in fact enhance economic growth in developing societies. There is evidence that government-directed development in Korea, Japan, and France helped organize capitalist firms and intervened in market processes (Wade 1990; Westney 1987; Johnson 1982; Djelic 1998).[1]

The question of whether bureaucratic elites in states can in fact produce stable market institutions and growing economies is complex. It is clear that some of the development projects of the past hundred years have been state led, as even the World Bank has acknowledged (1997). But many societies with dominant states have not developed, sometimes because national politics does not push a market-style development project, as in India during most of the postwar era. But even where governments have pushed such projects (in Mexico and Brazil, for example), those projects have not been entirely successful. To make progress on this issue of the effect of bureaucratic elites, one would need to clarify two aspects of state policies. First, do the policies provide stable market institutions in theory, and second, do the governments have the organizational capacity to implement the necessary regulatory apparatus in practice? Frequently the implementation of market institutions is difficult and can be resisted by local political authorities and organized groups of capitalists.

If a society's policy domains are entirely dominated by capitalists, the mechanisms for rent seeking shift, as presented in the second row of tables 3.1 and 3.2. Policy domains exist and governments have organizational capacity, but these domains are now captured by narrower capitalist interests. On occasion, government policy is made for an individual firm. But more normal is regulatory capture by the leading firms in a particular industry. The former situation can result in tension between individual firms that search for opportunities to rent-seek and other firms in a specific industry that want collective regulatory capture in order to promote collective rent-seeking by the industry.

Often dominant firms promote industry-wide rules that apply to all firms "equally." They do so for two reasons. Dominant firms want to restrict government officials' ability to directly intervene in any market, even when those officials more or less serve their interests. Government officials who are regulators cannot own firms or intervene in market processes to choose winners and losers. But dominant firms that have accomplished regulatory capture can have rules written and enforced that disproportionately benefit them. Thus, "fair" regulators appear to be enforcing rules for every firm, even if those rules benefit some firms (usually market incumbents) more than others.

In the case of property rights, capitalists prefer a clear set of rules giving power only to shareholders. They also prefer that states not own firms in any sector of the economy. This gives governments an incentive to take over firms in sectors in economic trouble and then return them to private investors after public funds are used to strengthen firm. A good example is the massive bailout of the savings and loan industry in the United States during the 1980s. Here the government sold bonds to pay off depositors in failed savings and loan associations. Then regulators took whatever assets were seized and sold them back into private hands. The federal government socialized the cost of the bailout to taxpayers and then made the assets available to private investors at attractive prices.

Firms' dominance also encourages governments to pay for investments firms want to make in plant capacity and technology while leaving profit making in private hands. Governments underwrite basic research but give firms opportunities to exploit new technologies commercially. So, for example, defense contractors have their costs underwritten but retain patents and use the results of research to make profits. This private ownership of property rights also ensures that patents allow firms to exploit a monopoly.

Capitalists also prefer legal forms of governance to control competition. Firms want rules that allow them to cooperate with their competitors to jointly produce new products, share markets, and set prices. Firms also prefer "fair trade" that makes predatory trade practices illegal. Fair trade implies that new entrants into a market cannot engage in predatory practices that might upset a stable set of arrangements. Rent-seeking firms attempt regulatory capture of agencies that control their ability to cooperate and compete. Firms do not want direct government intervention in problems caused by competition because that might result in public ownership of the sector or in one set of firms being favored over another.

Rules of exchange determine who can interact with whom and under what conditions. Regulatory capture would result in the easing of rules of exchange for dominant firms in an industry. To prevent rules from being written for a single firm, capitalists tend to want more general rules. So, for example, regulation that guarantees contracts and payment that provides for restitution if contracts are broken mean that no one has the incentive to cheat. Regulation that ensures product safety and quality prevents some firms from capitalizing on lower standards to sell cheaper products. However, rules of exchange can be used to thwart competitors (particularly foreign ones) by putting up barriers to entry in a given market. If outside firms have to put up bonds, pay tariffs, or meet extraordinary health and safety standards, their products are more expensive and easier to keep out. In this way, rules of exchange may become trade barriers to control competition.

Societies where capitalists are highly politically organized offer opportunities for dominant firms to create conceptions of control to ensure their stability without threat of government intervention. Capture of agencies and regulators who deal with governance structure ensures that arrangements to stabilize any given market may meet with success. In a society dominated by firms, we may expect a few large firms to divide a market in oligopolistic fashion. Competition is tempered by the recognition that if all prosper, all survive. Governments stay out of markets unless incumbent firms begin to fail. Under these conditions, incumbent firms may request government action. But the government's intervention is oriented toward returning conditions of profitability to the industry rather than reorganizing it or taking it over.

Domination of capitalist societies by workers is difficult to imagine. If workers really dominated a capitalist society, it would probably be more adequately described as socialist. If a worker-dominated state could exist in capitalism, it would create policy domains that favored using the government to own firms, protect jobs, and provide extensive benefits for workers. Private property rights would be severely curtailed. This would mean that, except for small businesses, effectively all businesses would be run by the state. Workers as rent seekers would act to preserve jobs and benefits rather than create "efficient" industrial structure. In the context of property rights, they would curtail capitalist social relations and favor state ownership. They would want workers to be represented on boards of directors. They would favor state intervention in competitive processes, particularly where such processes would likely result in the loss of jobs.

Rules of exchange would keep tariffs high and prevent capitalist competition from destroying jobs. Rules of exchange would also be structured to regulate transactions that threatened jobs or health and safety. One could expect extensive rules controlling conditions of work and the health and safety of products. Rules of exchange would make it difficult to import competitive products. Finally, the conception of control that dominated economic life would stress state preservation of jobs. In uneconomic industries, the state would intervene to restore financial strength and minimize job loss. Rules would make it difficult to fire workers and hard to close plants, even those that were clearly uncompetitive.

The socialist societies that have existed have had many of these attributes. Those societies, however, often had state managers who were unconstrained by workers' interests and therefore were able to engage in rent seeking. These societies were often lax in creating health and safety standards for products and work. Groups of workers were frequently exploited for redistribution of resources toward uses favored by state managers, such as defense expenditures. The social democratic countries, particularly in Scandinavia, embody a number of these tendencies of worker-dominated societies as well. But they are not pure cases of domination by workers, as much of the economy remains in private hands.

It is useful to consider how alliances between capitalists, workers, and government officials produce compromises in the structure of policy domains and the institutions that structure markets. I first consider the alliance between government officials and capitalists. In this situation, capitalists are not able to totally dominate the economy but instead must ally with state officials. Two historical trajectories can lead to such an alliance. First, for historical reasons, governments may have strong organizational capacity (Evans 1995). If capitalists are not sufficiently organized (which frequently occurs in the early days of industrialization) to take control of governments, governments can help to organize capitalists. Second, workers resist such attempts by firms to control states completely. If their political actions are turned back, governments and firms can work together to promote a capitalist order to strengthen capitalist control over economic processes. This means that repression of workers usually accompanies a capitalist-state coalition.

Such a compromise gives governments more ability to intervene in market processes and therefore control policy domains. Government bureaucrats can act to organize the interests of a particular sector of the economy if firms fail to do so. Firms try to keep governments from direct intervention and attempt to limit states to regulation. Table 3.1 sums up these arguments, showing that capitalist-state coalitions produce regulation, state-organized development, and worker repression.

Table 3.2 provides an analysis of the implications of this compromise for market institutions. State-led development implies that governments own certain sectors of the economy, such as utilities and finance. They do this because those industries are often essential to development, but often societies lack either capital or expertise to have developed private sectors. They also give government officials levers to control privately held firms. Generally, state-led development is done with limits on public ownership. There are clear rules about the conditions under which governments can intervene in the economy by the direct control of property rights. State-led development also causes governments to regulate competition and cooperation. States may try to protect certain industries in early stages of development, or longer if they are deemed crucial to the national market. At the same time, government officials may encourage firms oriented toward export markets to compete in world markets. Rules of exchange are used in the same way.

Capitalist-state coalitions often tread dangerously close to rent seeking. If powerful national firms ingratiate themselves with government officials, they may obtain official recognition of their status and protective regulation of their position. This means that the state will bail out declining firms or sectors. State officials can decide in the national interest to regulate a sector, and that comes close to equating the dominant firms' interests with the national interest.

Worker-state coalitions characterize some of the social democracies of Western Europe. Table 3.2 suggests that in such states officials organize policy domains but favor the interests of workers rather than capital in policymaking. Governments develop organizational capacities in many industrial sectors to directly intervene in the affairs of private firms in many ways. Extensive state ownership of firms and state protection of workers are likely. If firms begin to fail, governments take them over to protect jobs. Where private firms exist, they are subject to government scrutiny and are forced to adopt strict rules to make it difficult to lay workers off. Workers may also have extensive rights in the governance of the firm as well. Workers may be stakeholders who sit on boards of directors and help decide the strategies of the firm.

Generally, the regulation of competition and cooperation of firms are oriented toward protecting jobs. Governments encourage firms to merge and control competition to save jobs. Rules of exchange also are used to protect jobs. In the case of incumbents failing in an established industry, governments often soften rules to provide incentives for the reorganization of incumbent failing firms.

The final case to consider is a worker-capitalist standoff in society in general. Governments are then called upon to solve crises on a sector-to-sector basis. The nature of the intervention depends on which group has the upper hand in that sector. If no one dominates in a particular sector, groups may compromise, with state officials acting as brokers between sides. Where workers or capitalists are very powerful, they may dominate policy domains. Where both are weak, government officials dominate. Because of the complex politics of these situations, governments tend to have the ability to extensively intervene in economic life. This capacity may give government officials a narrow kind of autonomy, an autonomy that focuses on finding compromises and imposing them in specific situations.

Compromise situations can be stable in that groups maintain vigilance and promote and protect domains most important to their interests. All of the market institutions are open for intervention by state officials, and the form of that intervention reflects the crisis presented to government officials and the relative power of the sides. Governments are likely to own some firms, control the conditions of cooperation and competition, protect some sectors and jobs, and intervene as the particular crisis and the alignment of social forces determine (see Hart 1992 for a similar argument).

Political Structuring of Labor Market Institutions

Like policy domains, labor markets are organized around issues of property rights, governance structures, conceptions of control, and rules of exchange. In the context of labor markets, property rights refer to skills that one can claim in order to make profits. Usually the central issue is the process whereby states, workers, or firms control who can use credentials.

Governance structures refer to rules of social closure whereby groups can control the supply of labor. Credentialing can be used as both a property right and as a mechanism to control competition. If people cannot practice a certain occupation because they lack credentials, this controls labor supply. Rules of exchange concern the conditions under which labor is free to move. Rules of exchange guide hiring, firing, and pay and promotion. In specific labor markets, conceptions of control are such that organized groups structure market processes to benefit their members. Table 3.3 presents ideal-typical arrangements for labor market structures in a society.

Where the state predominates, labor market structures are likely to be nonexistent. The relative power of workers depends on clientelistic ties to governments. This dependence makes it difficult for groups of workers to enforce property rights, as individuals who know the right people may be able to circumvent any control. Neither firms nor workers' organizations can effectively control the supply of labor or the conditions that structure the rules by which firms and workers interact. Clientelistic relations to corrupt governments increase locally either groups of worker or firms that are best able to pay off local governments.

Where firms predominate, they tend to control labor markets. Firms create rules and structures for workers internally that allow them to reward and punish workers at will. Firms prefer workers who are not organized outside of the firm. (Dore 1973; 1997 shows how this works for Japan.) Competitive external labor markets with no minimum wage and few rules give firms the greatest leeway.

Firms may create forms of bureaucratic control to reward with careers workers who are important (Edwards 1979). Firms prefer workers to be disorganized and therefore want to keep property rights out of their control. Unions are weak or nonexistent, and professions are not fully successful at controlling certification. Finally, firms prefer to control work rules and do not want workers to be able to use work rules to affect the terms of exchange.

Workers prefer to control labor markets. Their means of control include strong unions and professions and trades that control certification and the supply of workers. Ideally, workers prefer to be able to offer to firms workers whom the firm has to accept. Thus, the supply of labor is under worker control. Finally, worker-controlled labor markets contain rules of exchange that control the movements of workers for their benefit and restrict firms ability to hire, fire, pay, or promote. Civil service systems that reward seniority and make workers difficult to fire reflect these principles.

Labor market structures that reflect dominance by firms and states allow firms to control many of their affairs but also protect the rights of individuals to get paid, move, or be certified for their credentials. State agencies are on the side of citizens because of an overriding commitment to fair

TABLE 3.3
Implications for Labor Markets of Domination by Different Groups

Dominant Group	Dominant Model of Labor Market	Property Rights	Governance Structures	Rules of Exchange
State as rent seeker	Corrupt	Difficult to attain and exploit	Groups with clientelistic ties can cooperate to attain labor market closure	Groups with clientelistic ties dominate
Capitalists	Firm-controlled labor markets	Unions outlawed/Professions weak	Firms keep labor markets competitive	Workers cannot use work rules to affect closure
Workers	Worker-controlled labor markets	Strong unions/professional/trades control over certification	Labor markets under worker control or closure	Workers prevent free movement of labor
Capitalist-state coalition	Firm-controlled labor markets, but laws protect individuals	Unions regulated; certification by state authorities that might be captured by professions	Labor markets mostly left to firm control; rules to protect individuals	Mostly free movement of labor
Worker-state coalition	Worker-controlled labor markets, but laws protect individuals	Unions powerful; professions and trades control certification under state regulation	Labor markets organized; rules to protect individuals	Workers prevent free movement of labor
Worker-capitalist stand-off; state autonomy	Mixed labor markets, some firm controlled, some worker controlled	Some unions; professions strong in certifying	Some worker controlled, some firm controlled	Movement of labor determined on case-by-case basis

competition and freedom of association. Unions are regulated and are most successful where skills need to be certified. Professions are most successful because of claims of individuals to profit from their training. Labor markets are mostly left to firms to control. Individual workers are offered protection from firms, but collective bargaining is highly regulated. While workers are protected from some forms of discrimination on the job, firms are largely able to hire, fire, promote whom they want and set rates of pay.

Where workers and state officials dominate, workers have a great deal of power in labor markets, but to some degree state officials also protect the rights of firms. This protection takes the form of promoting the rights of owners and managers as individuals to use their property as they see fit. Unions and professional associations are powerful and able to control certification of workers. While unions are able to organize workers, they have limited control over firms' hiring practices, and thus unions do not attain full closure over labor markets. State bureaucracies are organized to protect workers rights but also pay attention to the rights of managers and employers who are also citizens.

Where neither firms nor workers dominate a society's labor market, one expects many different arrangements across industries. Some labor markets are controlled by workers, others by firms. Some groups of workers attain the ability to certify workers and restrict competition among them; other groups of workers do not.

Policy Domains and Market Regulation in Real Societies

Real societies do not exhibit any one form of organization. This is because groups rarely control all institutions, and even more rarely are they able to do so over time because of the historical layering of governments' capacities for intervention in their economies. So, for example, one set of political and economic crises may lead to the triumph of capitalist-oriented political parties, which then limit the ability of both government officials and workers to regulate some economic feature of the society. But a subsequent crisis may sweep in a new political coalition more representative of workers' interests that expands the number of policy domains and the capacities of government officials for regulation and intervention on behalf of workers' interests.

The United States is the purest case of a society in which capitalist firms are able to use the policy domains of the state for their own interest. Government generally lacks the capacity to directly intervene, and, when it organizes domains or sectors, it is regulatory. Regulation of financial, ownership, and labor markets is minimal, almost always in the interest of firms, and is often captured by the leading firms in a sector. As for the property rights of firms, the United States is organized to maximize shareholder (i.e., those who own the stock) value (see chap. 7).

The United States is not a pure system. In terms of issues of governance, U.S. competition laws have traditionally prevented cooperation between firms, decreasing the power of firms to control markets directly (Fligstein 1990). Recently, however, these rules have been relaxed, and U.S. firms are being allowed to enter joint ventures with their major competitors, suggesting that even these limited rules of governance have tilted toward firms. The U.S. system of rules of exchange is a victory for capitalist firms. Rules protect such industries as textiles, sugar, and, for a while, automobiles and steel, while promoting exports by firms doing business on an international scale, such as manufacturers of computers or airframes.

Recognizing the degree to which American firms dominate the creation of market institutions and the regulation of those institutions helps make sense of two sorts of phenomena. When considering what market institutions may come out of a particular crisis, one must always bear in mind that government will tend to intervene to protect capitalist interests. Thus, analyses of market crises should begin and end with understanding that governments intervene for incumbents so as to preserve private capital. A comparison of market institutions across societies and of the responses by governments to similar crises shows that the U.S. federal government always acts to preserve and enhance firms, while other governments may pursue policies oriented toward protecting other social groups.

Japan appears to be a case where capitalists and state officials share control over the policy domains of the economy. The Japanese economy is organized to protect small business and agriculture in the home market while supporting big business in exporting around the world (Dore 1973, 1997). This set of relations may appear to be an example of dominance by capitalists, as in the U.S. model. But government officials have had the power historically to intervene in product markets directly, and, in particular, to direct investment toward firms engaged in exporting. MITI has directed capitalist development when the capitalists themselves have not been strong enough to do it (Evans 1995). The government has been deeply involved with directing investment and controlling trade (Johnson 1982). Business is also powerful, having local markets protected and being able to cooperate across firms (Aoki 1988; Gerlach 1992). Workers have been systematically disorganized by the Japanese government since the early 1950s (Dore 1973). In the economic crisis of the 1990s, the Japanese government tried many strategies to promote a recovery. It propped up banks and injected huge amounts of money into public infrastructure projects. It did not force a reorganization in the keiretsu structure, the families of firms with interlocking ties of ownership across different industries.

The Scandinavian welfare states appear to be the real societies closest to the ideal type of dominance of workers with the assistance of state actors. Governments own some firms, although important parts of the economy remain privately held. The economies are export-oriented but internal consumption is heavily regulated to protect the internal markets and jobs. Wages and benefits are high, and inequality is low. The government intervenes in many features of economic life (Lawrence and Spybey 1986), mostly to protect workers and save jobs. There are extensive work rules, unemployment benefits, and health benefits. Governments legislate paid vacations, sick pay, and maternity leave (Esping-Anderson 1990). If firms lay workers off, governments attempt to retrain workers and find them new jobs. An extensive public sector engages in public works as well.

The German system is a political compromise between capital and labor, although, in many domains, labor appears to have the upper hand. Officials in the federal German government have relatively little capacity to organize policy domains or directly intervene in industrial sectors (Ziegler 1997). The German states, called Lander, do have more capacity to intervene in labor markets and product markets. Many of the Lander own stock in their largest firms. With employers they organize the training of workers and the retraining of workers if industries decline. Until recently, workers and firms were organized into large corporatist organizations that settled many important economic issues (Streeck 1984, 1995). Workers sit on boards of directors and are involved in firms' decision making (Lane 1989; Kocka 1980; Cable, Palfrey, and Runge 1980). Extensive labor market protections are in place. Workers enjoy countrywide collective bargaining. They also have generous benefits.

While German firms are subject to more collective arrangements than in Japan or the United States, there is less public ownership of firms in Germany than in Scandinavia. A number of private large and extremely diversified corporations, such as Daimler-Chrysler, exist. A large number of much smaller firms, are oriented toward market niches and export (Herrigel, 1996). Firms are allowed to cooperate in markets that involve foreign trade. The core of the German economy is export oriented and privately held.

The French system has produced an interesting hybrid that may have the strongest control by state actors of any of the OECD countries. One of its most interesting features is a highly interventionist government. One could argue that French society fits the ideal-typical model in which capitalists and workers are balanced and the state plays an autonomous role vis-à-vis both groups (Crozier 1973). This standoff means that the French state intervenes on whichever side has the most power in a particular domain.

The French government, historically, has owned firms, directed investment, and controlled the financial system. It underwrites research, and the top of the French management system has a symbiotic relationship with the government (Green 1986; Barsoux and Lawrence 1990; Bourdieu 1996; Djelic 1998). French workers also have extensive welfare benefits and work rules. The government responds to crises in various sectors by direct intervention. If workers are more organized, then the state builds policy domains and organizational capacity to aid workers. The policy domains of the French government appear to be dominated by the interests of workers. But state officials have set themselves up as cadres with similar social background and educational credentials (Bourdieu 1997; Boltanski 1987). This implies that government officials are somewhat independent of workers' interests.

The ideal types just described can be used to make sense of the policy styles and domains of existing capitalist societies. Once those styles are characterized, it is possible to predict what kind of new state capacity is likely to be built in a political or economic crisis. So, for instance, government intervention into market processes is more likely in France or Scandinavia than in the United States or Great Britain. Since workers are much less protected from market crises in the United States, one expects them to bear the brunt of market crises more systematically.[2] This means that the same economic crisis will be met with entirely different policy responses by different governments. So, for example, the slow economic growth of the 1970s was met in the United States by public policies that favored deregulation of the economy, while the French and German governments were more concerned to ensure social solidarity and protect benefits and workers' rights. One important result was that income inequality increased substantially in the United States while it changed little in France, Germany, and Scandinavia.

Over time, crises tend to reinforce a given set of institutional rules and build organizational capacity of a certain variety. Even in the era of so-called globalization, national political systems continue to matter. Groups of capitalists and workers interpret crises in terms similar to those they have been using all along. When they go to established policy domains, they expect the existing configuration of power and style of intervention to produce an accurate interpretation of the crisis and a solution. So, in the United States, every economic crisis calls forth the response to deregulate and to reduce government and worker influence, while in France, government officials are called upon to act in the "public interest."

Stability and Complexity

Recently, Chandler, Amatori, and Hikino (1997) have compiled a volume of papers oriented toward understanding the role of big business in economic growth. They assert that big business has been the engine of economic growth across capitalist societies because of the investments managers make in economies of scale and scope. Their argument is that societies where there are large firms have experienced sustained economic growth, while societies that have not managed to create large corporations have less growth. The central problem with the argument is that the papers in the volume, which consider various societies in Western Europe, Asia, and North America, reach a remarkable conclusion that is at odds with the central assertion of the editors. The most important factors for long-term economic growth appear to be stable state-society political arrangements, formal mediation of class struggle between workers and capitalists, and a history free from war, invasion, or victimization by imperialism (Fligstein 1998). Large corporations, from the perspective of most of the papers, are endogenous to this process.

This conclusion, of course, dovetails nicely with the political-cultural approach. Capitalist development depends on the production of stable institutions and the creation of solid frameworks to guide the interactions between workers, capitalists, and states. I would like to develop this insight more explicitly.

Proposition 3.1. Sustained capitalist economic growth requires the political resolution of worker-owner-state conflicts and the creation of rules to govern those conflicts by producing property rights, governance structures, and rules of exchange.

The literature on comparative capitalisms has shown us that there are many ways to attain these stable forms. In some societies, capitalists dominate, while in others, workers or state managers play a stronger role. The degree to which this domination spills over into the logic of employment systems explains how jobs are created and how far workers are able to influence rates of pay. I want to make a strong assertion here. Unless there is substantial rent-seeking, all of these possible patterns of relative strength produce stable institutional conditions for economic growth over the long term.

Now the central claim of economics is that there are more or less efficient ways to set up institutions to promote economic growth. It is correct in that, at certain extremes where rent seeking is unchecked, we are less likely to observe positive outcomes. For example, in African, Middle Eastern, and some Asian societies (India and Pakistan) in the past 30 years, rent seeking has constricted economic growth. Economics has a tougher case to make where institutions are more socially balanced. I want to argue that once stable institutions are in play, their impact on highly aggregate outcomes such as long-term economic growth and employment growth may be similar, regardless of the particulars of the institutions.

The basic idea for economists is that societies make institutional trade-offs between the efficient allocation of resources and the equitable distribution of goods and services. But the empirical evidence for this assertion is difficult to gather. Economists who study long-term economic growth are often struck by the importance of state investments in infrastructure, education, and political stability (Barro 1990; Maddison 1995; Aschauer 1990; North 1990). While we can examine rates such as GDP per capita as long-term measures of economic growth, it is difficult to show that differences in such rates result from different institutions. So, if one examined economic growth in Germany from 1950 to 1975, one might conclude that the German system, which favored workers, was more efficient than the American system, which favored capital. If one examined economic growth from 1990 until 2000, one might view American institutions as more effective. Of course, one could only draw this conclusion if one ignored the costs of German unification and the decision to create the single currency in Europe.

It is very difficult to assess the relative effects of institutional arrangements when they change relatively infrequently and economies go through business and political cycles that affect economic growth according to their own dynamics. This does not prevent scholars and policymakers from engaging in comparative institutional analysis on the basis on long-term economic growth. For example, edited volumes by Berger and Dore (1996), Boyer and Drache (1996), Crouch and Streeck (1997), and Hart's monograph (1992) start with the idea that one can assess the relative effects of economic institutions on economic growth. But the analytical weaknesses do suggest that consumers of such analyses should take them with a grain of salt.

This is the lesson the political-cultural approach offers reformers in developing societies, particularly the formerly socialist societies. The critical problem for these societies is to build reasonable political coalitions between workers, capitalists, and governments that reflect the real concerns of the organized forces in those societies. Those groups must help produce legitimate states that have the capacity to intervene in market processes in order to produce stable outcomes for firms and workers. Without the building of such a political consensus, these societies may be doomed to long periods of rent seeking on the part of government officials or former government officials who control the largest firms. Economic growth is not just a matter of freeing up prices and unfettering markets. It is a matter of creating rules of stable interaction such that rent seeking is avoided, exchange is possible, and varied groups are represented.

There is much political pressure (particularly from Western agencies such as the World Bank and the IMF) on developing societies to favor capitalist interests over worker interests. But it is not totally clear that this has been the surest path to economic development. The history of development of the industrial societies shows that as development proceeded and democracy spread, political parties that reflected the interests of workers became more prevalent. These political parties were the strongest in Western Europe, and they helped create more equal and just societies. The overall effect of these reforms on long-term economic growth is difficult to measure. The most important features to promote economic growth appear to be related mostly to the production of rules and laws that did not allow extreme forms of rent seeking on anyone's part and investments in physical and social infrastructure. Redistributive policies that produced, for example, more equal income distributions and universal pensions and health care do not appear to have negatively affected long-term economic growth in societies that were more developed.

The political-cultural approach supplies scholars interested in economic growth with insight into the forms of stability and instability in modern market economies. The political and institutional stability of societies plays a huge role in their economic stability. Governments in industrial societies play a role in investment and mediating the class struggle as well. The actions of managers and entrepreneurs are framed around these forms of stability. They can create new industries using government support to invest in uncertain technologies. They can diversify their risks in their firms to produce stable identities for firms.

Implications for Research

Three sorts of studies are suggested by the political-cultural approach. First, scholars may focus on the political processes that generate particular market institutions and the roles of various groups in those processes in a given society. This type of work examines the production of particular laws, shared agreements over ways to intervene and regulate market processes, or the decision-making process by which laws are interpreted by courts. Many excellent studies exist that consider such political decision-making processes (Thorelli 1955; Evans 1995; Ziegler 1997).

One may also extend the model to analyze trade agreements between societies. The World Trade Organization, NAFTA, and the European Union all require agreements over economic rules for exchange. Therefore, they can be analyzed according to what kind of rules have been written (property rights, governance structures, rules of exchange) and which groups have had the largest say in their nature (for such an analysis of the European Union's Single Market Program, see Fligstein and Mara-Drita 1996).

Second, studies may focus on the emergence, stability, or transformation of a particular market, holding constant market institutions. This kind of work has already produced rich understandings of particular industries (for examples, see Baker, Faulkner, and Fisher 1998 for advertising; Baker 1984 for the Chicago Board of Trade; Podolny 1993 for investment bankers;

Baker and Faulkner 1991 for Hollywood producers; Uzzi 1997 for clothing manufacturers; and Biggart and Guillén 1999 for automobile manufacturers). In the next chapter I provide some tools for analyzing transformation of particular markets and offer examples of these processes.

A third set of questions is also opened by the political-cultural approach. One of the most important tasks is to offer analytic tools that bring together action in a particular market or set of markets and political institution-building. Interactions between these two domains work in two ways. First, a given market-building process can feed into policymaking, thereby shaping the production of institutions. Once large firms emerge in capitalist economies, how do they compete and cooperate? Economic crises caused by the oversupply of goods drive firms to try to control competition. Government interventions to produce governance structures follow. Across societies, the political responses to crises produced by too much competition have resulted in different solutions depending on the relative power of social actors.

In the United States, for example, the Sherman Act (1890) prohibited cartels as restraints of trade, but did not prohibit large firms from controlling huge market shares and using their size to threaten competitors (Fligstein 1990). By 1896, cartels were illegal, but joining together the assets of a large number of competitors was not. It is not surprising that the major participants in the 1898–1904 merger movement engaged in the horizontal integration of their industries. This joining of production became an accepted tactic to deal with competition.

This is a way in which political institutions and actions in markets interrelate second. Preexisting market institutions determine what possibilities exist for entrepreneurs organizing new markets. These institutions open up new opportunities and foreclose others. If governments set tariffs to protect particular industries, other industries are tempted to get governments to do the same for them. Alternatively, government policies can have unintended consequences. So, for example, a government policy that defines legal and illegal forms of competition forecloses opportunities to form conceptions of control based on illegal forms of competition. It does not end the search for conceptions of control but pushes the owners and managers of firms to find new ways to control their problems of instability. We have studies of how changing the rules for an industry has greatly affected the founding and survival of new organizations (Ranger-Moore, Banaszak-Hull, and Hannan 1991 on the insurance industry; Haveman and Rao 1997 on banks). Djelic (1998) has done a fascinating study of the use of the Marshall Plan to push European governments to reorganize their largest firms after World War II.

Another spectacular example of this process in the United States is the so-called separation of ownership and control that operates in the largest corporations. Currently, agency theorists in economics argue that the separation of ownership from control exists because it is the most efficient way to organize property rights (see, for instance, Fama and Jensen 1983a). Yet Mark Roe (1994) has shown that the separation between ownership and control in the United States was primarily a political, not an economic, project. During the Great Depression of the 1930s, the widespread economic crisis brought the federal government to change the laws regulating which economic activities banks, brokerage firms, and insurance companies could engage in. Banks had to choose between lending money and owning firms. Brokerage firms had to focus on selling securities. Insurance companies were kept from holding controlling positions in firms.

These rule changes were an effort to prevent bank failures. They were also motivated by populist concerns with the concentration of ownership and wealth. Roe (1994) documents that the development of large equity and debt markets subsequently was the outcome of firms' search for capital. Since federal regulators would not allow firms to be owned by banks or other financial organizations, firms were forced to find other ways to raise funds. Roe argues that part of the reason the United States developed sophisticated capital markets in the postwar era was because there was a huge demand for capital, yet relatively high interest rates offered by banks.

The connections between states and markets depends on where one cuts into a particular market process. It is, of course, possible to study market processes without reference to governments and the more general rules that enable firms to exist. But analysts always need to be sensitive to the role of governments in the formation of new markets. Governments can provide funding for new technologies, underwrite standards, produce regulation with intended and unintended consequences, and engage in many forms of direct and indirect intervention.

If one is focusing on some innovation in market rules, then one studies how crises in markets spilled over into politics. One is interested in which groups supported what project and which group won out. Alternatively, if one is interested in how sets of rules enabled or constrained subsequent market actors, one sees how rules were interpreted by entrepreneurs to produce new markets or transform existing ones.

Conclusion

When scholars observe the structuring of product, capital, and labor markets across industries and societies, they are struck by the plethora of arrangements. I argue that this variety reflects two forces: one historical and the other systemic. Because of their unique trajectories and entry into capitalism, societies have found different ways to organize their property rights, governance structures, and rules of exchange. While there are real cultural differences at work in different societies, I want to argue that many of the differences reflect the particular power arrangements that exist as societies enter industrialization. The relative power of state, capitalist, or worker groups as state building proceeded is inscribed in government capacity and in who the benefits from a certain set of arrangements. Arrangements that favor one group over another promote the life chances of that group and work to disorganize others. In "normal" times, the crises of a given society are in fact the crises of whoever has privilege at the moment. Those in power use the mechanisms they have developed to maintain that power.

Only in a more widespread societal crisis (war, depression) does the possibility for real institutional reform occur. This is because the current power arrangements and the rules that support them are no longer able to reproduce those groups. New social groups can be swept into power and create new government capacity, oriented toward their interests and interventions in their favor. These new groups create domains that overlay or replace existing ones. Market organization is thus a mix of the historical and the political. The chosen solutions for organizing for markets depend on who writes the rules and how these rules help a given set of actors.

But rules can have unintended consequences. New social groups may use rules in ways their framers did not intend. These new actors may then push for modernization of the rules under the guise of making the old rules relevant for new circumstances. Thus, new rules can reflect an unusual mixture of the past and present. They constrain and reinforce systems of power but also enable new social actors and eventually may be transformed to serve in new contexts. Rules can be borrowed, not just from one's own society, but across societies. As markets integrate across national borders, new conceptions of control become possible. These conceptions can be borrowed for use in existing national markets as well.

Modern markets defined as structured exchange are difficult to imagine without the existence of modern governments. Governments are implicated in modern capitalist economies in two ways. First, their current policy domains are constituted to intervene, regulate, or mediate in product, capital, and labor markets. These structures are not innocent but bear the marks of control by dominant social groups. Thus, in economic crises, organized groups of firms or workers quickly take their grievances to governments if their group controls the domain.

Second, rules and understandings built around property rights, governance structures, rules of exchange, and conceptions of control create the possibility for new markets to emerge by providing social-organizational vehicles for entrepreneurs to take advantage of selling new products. This implies a somewhat more passive role for governments, but it is important nonetheless. Accepted rules by which entrepreneurs can be organized and legally defined means to control competitors give entrepreneurs the chance to exploit opportunities to capture profits. It is to the building of market structures that I now turn.

4

The Theory of Fields and the Problem of Market Formation

MY GOAL in this chapter is to develop a general sociological view that makes sense of social structures in a particular market (for a compatible approach, see Baker et al. 1998). This requires two main elements: (1) a sociological model of action that describes what entrepreneurs and managers try to do in a market, and (2) a theory of market formation based on the theory of fields. I use this conceptual framework to develop propositions about the dynamics of the formation, stability, and transformation of markets.

I then use this framework to explore the production of stable markets and market institutions in the United States and some of the current efforts to construct market society in the former socialist countries. I take up the question of what it means to say that a market is globalized from the perspective developed here and consider what the implications are for the problem of forming globalized market institutions. Finally, I consider how, as market society grows and expands, economies become more stable as firms diversify and markets multiply.

Markets as Fields

Most key insights of the sociology of markets have been framed as reactions to neoclassical economic views of the functioning of markets. White (1981) suggested that stable production markets were possible only if actors took one another into account in their behavior, contrary to the basic assumption of the neoclassical economic view, which stresses anonymity of actors. Granovetter (1985) extended this argument, suggesting that all forms of economic interaction were centered in social relations, what he called the "embeddedness of markets." Various scholars have presented evidence that market embeddedness produces effects that economic models cannot predict (Burt 1983; Zelizar 1983; Baker 1984; Fligstein 1990; Uzzi 1996, 1999; Baker, Faulkner, and Fisher 1998).

The empirical literature has failed to clarify the precise theoretical nature of the social embeddedness of markets. Granovetter (1985) argues that network relatedness is the most important construct. Burt (1983) proposes that networks stand in for resource dependence. Podolny (1993) uses networks as a cause and consequence of the creation of a status hierarchy. Uzzi (1996, 1997, 1999) and Gulati and Gargiulo (1999) have focused on trust relations in repeated market transactions. Fligstein (1990) and Fligstein and Brantley (1992) argue that the social relations within and across firms and their more formal relations to the state are pivotal to understanding how stable markets emerge. Campbell and Lindberg (1990) and Campbell, Hollingsworth, and Lindberg (1991) take a similar approach and focus on the emergence of what they call "governance structures" in industries. Institutional theory in the organizational literature implies that institutional entrepreneurs create new sets of social arrangements in organizational fields with the aid of powerful organized interests, both inside and outside of the state (DiMaggio 1988; DiMaggio and Powell 1991).

These latter perspectives have been buttressed by studies on comparative industrial organization (Hamilton and Biggart 1988; Chandler 1990; Gerlach 1992; Whitley 1992; Wade 1990; Amsden 1989; Dyas and Thanheiser 1976; Mueller 1980; Stokman, Ziegler, and Scott 1985; the papers in Chandler, Amatori, and Hikino 1997) that show how state-firm interactions in various societies produce unique cultures of production. Industrial countries are not converging toward a single form (Fligstein and Freeland 1995). Instead a plurality of social relations structures markets within and across societies. These observations have challenged the neoclassical economists' view that markets select efficient forms that, over time, converge to a single form.[1]

To push this debate forward, I want to develop a new view from the existing literature. The basic insight is to consider structured exchange (i.e., markets) as a field. The social structure of a field is a cultural construction whereby dominant and dominated coexist under a set of understandings about what makes one set of organizations dominant. This is similar to what Podolny (1993) has called a "status hierarchy." The interactions of firms are cultural constructions that are understood by participants. Both are locked in a "game" in which the goal of dominant actors is to reproduce their advantage and the goal of the dominated is to either directly challenge the dominators or accept a lesser role, albeit one in which the dominated too are reproduced on a period-to-period basis.

To apply the theory of fields to markets, one must focus on the behaviors of the organizations that produce the goods or services in the market. The incumbent firms are defined as those who dominate the field by being big, defining the product, and undertaking moves to reproduce their position vis-à-vis smaller, challenger firms. The basic idea is that the price mechanism in a given market (i.e., the balance of supply and demand) tends to destabilize all firms in a market. This is because it encourages all firms to undercut the prices of other firms, and this threatens the financial stability of firms.

The goal for dominant firms is to provide a set of understandings for themselves about how to cope with this potential destabilization. Firms frame their behavior vis-à-vis one another with the goals of convincing incumbent firms not to directly challenge one another and of ensuring that challenger firms decide not to compete directly over prices. The social structures of markets are, therefore, fundamentally systems of power whereby incumbent (dominant) firms use tactics and strategies to stabilize themselves and reproduce their position over challenger (dominated) firms.

From this perspective, the networks formed among customers and suppliers and among competitors function to solve the problems of competition and uncertainty for firms. They provide information on the behavior of other firms. In the case of long-term supplier relations, they ensure that suppliers do not defect to competitors. They also ensure that suppliers remain favorable to long-term customers. In the case of alliances or joint ventures between competitors, they link the fortunes of firms together. This interdependence has the effect of stabilizing outcomes for firms that might normally be competitors and reduces the competition between them (Gulati and Gargiulo 1999; Kogut, Shan, and Walker 1992).

These tactics and strategies are not always successful at preventing price competition. Stable markets do not always emerge, and firms can always challenge one another by cutting prices. But firms' tactics to control competition are not limited to holding prices at a given level, as they are in neoclassical economics. Many kinds of strategic games can be played by incumbent firms or coalitions of firms to gain advantage and stabilize their situations.

Two related sets of social relations, what can be called "control projects" (White 1992), are implicated in market building. First, a firm's internal power struggle must be resolved. The internal power struggle is about who controls the organization, how it is organized, and how ongoing situations in the product market are analyzed. Second, actors in incumbent and challenger firms must recognize the social stabilizing effects of the current relations between firms. This understanding structures their interactions by providing them with interpretations of other firms' behavior (White 1981).

The winners of the internal power struggle are those with a compelling vision of how to make the firm work internally and how to interact with the firm's main competitors. I introduced the idea of a "conception of control" to summarize this worldview and the real social relations that exist between firms. In this way, a conception of control is a story about what the organization is and its location vis-à-vis its principal competitors. It is also an interpretive frame used to interpret and justify actions vis-à-vis others.

The production of market institutions is a cultural project in two ways. Property rights, governance structures, conceptions of control, and rules of exchange define the social institutions necessary to make markets. These organizing technologies provide actors with tools to engage in market activity. Market worlds are social worlds; therefore, they operate according to principles like other social worlds. Actors engage in political actions vis-à-vis one another that reflect local cultures that and define social relations, who is an actor, and how actors can interpret one another's behavior (Geertz 1983).

The Goal of Action in Stable Markets

The purpose of action in a given market is to create and maintain a stable world within the firm and produce social relationships across firms in order to allow them to survive. Dominant firms set the rules and agendas for others. Challenger firms can help their survival by finding ways to fit into the dominant scheme. I have defined conceptions of control as understandings that structure perceptions of how a market works and allow actors to interpret their world, and as the real social relations that produce that world.

The key insight of the perspective I propose here is that there are two forms of potential sources of instability in markets: (1) the tendency of firms to undercut one another's prices, and (2) the problem of keeping the firm together as a political coalition (March 1962). Market actors try to control sources of instability to promote the survival of their firm (see Baker, Faulkner, and Fisher 1998 for an example).

The goal of a conception of control is to erect social understandings whereby firms can avoid direct price competition and can solve their internal political problems.[2] These challenges are related, and the solution to one is often part of the solution to the other. Actors in the firm who can claim to stabilize the relations of the firm to its principal competitors argue that their version of how the firm should work internally is the cause of the firm's success.

My major point is not to suggest that competitive processes do not matter to market structure or survival of firms. Nor am I saying that the control projects of actors in firms are always successful. Price competition always has the potential to undermine market structures. In some classically competitive markets, such as restaurants and barber shops, stability has never emerged.

My point, rather, is that we can get a great deal of analytic leverage over what is going on in a particular market if we assume that entrepreneurs and managers construct their actions so as to avoid price competition and stabilize their position vis-à-vis other competitors. This effort involves attempts to co-opt different kinds of resource dependencies, such as the need to find out information about what competitors are doing and maintain relations to key suppliers and customers. But the effort also involves positioning one's firm vis-à-vis one's principal competitors. Even in markets that are highly competitive, actors try to differentiate their products to form niches to protect themselves from price competition (for example, restaurants serving high-priced California cuisine, or hamburger chains; see White 1981 for a compelling mathematical demonstration). My claim is not that actors in firms are always successful at creating stable shelters from price competition, but that the price mechanisms in markets push them to do so. In markets, the goal of action is to ensure the survival of the firm. It is very difficult for actors to know a priori if a given set of actions will stabilize a firm's market position vis-à-vis its competitors. Put rhetorically, no actor can determine which behaviors will maximize profits (either a priori or post hoc), and action is therefore directed toward the creation of stable worlds.

Issues of internal organization revolve around producing stable (reproducible) social relations. The intraorganizational power struggle is about actors within the organization making claims to solve the "critical" organizational problems (Pfeffer 1981; March 1962). Actors need to have a coherent view of organizing that allows them to simplify their decision-making processes. Those actors that convince or defeat others are able to define, analyze, and solve problems in their own terms. They will also be the leaders of the organization (Fligstein 1987). Once in place in a market, the conception of control dominating the market figures into how the leaders of firms operate to structure its corporate culture.

Conceptions of control function in two ways. They define the nature of the social relations between incumbent and challenger firms. In this way, they are a local set of understandings about who is powerful and why. They also function as cognitive frames through which the leaders of the firm interpret the actions of others. This means that a given strategic move of a competitor is interpreted in terms of the relationship between two firms (i.e., who is an incumbent and who is a challenger) and more broadly within the framing of how the market works.

There are a large number of possible conceptions of control because the unique history of markets means that clever entrepreneurs and managers can produce myriad cultural solutions to their collective problems of price competition. To understand a given conception of control, one must have practical knowledge of a particular market. Although conceptions of control are often unique, it is possible to note that firms liberally borrow conceptions of control from other markets, particularly nearby ones. Thus, markets founded at a similar moment in time are likely to use similar conceptions of control.

It is useful to consider an example. One common conception of control in high-technology markets is the attempt to make one's product an industry standard. This is a tricky thing to do. If one tries to be too proprietary about creating a particular standard, other firms will resist. In order to produce a standard, one must make the standard open to all potential users. A firm that is fortunate enough to have its technology be adopted as the industry standard can be characterized as having a kind of monopoly. Where did the idea for this conception of control come from?

Before 1980, the personal computer industry was fragmented. The most dominant firm was Apple Computer, which had a proprietary operating system and computer chip running the machine. IBM decided to enter the market for personal computers. In order to get to market as quickly as possible, they decided to buy computer chips and an operating system from other suppliers. IBM's choice on entry had several unintended consequences. First, by entering the personal computer market, IBM legitimated these machines for business use. This meant that what had been essentially a small market for hobbyists all of a sudden became a large market. Second, because they chose to enter the market using technologies that were owned by other firms, they quickly spawned an industry of "clones." At the core of this new industry were the producers of the operating system, Microsoft, and of the main computer chip that functioned as the brain of the machine, Intel. Both Microsoft and Intel sold their products to whoever wanted to buy them. Microsoft and Intel became the standards for anyone wanting to make hardware or software for the personal computer. The huge growing market and the proliferation of firms involved in various aspects of the market meant that the Microsoft operating system and the Intel computer chips were in an outstanding position to dominate these markets.

It was never IBM's intention to make Intel or Microsoft into industry standards. This was an unintended consequence of the way the market evolved. Apple Computer with its proprietary operating system and computer chip was not able to compete with the open architecture of IBM and its clones, and the firm has been relegated to a small niche in the overall market. The lesson that high-technology firms have taken away from this case is that trying to become an industry standard by licensing or selling your technology to anyone is a conception of control that leads to success. Trying to dominate the market by maintaining strict control over a technology is likely to lead to others finding a product with more open standards. This is now the "conventional wisdom" that can be used to organize new technology markets (Edstrom 1998). It is a conception of control that came from experience that can now be mobilized to organize new markets.

Firms can move into existing markets and impose successful conceptions of control on other firms. I have argued that merger movements can be understood in this way (1990, chap. 7). During the 1960s, for example, financial managers realized that they could increase the size and diversity of their firm by purchasing other firms. During the period 1965–67, fully 40% of the assets of the five hundred largest corporations were bought up. In essence, firms either became merger targets or else pursued other firms in order to avoid being a target. This financial conception of control came to dominate the world of large corporations in the United States. Davis and Thompson (1994) and Stearns and Allan (1996) make the argument that mergers in the 1980s were a kind of social movement that reorganized the world of the largest corporations, an argument I take up in chapter 7.

In spite of the historical uniqueness of conceptions of control, it is possible to understand the general strategies that firms use to cooperate with competitors in order to share markets. Cartels, publicized prices, barriers to entry, limited production, patents, licensing agreements, and joint ventures in marketing and production are all tactics that firms use to divide markets. One way to produce stable markets is to get the state to intervene to restrict competition. Involving the state in regulation or protective legislation that increases the odds of survival is a normal strategy for dominant firms. Finally, forming relations through networks to principal suppliers, customers, or competitors gives firms the opportunity to co-opt their world (Gulati and Gargiulo 1999; Kogut, Shan, and Walker, 1992). Such networks give firms access to information and secure valued inputs and outputs.

Actors use two internal principles of organization to indirectly control competition: (1) integration and (2) diversification, which, in large firms, is often accompanied by producing multiple divisions in the organization. Integration can be vertical (the merger of suppliers or customers) or horizontal (the merger with competitors). Vertical integration prevents others from threatening valued inputs or outputs. Spot contracting for inputs suggests that there is ample supply of valued inputs. But if that supply is threatened, firms can switch from spot contracting to long-term network relations, and, if those fail, they can engage in acquisitions.

Similarly, firms can continue to directly compete with their main rivals. They can also try various means of co-optation, such as forming joint product alliances or else pursuing nonprice forms of competition. The integration or merger of a large share of an industry means that a few firms can control the market by tacitly agreeing not to threaten one another's position through a price war. Firms in these situations often publicly announce pricing and production decisions so that other firms can follow suit (what an economist would recognize as an oligopoly).

Diversification implies entering new markets to increase the probability of the firm's survival. It begins with the differentiation of a single product on the basis of quality or price (White 1981). To the degree that firms do not compete because their products differ, price competition does not threaten firms' existence.[3] As I already noted, this explains why small firms, such as restaurants, specialize according to cuisine and price.

A firm can produce multiple products that reduce their dependence on any one product and, hence, increase the likelihood that the firm will survive (Kay 1997). This practice allows the firm to grow larger, which increases its stability as well. Firms search for new markets because huge gains can accrue to the first mover in a growing market. Such gains help stabilize the firm. If markets fail to materialize or market conditions deteriorate, a diversified firm can exit a failed market without threat to the larger corporate entity (Kay 1997). On the other hand, the production of multiple products introduces internal control problems, and actors are constantly reorganizing around variations of the holding company and multidivisional form (Fligstein 1985; Prechel 1994).

My perspective may seem antithetical to two perspectives that dominate the current literature on business firms: organizational population ecology and the literature that emphasizes organizational learning or adaptation. Organizational population ecology argues that competition produces selection pressure on firms and that many fail (Hannan and Freeman 1989). My argument is not that firms do not fail in spite of the best intentions of managers. Nor is my argument that "control" projects always work. My main idea is to examine market processes by trying to understand what owners and managers of firms try to do in the face of competition. If they succeed, they do so in the face of selection processes and competition. What my framework is intended to explain is exactly what kinds of tactics are available to managers and owners and which ones work (or don't work!). When we see a stable market with social relations, we can study its history to understand which tactics were attempted and which succeeded.

The other main thrust in the literature focuses on processes of organizational learning and the role of networks within firms and across firms in this endeavor (for example, see the papers in Nohria and Eccles 1992; Kogut, Shan, and Walker 1992; Powell and Brantley 1992). The idea of organizational learning often reflects an ideological stance. It suggests that actions of firms to scan their environments and make adjustments in their products and processes are an adaptation to market conditions (see Gulati and Gargiulo 1999 for example). But one can easily make the case that much of this learning is more focused on mitigating the effects of competition. So, for example, joint ventures are not only an opportunity for learning about a new production process but an attempt to co-opt potential competitors.

Powell and Brantley (1992) have postulated that the network and alliance structure present at the founding of the biotechnology industry were a form of "learning." One could easily interpret those relationships as risk spreading and information gathering. Alliances are a form of risk spreading or product diversification whereby firms do not put all of their eggs in one basket. By cooperating with competitors, one competes less, by definition. By sharing information, one finds out where opportunities are and what opportunities have been foreclosed. Thus, this learning can easily be interpreted as an attempt to find ways to stabilize one's environment.

Another example is provided by Uzzi (1999), who shows how firms form relationships to various financial organizations and that, once relationships are established, firms are able to raise capital more readily. I would argue that this pattern shows the co-optation of suppliers and the attempt on the part of managers and owners to control their future by securing supplies of capital. These actions affect the stability of the firm that receives financing, but it also could affect the fortunes of firms that did not receive financing. In this case, networks help co-opt a resource dependence. But for firms that fail to secure relationships with financial organizations, their legitimacy is undermined. Either way, these financial relationships can be interpreted as a stabilizing tactic.

Conceptions of control refer to broader cultural conceptions in which these tactics are embedded. Actors in two different firms may use product diversification, but one may view it as diversifying the financial portfolio (a financial perspective), while the other may see it as carrying a full line of goods (a marketing perspective) (Fligstein 1990). Conceptions of control also allow actors to interpret the meaning of a particular strategic move by competitors. Actors stick with the conception of control they believe works. After some period of time, others, in either a given market or related markets, recognize some key set of factors and begin to imitate them. But these factors are rarely articulated before the fact; they become accepted only after they operate to produce stability for some firms. Such tactics and conceptions create cultural stories that can be used over and over again to justify an action or produce a new one.

The Problem of Change and Stability in Markets

There are three phases in market formation: emergence, stability, and crisis.[4] My concern is to specify how actors' perceptions of the current social structure affects the tactics they use to seek stability for their firms. In any market, participants can usefully be distinguished in terms of their size relative to their market. Large firms control more external resources than small firms, including pricing from suppliers, financial assistance, and legitimacy, and they may possess control over key technologies or large customers (Pfeffer and Salancik 1978; Burt 1983). As a result, it makes sense to distinguish market participants as incumbents and challengers (Gamson 1975). Incumbent firms are large, and actors in those firms know their major competitors and model their actions on other large competitors. Challenger firms are smaller and frame their actions in reaction to the largest firms. But they experience the world as a given—one out of their control.

Differing conditions of market stability produce different kinds of politics. A stable market is defined as a situation in which the identities and status hierarchy of producer firms (i.e., who are the incumbents and the challengers) is well known, and a conception of control that guides actors who lead firms is shared. Firms resemble one another in tactics and organizational structure. Politics reproduce the position of the advantaged groups.

In new markets, the politics resemble social movements. The conditions in the market are wide open and fluid. Lots of firms are forming, each with different conceptions of what the market will be. The problem is that, in fluid situations, it is not clear how to control competition. Actors in different firms are trying to convince other firms to go along with their conception of the market. If they are powerful enough, they try to force their view. If there are many different firms of equivalent size, then alliances around conceptions of control are possible. Networks form between competitors, suppliers, and consumers that are oriented toward making sense of what others are doing (reducing information costs) and toward co-opting resource dependencies (Gulati and Gargiulo 1999). Conceptions of control may become political compromises that bring market stability to firms. This is just the way social movements work. They create collective identities for disparate groups that push forward political coalitions for change. (Tarrow 1994)

Markets in crisis are susceptible to transformation. On rare occasions, the push for change may come from within the firms in a market. More frequently, firms invade the market and transform the conception of control. This can look like a social movement, in the sense that the invading firms are trying to establish a new conception of control and in doing so are likely to ally themselves with some of the challengers or existing incumbents.

The most fluid period in a market is during its emergence. The roles of challengers and incumbents are yet to be defined, and there is no accepted set of social relations. It is useful to explore the metaphor of a social movement and its application to an emerging market. The ability of groups in a social movement to attain success depends on factors similar to firms trying to produce a stable market: the size of groups, their resources, the existence of a political opportunity to act, state actors willing to negotiate grievances, and the ability to build a political coalition around a collective identity (Tarrow 1994; Snow et al. 1986; McAdam 1982).

A new market spawns the growth of new firms as well as entrance of firms operating in other markets, just as a political opportunity creates new social movement organizations. Firms try to take advantage of a market opening in the same way that organizations in social movements try to take advantage of a political opportunity. In a new market, the situation is fluid and is characterized by multiple conceptions of control proposed by actors from various firms. A stable market requires the construction of a conception of control to promote noncutthroat ways to compete that all can live with and that state actors can accept. A conception of control operates as a kind of collective identity that many groups can attach to in order to produce a successful market.

Proposition 4.1. At the beginning of a new market, the largest firms are the most likely to able to create a conception of control and a political coalition to control competition.

At the origination of a market, all interorganizational relations must be constructed. Markets are the outcome of an institutionalization project that is the equivalent of discovering a conception of control (DiMaggio 1988). In this way, markets are social constructions. Making these institutional projects successful is inherently a political project. Actors need to find conceptions of control to signal to other firms in the moment of market formation what their intentions are. One can predict that the largest firms in an emerging market are likely to create a conception of control and persuade others to go along with it because of the perceived advantages of size.

Proposition 4.2. Power struggles within firms are over who can solve the problem of how to best organize the firm to deal with competition. The winners of the struggle impose their organizational culture and design on the firm.

A firm's internal power struggle depends on actors coming up with coherent conceptions of control that they can impose on others within the firm. The internal power struggle is likely to be most intense during the emergence of markets. Different groups believe that they hold the solution to the problem of how to organize the firm to best deal with competition. Those actors that win impose their organizational design and culture on the firm. Internal firm structure and who controls the firm result from the conception of control that deals with the problem of market competition. These conceptions of control are available to other firms and help produce a stable status hierarchy of firms.

Proposition 4.3. Through intended and unintended actions, states can thwart the actions of firms to create stable conceptions of control.

All conceptions of control are built around current understandings of legal and illegal market behavior. Firms avoid conceptions of control that are illegal, but occasionally find themselves scrutinized by government officials. More frequently, state regulation of economic activities changes the balance of power in a market away from one conception of control and toward another. This occurs in regulated markets such as drugs, food, telecommunications, utilities, banks, and media.

Proposition 4.4. The "liability of newness" in new markets reflects, in part, their lack of social structure and a conception of control; that is, it reflects participants' inability to control competition.

It is at the emergence of markets that competition and price mechanisms exact their greatest toll. With no established conception of control to structure nonpredatory forms of competition, price has its strongest effect (Stinchcombe 1965; Hannan and Freeman 1977). Business failures are often blamed on a lack of resources or the inability of managers to construct organizations that reliably deliver products. I argue that part of the difficulty is the lack of a social structure to control competition. Markets in which a conception of control never emerges continue to have relatively high death rates of firms, while markets that produce conceptions of control stabilize at lower death rates.

Proposition 4.5. New markets borrow conceptions of control from nearby markets, particularly when firms from other markets choose to enter the new market.

New markets are born in close social proximity to existing markets. Earlier, I argued that diversifying products is a way to produce more stable firms. Entering new markets does not require confronting entrenched interests and does not directly threaten the stability of the firm. If new markets succeed, then the firm's stability is enhanced. The differentiation and creation of new products is most frequently the spin-off of existing products. The start of a new market is not random but is shaped by existing conceptions of control, legal conceptions of property and competition, and the existing organization of related markets.

To illustrate these principles, it is useful to consider examples. The creation of the U.S. steel industry is a clear case of firms struggling to create a social structure to control competition.[5] In the nineteenth century, steel companies faced huge price swings because of the companies' role in the railroad industry and building trades, and these price swings were devastating because of the large amounts of fixed capital invested in the industry.

There was a great incentive to find legal mechanisms to stabilize prices (Hogan 1970). The basic problem for the steel industry was to discover a conception of control that limited competition. Cartels and monopolies were illegal in the United States (Thorelli 1955). The choice that remained was to integrate firms to control the market. My proposition (4.1) that the largest firms in the market are the leaders in such efforts is historically accurate in this case (Hogan 1971).

During the turn-of-the-century merger movement, the largest industrial corporation in the world emerged: U.S. Steel. The merger created a large corporation that controlled inputs into the steelmaking process as well as divisions that produced outputs for every segment of the market. The company controlled more than 65 percent of the market for steel and 75 percent of the industry's iron ore reserves (Hogan 1970). In spite of this strong position, the firm found itself confronted by wild swings in product demand and unstable prices well into the twentieth century. It faced a dilemma in enforcing its position against its competitors. If the firm vigorously pursued price-cutting to gain monopoly control over the industry, it would find itself a target of antitrust authorities; if it did nothing, its large investment was threatened.

U.S. Steel began to pursue an alternative tactic. It posted its prices and production schedules and defended them by decreasing production in the face of aggressive competitors (Fligstein 1990). U.S. Steel tried to cajole others into going along with its prices by threatening to use its control over inputs and its huge capacity to produce. If all behaved "reasonably," then some price stability could result. This strategy worked to stabilize steel prices from 1904 until the depression in 1929 (Kolko 1963).

U.S. Steel's strategy of integrating production, setting prices, and daring others to undercut them was ratified as a legal way to control competition when it won its antitrust lawsuit in 1920. This conception of control spread in social movement–like fashion during the 1920s merger movement, when oligopoly structures emerged in all of the core metal-making and petroleum industries (Eis 1978). This structure proved durable in the U.S. steel industry and lasted until the 1960s (Hogan 1971).

It is useful to examine an emerging industry when there is not yet a conception of control, applying the perspective advanced here to predict an outcome. The biotechnology industry has sprung up from common technologies that developed at major universities. To figure out which conceptions of control are contenders for organizing the industry, one asks: "What problem of competition would a social structure need to resolve?" One way to control competition is patent laws. Firms that discover a product first can extract monopoly rents from their investment in that product, thereby avoiding competition. The game is to find new products that can be patented. Two competing conceptions of control can be identified to take advantage of patent laws.

Powell and Brantley (1992) have argued that the critical problem for biotechnology firms is to control the supply of scientists who have the knowledge about the products. They view a network organization as a stable conception of control because it is a political compromise in which scientists may be able to leave a firm with knowledge of products, but firms have extensive organizational ties so that they will not have to depend on just one or two scientists for information or products. If the arrangements one firm has with other firms are alliances, then the collapse of any given alliance will not necessarily lead to a collapse of a given firm, by denying it either products or information. If a given scientist leaves, firms presumably have other scientists or alliances who can take up the slack. In this way, a networked firm oriented toward producing patents to control competition may prove stable.

Two other features of the biotechnology industry imply an alternative conception of control (Barley, Freeman, and Hybels 1992; Powell and Brantley 1992). Most biotechnology products must undergo extensive testing by the Food and Drug Administration. Firms need money to survive this period of testing before bringing products to market. Thus, the state, through FDA regulation of the market, shifts the competitive conditions in the market from the discovery of new products to the ability to survive the testing and approval process. Once through the testing phase, firms have to reliably produce, market, and distribute the product. This creates a second arena of competition that relies on production and marketing expertise.

These two competition problems imply that a different conception of control may emerge. I suggested earlier that one source of conceptions of control was nearby markets. The drug industry has extensive experience with the same testing and production processes used by the biotechnology industry and is built on the creation, production, and control of proprietary drugs. I predict that, to the degree that surviving the testing process and producing and marketing the product are pivotal, biotechnology firms will be tempted to form alliances with drug companies. Moreover, drug companies will be tempted to buy out the most successful of the biotechnology firms. The drug companies' conception of control (integrated firms that produce drugs with monopoly patent rights to eliminate competition to gain back the cost of producing the drug) will dominate.

A more hybrid form could emerge that would focus on maintaining the network organizations by keeping the discovery of products separate from the production and distribution of those products. This arrangement has advantages for both drug companies and biotechnology firms. The biotechnology firms maintain some control, while the drug companies lower their risk.

There is evidence that all three conceptions of control are practiced (Barley, Freeman, and Hybels 1992; Powell and Brantley 1992). My model would predict that the most likely outcome is a merger between the two industries, whereby large biotechnology companies become drug companies or divisions thereof. The largest players in the market are the drug companies; their conception of control solves competition problems in the pharmaceutical industry; they already have negotiated the legitimacy of that solution with states. My fallback position would be to argue that biotechnology firms remain fundamentally research organizations then license products to pharmaceutical companies. The problem of controlling the defection of scientists is more ephemeral than the problem of getting products through the patent process.

Proposition 4.6. In markets with stable conceptions of control, market participants widely agree on the conception of control and the status hierarchies and strategies it implies.

Once a stable market emerges, the roles of incumbents and challengers are defined and the power structure of the market becomes apparent. Actors in firms throughout the market are able to tell observers who occupies what position and what their central tactics are. They will be able to make their actions contingent on their interpretation of those tactics.

Proposition 4.7. Incumbent firms pay attention to the actions of other incumbent firms, not challenger firms, while challenger firms focus on incumbents' behavior.

A stable world depends on social relations between the largest firms. The central players ignore challenger organizations under most circumstances because they pose little threat to the overall stability of the market. If these organizations live up to their name and begin to challenge the existing order, incumbent organizations confront them and attempt to reinforce the governing conception of control.

Proposition 4.8. Firms in stable markets continue to use the governing conception of control, even when confronted with outside invasion or general economic crisis.

The major force that holds a market together over a period of time is the ability of the incumbent firms to continue to enforce a conception of control vis-à-vis one another. Incumbents are constantly trying to edge one another (and challengers) out for market share, but they refrain from direct confrontation that might prove the ruin of all. These actions are guided by the existing conception of control (i.e., the conception of what is a reasonable action). This requires actors to frame action for their firm against their competitors and to have the resources (power) to make it stick. They know the identity of the important firms in the market, they try and make sense of their moves, and they respond to those moves.

This accounts for the relative stability of established markets, in both the identities of the participants and their tactics. To produce a stable order where firms survive is a relatively difficult problem. Once stability is attained, actors in firms are loathe to engage in actions that undermine their incumbency. If challengers shift tactics or invaders come into the market, incumbent firms continue the same kinds of actions that produced the stable order in the first place. Incumbent firms may allow some redefinition of who is an incumbent and who is a challenger, but they will remain committed to the overall conception of control that lessens competition. To break down the stable order could bring more chaos than would enforcing the "way things are done." Actors are also cognitively constrained by a conception of control. Their analysis of a crisis is framed by the current conception of control and their attempts to alleviate the crisis by applying "the conventional wisdom."

The case of the Japanese keiretsu illustrates how a stable conception of control has withstood both political and economic assaults. Japanese keiretsu are families of firms in different industries that share ownership ties. The overall structure of the keiretsu is to cement important interdependencies and allow various keiretsu members to survive economic downturns. Often banks are at the center of keiretsu, and they function as an internal capital market for the firms.

The keiretsu show high growth, high investment, and relatively low, but stable, profits (Aoki 1988). In economic downturns, keiretsu structures allow workers to be transferred across firms rather than being laid off (Lincoln, Gerlach, and Takahashi 1992). This exerts downward pressure on profits but secures employees' loyalty. When firms within the structure are experiencing economic troubles, managers in other firms respond by helping to reorganize the troubled firm (Gerlach 1992).

After World War II, keiretsu were reformed from prewar economic conglomerates (zaibatsu) that were family controlled. The zaibatsu were broken up during the American occupation but began slowly to reform in a looser manner (Hadley 1970). Since World War II, they have been directed by state actors to enter new markets, and they have proved adept at producing new products (Johnson 1982). The keiretsu structure contains firms with activities spread across a wide spectrum of industries and markets. The keiretsu structure, as a conception of control, does not directly restrict competition in a given market. Its advantage is its capacity to stabilize competition across markets. It has been noted that within given product markets, the firms from different keiretsu compete quite vigorously (Aoki 1988).

The keiretsu structures operate to mitigate competition across markets in a number of ways. First, firms tend to purchase goods and services from inside the keiretsu. This means that some markets are captive and price competition is held down. Second, if a given firm faces an economic crisis, the other firms attempt to support it. Management expertise, capital, and the ability to place workers with other firms during slumps mitigate short-run competitive processes. Third, the focus on market share implies that firms invest for the long run and that expectations for short-run profits are not high, which gives managers latitude in dealing with competitive conditions. Fourth, because of the ownership relations between firms and banks, the cost of capital tends to be lower (see Gerlach 1992 for a review of the literature). One can see the intimate connection between the problem of trying to control competition externally and the internal social organization working to solve that problem.

Recently, two forces began to close in on the keiretsu. First, the U.S. government applied pressure to open up Japanese markets, an effort directed in part against the keiretsu structures (Gerlach 1992). The United States wanted to break open the procurement arrangements of the keiretsu and demanded that the Japanese open their financial markets and allow a market for corporate control to develop. Second, the economic downturn of the 1990s put pressure on the permanent employment system of the keiretsu. It became more difficult to pass workers onto other firms in the keiretsu. The managers who controlled the keiretsu have been able to use their traditional methods to fight off these attacks. They were well enough connected politically to fight off reforms within Japan and strong enough economically able to endure a long recession (Gerlach 1992).

Proposition 4.9. Market crisis is observed when incumbent organizations begin to fail.

Crisis comes to markets when the largest firms are unable to reproduce themselves from period to period. This can be caused by three kinds of events (alone or in combination): (1) decrease in demand for the firm's products can result from bad economic conditions or a shift in buyers' preferences, (2) an invasion by other firms can upset the conception of control and introduce procedures that force a reorganization of the market, or (3) the state can intentionally or unintentionally undermine the market by changing rules.

Incumbents rarely become innovators because they are busy defending the status quo; market transformation is precipitated by invaders. The reorganization of a market around a new conception of control resembles a social movement and is very much like the formation of raw markets. Invading firms can form alliances with existing firms around a new conception of control or a compromise conception of control, and this makes the reorganization of the market more predictable than it was at market formation.[6]

Proposition 4.10. Transformation of existing markets results from exogenous forces: invasion, economic crisis, or political intervention by states.

One of the key features of capitalist society is the dynamic interplay of markets, in which some markets are emerging, others are stable, and still others are in crisis and undergoing transformation. I propose an exogenous theory of market transformation that views the basic cause of changes in market structure as resulting from forces outside the control of producers, due to shifts in demand, invasion by other firms, or actions of the state. Incumbent firms respond to these destabilizing forces by trying to reinforce the status quo. Markets are connected in a wide variety of ways. Firms rely on suppliers, capital markets, labor markets, and customers as well as on states for their stability. It follows that these market and state forces are always interacting and thereby producing potential problems for an existing conception of control. Crisis in relations across markets can undermine existing agreements by threatening the well-being of all firms, either by withholding key resources or through the direct invasion of firms from nearby markets.

Proposition 4.11. Invaders are more likely to come from nearby than from distant markets.

This proposition parallels the argument about where new markets come from. Firms seek stability by finding new markets. The invasion of an existing market can occur in a couple of ways. First, firms in closely related markets enter existing markets, where they can successfully introduce a new conception of control to increase their advantage. Second, firms may enter the same product market in different geographic areas, thereby undermining a local stable order.

Proposition 4.12. When firms begin to fail, the intraorganizational power struggle heats up, leading to higher turnover of top personnel and greater activism by boards of directors and nonmanagement shareholders. New sets of organizational actors attempt to reconstruct the firm along the lines of the invaders.

Conceptions of control are used by actors in incumbent firms to ward off market crises. The power struggle internal to the firm becomes more intense as market crises become more pronounced and the reigning conception of control proves inadequate to the crisis.

Consider the example of the transformation of the finance conception of control as the guiding principle in the market for corporate control in the United States during the 1980s (an issue I will take up more systematically in chapter 8). The financial conception of control dominated the actions of many large U.S. firms between 1950 and 1970 (Fligstein 1990). This view held that firms were composed of assets that could be deployed and redeployed by financial actors within firms in order to promote growth. The major tactics of this conception were the use of financial tools to internally monitor divisional performance, and the use of mergers to buy and sell divisions that produced diversification for firms (Fligstein 1990). These tactics solved the competition problems of large firms by allowing them to exit and enter businesses and stabilize the overall corporate structure. Firms were the principal actors in the market for corporate control as they used the stock market to add to or subtract from their "portfolios."

What crisis made this conception of control no longer viable for large corporations? High inflation rates during the 1970s meant that interest rates were high, stock prices were low, and the value of assets was inflated, thereby making returns on investments poor (Friedman 1985a). The financial conception of the firm, with its focus on the profitability of product lines and market diversification, suggested that "good" managers would deal with these problems by keeping debt low and funding investments from cash generated internally. The market for corporate control was in crisis because managers were not reorganizing their assets, even though corporate profits were low. This presented a new opportunity for actors to seek a new rationale to reorganize the market for corporate control.

What was this "new" conception of control, and who were its proponents? Davis and Thompson (1994) have argued that the language of "shareholder value" and the discourse that blamed managers for being ineffective spread among institutional investors in social movement fashion in the early 1980s. The financial strategy of holding undervalued assets, funding investment internally, and keeping debt low was viewed as a problem. The idea of maximizing shareholder value was allied with "agency theory" from economics (Jensen 1989) to emphasize that if managers were not going to maximize shareholder value, then they should be replaced by management teams who would.

Institutional investors are a heterogeneous group that includes investment bankers and representatives from pension funds, mutual funds, and insurance companies. In the 1980s they were from a closely related industry, financial services, and they invaded the turf of financial managers who controlled the largest U.S. corporations. Their goal was to force these managers to redeploy their assets to reflect the effect the 1970s had on their balance sheets. They wanted managers to sell off overvalued assets, assume debt to keep firms disciplined, and to remove layers of management to save money. They also forced managers to focus their business by buying up competitors and selling off their most diversified assets (Davis, Dickmann, and Tinsley 1994). They, of course, benefited by making money on organizing and executing mergers.

Research shows that firms that were merger targets tended to ignore financial reorganization to increase "shareholder value" (Davis and Stout 1992; Fligstein and Markowitz 1993). Useem (1993) has shown how managers began to use the language of shareholder value and engage in the behaviors that the perspective implied. The merger movement of the 1980s resembled a social movement in that some financial executives and the various actors within the financial services industry discovered a common language and produced a conception of control to reorganize the market for corporate control.

The federal government played both direct and indirect roles. The Reagan administration passed a huge tax cut that produced windfalls for corporate America in 1981. The administration expected firms to reinvest that capital in new plants and equipment, but instead firms bought other firms. The administration also announced that it would not vigorously enforce antitrust laws (Fligstein and Markowitz 1993). Davis and Stout (1992) argue that the Reagan administration became a cheerleader for the shareholder value conception of control. The shareholder value conception of control is related to the finance conception of the firm, but it uses a stark discourse that only recognizes the rights of one group: those who own stock. All other concerns are subordinated to maximizing the returns for owners. The attention of top managers is focused on evaluating their product markets, but more importantly on how the financial markets evaluate the firm's stock price.

How does this new conception of control affect competition in the market for corporate control? If managers pay attention to shareholder value in a narrow sense, they are less likely to become merger targets. To the degree that the "game" is to avoid becoming the object of acquisition from outsiders (i.e., mergers), managers with a narrow focus are likely to maintain control. I hypothesize that the managers who win the internal power struggle will be those who can claim to maximize shareholder value. This process explains the spread of these tactics to most large firms during the 1980s.

Links between Market Formation and States

In the last chapter, I suggested some general propositions about the links between market building and state building. I argued that many groups in society had interests in creating general market institutions in order to stabilize economic growth. But because these interests are often opposed, I described how various political coalitions between state managers, workers, and capitalists provide different tools state managers, entrepreneurs, and managers can use to organize markets. The earlier discussion explained that the policy domains of the state oriented toward market building were the outcome of the political organization of important groups in society. The current discussion is about how entrepreneurs and managers actually engage in market building within new and existing markets. It is useful to bring these discussions together in two ways. I would like to consider why the initial transition to capitalism is so important for varying societies. Then I will discuss how to think about the concept of "globalization."

The central insight of this chapter is that market instability mobilizes entrepreneurs and managers to build internal organization and external social relations to their principal competitors. Now imagine the situation where an economy is rapidly growing and there are a great many competitors across a large number of markets, all searching out ways to control competition. Their "local" problems of instability cause many of them to look wherever they can for ways to produce stability. Managers and entrepreneurs widely search for stable conceptions of control. Firms in particular markets that find ways to stabilize their interactions are immediately copied. One can get a kind of lock-in for a given conception of controls across many industries if these solutions are sufficiently general.[7]

To the degree that workers, firms, and government managers become involved in this process of defining stable conceptions of control by building state capacity to regulate social action in markets, this lock-in can occur in the institutions of the state as well as the particular markets. Such market institutions are also readily available for entrepreneurs in new markets seeking to find stable solutions to their problems of control.

One major implication of this process is that distinct national "cultures" of control develop at the moment of entry into capitalism. These national ways to legally control competition are inscribed in the institutions of the state and in the ways that firms pursue their tactics in markets. This theory helps explain why scholars who try to understand distinct national systems of governance often conclude that the history and politics of a given society matter a great deal for a distinct set of practices by firms.

The process also implies that these institutions only become unstuck under the most dire circumstances. At any given time, there are crises in many markets in a given society, and thus the possibility for new conceptions of control exists. But local crises do not bring about systemwide transformation because many other markets remain quite stable with incumbent firms that are happy with the status quo. It is only under extreme circumstances that wholesale changes in the rules occur. More frequent are crises of particular sectors, followed by reorganization.

These insights illuminate the kinds of problems confronting the latecomers to capitalist social relations in Eastern Europe. Attempts to "marketize" are met by three difficult problems. First, governments there have little or no capacity to intervene effectively in capitalist societies. Second, the international organization of markets means that firms in developed product markets are poised to invade these societies and take over the local product markets, thereby undermining efforts on the part of local firms to adjust to changed circumstances. Third, there exist few market institutions, such as property rights, governance structures, or rules of exchange, to guide actors in new firms (Stark 1992, 1996; Burawoy and Krotov 1992). In essence, these societies are attempting to cram two hundred years of market and state building into a short period of time.

It is interesting to consider how this process appears to be going in Hungary. Lacking the ability to regulate a capitalist economy and lacking an indigenous entrepreneurial class of managers, the Hungarian government nevertheless initially tried to cultivate a capitalist class by privatizing state-owned firms. The market reformers in government tried to cultivate such a class by producing a market.

The property rights issue was initially dealt with in the following way. Stark (1992, 1996) found that state actors in Hungary turned state-owned ministries into corporations. The government, however, held the bulk of stock in these corporations, although control appears to have devolved to managers. Eventually, state managers appeared willing to have firms sold off to private interests, including foreign corporations. Complicated patterns of shareholding have developed whereby the state owns all of some firms and parts of others.

In this context, it is particularly interesting to consider how managers have responded to the problem of competition. Stark (1996) documents that managers have reorganized firms into complex structures in which large firms incorporate satellites of smaller firms in which the large firms hold equity shares. Firms have taken up two tactics. First, they have taken ownership stakes in firms producing similar products and have tried to control both the inputs and outputs of production. Second, groups of firms with related and unrelated products have joined together. These are the two tactics, integration and diversification, I earlier described that are used by firms to avoid direct competition.

Pushing firms to behave competitively, state actors have forced Western-style accounting standards on firms to attract Western investment. This, in turn, has pushed many firms into bankruptcy (Stark 1996). Western-style investors have, so far, not been attracted to Hungarian partners. Western firms prefer to directly sell their goods to Hungarians. The state is the holder of equity and debt, and, thus, if firms fail, their bankruptcies drain the state's coffers. Moreover, there is political pressure to maintain jobs and keep firms from failing.

It is not clear whether integration and diversification within Hungarian firms will produce stable outcomes. These strategies may not be able to stand up to invasion by Western firms, particularly given the financial problems firms face. Eyal, Szelenyi, and Townsley (1998) have found that Hungarian managers, not surprisingly, refuse to purchase the firms they run. They prefer to be paid straight salary since they know better than anyone else how precarious firms are. Thus, the indigenous capitalist class that market reformers have hoped to cultivate does not want to play the part.

While my approach cannot say how these transformations will turn out, it does suggest that one can expect more demands to be placed on the government. The policy domains of the state that will directly deal with questions of ownership, financing, and employment are still being built. Market reformers will have a difficult time producing these institutions without an indigenous entrepreneurial and capitalist class that proposes how to do so. Eventually, the people who run the government will have to realize that they own the biggest firms in the economy and that they must decide what to do. They will have to provide capital for firms directly, keep firms alive by subsidizing employment, and consider ways to mitigate competition with firms outside of Hungary. If this proves to be untenable, then one can expect that they will continue to try to sell off assets to foreign firms. In essence, unless strong capitalist groups emerge with a positive agenda to produce different rules and economic growth, one can expect that the rules produced will likely be designed to protect jobs.[8]

Some Macro Implications of the Theory of Fields

The imagery suggested by the theory of markets as fields is useful to explore. The economic sociology of capitalist societies is concerned with the construction of massive numbers of markets operating with different conceptions of control and massive numbers of fields of government connected to these markets. The interesting questions concern not just the internal dynamics of particular markets but the interactions of markets and states more generally. The view of markets as fields proposed here captures the two key dynamics that are attributed to the world of firms. First, the largest firms are seen as very powerful, and within their markets they maintain an order that benefits them. If one cuts into a given market, one is likely to find a hierarchy of power whereby a set of firms rules the market with a set of practices. But there is a second dynamic at work here as well. As markets are formed or are invaded and transformed, no one player has power and who will survive is up for grabs. Competition is the driving force at these moments, and even the most powerful are vulnerable if the analyst cuts into the market at the point where transformation is coming.

Stable markets are like sand castles. They are built up, last a while, but in the end are transformed. Unlike like sand castles that survive only for a day, stable markets can last sixty to eighty years. This spans several human generations and shows enormous stability. But, ultimately, even the most stable markets (such as steel, automobiles, and chemicals) have been transformed.

For a huge number of markets as fields, a period-to-period stability is induced by the ability of the largest firms to reproduce their role structure by playing the game against one another and the challengers. But there are also dynamic parts of the economy where new firms are emerging and no order exists, and others where transformation of an existing order is happening. The imagery of markets as fields and of fields as connected to and part of governments stresses both continuity and change.

It is interesting to speculate on conditions that produce massive changes within and across markets. Clearly, the number of markets and their social relations have increased dramatically since World War I. Moreover, since the worldwide economic depression of the 1930s and the devastation of World War II, the world's capitalist economies have grown incredibly as governments learned how to stabilize markets by regulation, controlling the money supply, fiscal policy, and mediating in interfirm relations and worker-firm relations. One of the most interesting features of these changes is that since the 1930s, there have been no large-scale worldwide depressions. Why is this the case?

There are three possible sources of instability in a given market: conditions within the market, conditions across markets, and relations between the state and firms. A given market may become unstable because demand for its product decreases, the invaders enter it, or the government intentionally or unintentionally changes rules. If a given market is unstable, instability may spread to adjacent markets. For example, if there is a downturn in the automobile industry, one expects the suppliers of the materials consumed by the industry to be affected as well. If demand for a product drops precipitously, a dependent market may actually disappear.

The interesting question is how far and how deep instability may spread. One can make one of two arguments about the increased number and complexity of markets. First, more complexity has increased "tight coupledness" of markets, implying that a breakdown in one is likely to have profound effects on many others. Markets that are more centrally linked to many markets thus have the possibility of having much larger effects on a complex society. So, for example, one can argue that financial markets are pivotal to capitalist economies. Bank failure or stock market collapses are likely to affect the conditions in many markets and possibly induce recession.

Alternatively, one can argue that the increase in the number of markets means that markets are only loosely dependent on one another. Thus, a crisis in a given market may have effects on nearby markets, but those effects may be quickly dampened. Since there are so many markets, many are not affected, and the crisis is "locally" devastating, but "globally" not so large. Moreover, there are always new and growing markets, and these can offset some of the negative effects of crisis elsewhere.

So, for example, in the 1980s in the United States, the entire savings and loan industry went bankrupt. But the federal government intervened, and while certain markets were affected, there was no financial meltdown and the economy did not even go into recession. In 1987, a huge stock market crash also did not produce an economic recession. This crash was followed by the Federal Reserve Bank's increasing money available to prevent a more general liquidity crisis. Neither crisis made it harder for firms to borrow money or make investments, thus showing that the underlying economy was not as dependent on the financial sector as one might have speculated.

These examples point out that action by government coupled with a large diversified economy makes deep economic depressions less likely as capitalism develops. This does not mean that recessions do not occur nor that crises within particular markets are not always going on. But it does suggest that, overall, the growing complexity of markets and market arrangements makes the whole system more, not less, stable. Thus, advanced market societies can be highly dynamic in the sense that markets are always forming and being transformed. But the overall effect on economic growth and stability across markets can be dampened. Particular market crises do not spread very far, particularly if governments intervene.

Proposition 4.13. Complexity in market structures and a growth in the size of markets tends to produce stability, not fragility, in societal economic growth. This is because the diversification of products of firms and the diversification of economies makes firms and economies more stable.

The largest corporations have become diversified in their product lines. This means that they have, by and large, found ways to stabilize the overall identity of the firm. It also means that managers and entrepreneurs can choose to exit slow-growing or declining industries and devote resources to fast-growing industries. The general effect is that in an economic downturn in a particular market segment, corporations have strategies for coping apart from laying off vast numbers of workers. They can redeploy workers in the short term and capital in the middle term. They can concentrate on products less affected by economic downturn and can promote fast-growing products.

Governments have helped firms make these investments through tax policies, direct ownership, subsidization of research and development, industrial policies, and military expenditures. Almost all of the important new technologies of the postwar era have been funded directly or indirectly by government spending on education research organizations or on, corporate research and development or as spillovers from military applications. Firms have been the principal beneficiaries of these policies.

Governments also have intervened in their economies during economic downturns to even out the worst effects of recessions on consumption through Keynesian deficit spending and spending on unemployment benefits and public works projects. Political intervention in labor markets has varied across industrial societies. To the degree that class struggle has been stabilized, governments have bought themselves political peace.

In the Western industrial societies, the main effect of the production of stable market systems is to provide stable political conditions for entrepreneurs and managers. This encourages them to invest in new product lines. The development of new industries, particularly those that rely on science-based investments, has been possible primarily because of the stabilizing influence of governments on general economic growth and political conditions.

The overall effect of these three forces is to encourage more diversification of the economy by the production of new products and markets, more stability for the largest firms by the diversification of product lines, and less dependence of the total economy on any given industry. The lack of economic depressions in the postwar era is a testament to the positive feedback produced by these stabilizing processes.   ·

Proposition 4.14. Economies that are large and diversified experience more stability and less severe economic downturns. This is because their diversity makes them less dependent on any one source of economic growth and therefore less prone to extreme swings.

If diversity and complexity have produced stability, then lack of diversity and dependence on a small number of products is likely to produce more instability. In small economies that are highly dependent on a small number of products, fluctuation in prices for those products has big effects on the economic growth of that economy. This, of course, is one of the insights of dependency theory (Frank 1969).

Proposition 4.15. The complexity of markets does not lead to tighter connections between them, but weaker connections. The overall effect is that a recession or depression in a particular market is likely to affect economic conditions in nearby markets, but these effects are quickly dampened and do not spread across the economy.

This follows from our argument about complexity. If a society contains a great many markets, some of those markets are forming and growing quickly, some are mature, and others are declining. Rapid changes in demand for the products of some products, whether brought about by too many producers (or the invasion of "foreign producers"), a downturn in demand, or technology obsolescence, could have huge effects for those firms or geographic areas that are highly connected to the production of a given market. We would expect for those effects to spread across competitors and to suppliers. But the degree to which a downturn in a single market or set of markets has larger effects depends on a number of factors. First is the degree to which firms in a given market are dependent on that market for their existence. If they are sufficiently diversified, then they may be able to exit a given market over a period of time and invest themselves in other markets. Second, the size of the market is consequential as well. Crises in markets that do not affect a lot of other producers or consumers are not likely to cause more general crises. Third, the degree to which connected markets are dependent on a particular market for resources matters. If connected markets are not totally dependent upon a small number of customers, then they are able to shift their sales to other markets.

As economies grow, they produce more markets, more complexity, and less general interdependence. Taken together, these forces suggest that the larger and more diversified the markets are in a given society, the more able it is to withstand an economic downturn in a single market or related markets. The negative effects of downturns in those markets are likely to be dampened quickly to the degree that dependent suppliers and customers are themselves diversified. Thus, stability breeds complexity and loose coupling.

This set of insights can be brought to bear on issues of globalization and world trade. To the degree that societies have diversified economies and to the degree that participation in the world economy provides new markets and hence a more stable set of customers and suppliers, increases in world trade for a particular society are likely to have stabilizing effects. World trade is most threatening to societies that are small economies that are not diversified in their products. This makes them more vulnerable to fluctuations in demand for their products. But, even here, having more customers and suppliers may increase the size of firms and the diversification of their products.

Recently, we have seen the destabilization of currencies produce deep recessions in less-developed societies such as Mexico, Korea, Indonesia, and Thailand. Clearly, the relatively small size of these economies is one of the principal causes of their collapse. But equally responsible is the way in which foreign investment has entered these societies. These economies were encouraged by international organizations, such as the World Bank and the International Monetary Fund, to liberalize their financial systems in order to allow foreign investment. The problem was that those who encouraged this deregulation did not realize that many governments lacked the capacity to regulate their banking systems. This meant that they had little ability to understand the real financial situation in their society until it was too late.

Globalization and Market Processes

One potential objection to my focus on states is that it fails to deal with the fact that the world economy is now truly global. But I believe that this political-cultural approach centered on state and society is quite useful in analyzing so-called global markets. I show in chapter 8 that comparative empirical analysis of the organization of firms' activities supports the view that national capitalisms persist. There are two important reasons why this is. First, firms depend on national institutions to organize themselves. These institutions produce stability and, hence, wealth for the owners and managers of firms. The owners and managers of firms still turn to their national authorities for help. Second, most consumption remains national, not international. In 1996, about 83% of the $35 trillion world economy was national (WTO 1997). Globalization cannot be in all markets. I will explore these themes in chapter 9.

Here, I want to pick up some alternative themes that follow from the discussion in this chapter. My main insight is that the only difference between a global market and a local one is geographic spread. The definition of a market provided here, a reproducible role structure, can be applied to globalization in a straightforward way. A market is "globalized" if there are a small number of participants who form an incumbent-challenger structure and operate across countries with a common conception of control.

It is an empirical question as to how many world markets are truly global in this sense. Moreover, it may be the case that some markets are partially globalized in that some regions are dominated by firms that know each other, but other parts of the world market are protected or local. How many globalized markets are there? Given that 83% of world economic activity is national, it is safe to say that there are fewer than many observers believe. Of course, many of these markets are for important products such as automobiles, chemicals, airframes, computers, software, pharmaceuticals, and some business services such as accounting and consulting. Industries that are partially global include telecommunications and some financial services, such as investment banking.

How do we tell if a market is being globalized? That is, when do foreign firms become invaders that transform a stable national market with a conception of control? The model developed here suggests a national market is upset when invaders arrive with a new conception of control. When this happens, the model predicts that the incumbents will respond by (1) reinforcing the old conception of control, (2) getting their governments to intervene to protect their local market, (3) co-opting invaders by forming alliances or joint marketing or production arrangements. If these fail, it is possible that the national market is absorbed into the international market, whereby firms adopt the new conception of control either by adopting the "new" methods for competition or through merger.

This brings up a more systematic consideration of what governments do in the face of globalization. One can conceive of the problem in the following way. Divide a country's main markets into those involved in exporting and those not involved in exporting. Consider the situation where firms either are or are not experiencing pressures from exporting firms from other countries. Firms in markets that are not exporting and are not being threatened by exporters will not pressure their governments to do anything about trade. Firms that are exporting and are not threatened by other firms (i.e., those already in globalized markets under my definition) are also unlikely to put pressure on their governments to keep foreign firms out.

Firms that are not exporting but suddenly find themselves under assault by those who have invaded their home market will try to get protectionist measures passed by their governments. Firms that are exporting and are feeling pressure from other exporters may put pressure on their governments to help them open up foreign markets, particularly those of their main competitors. This implies that it is not schizophrenic for governments to simultaneously pursue the opening of some markets abroad while protecting some of their own markets at home. So, for example, the U.S. government continues to support the textile and sugar industries domestically while it tries to force the internal market in Japan open for cars and other American products.

Proposition 4.16. The emergence of global markets depends on cooperation between firms and states to produce rules of exchange, property rights (i.e., guarantees that firms can expropriate profits), and governance structures (i.e., ways to compete). One hypothesis is that increases in world trade produce demand for more of these agreements that produce more extensive cooperation between governments.

The European Union, NAFTA, and the recently completed GATT treaty, which founded the World Trade Organization, can all be analyzed according to whether or not they provide common rules for property rights, governance structures, and rules of exchange. They can also be broken down by sectors that involve or do not involve exporters to see if rules tend to apply more or less exclusively to those sectors (Fligstein and Mara-Drita 1996). These agreements have so far been primarily concerned with rules of exchange that facilitate more trade.

One implication of this proposition is that the creation of global markets will depend on states and will in fact be limited by states. There are two kinds of projects that states can undertake in opening markets. First, they can remove trade barriers between societies. This eliminates many kinds of rules that prevent market access. This is a negative integration project. But there are limits to this kind of market integration. Without common rules to guide interaction, market opening will not involve creating a true world market (i.e., one where a small number of firms make investments around the world in response to one another's actions and market opportunities). Thus, trade and the benefits to trade will be limited. To get single markets for a particular commodity requires that extensive rules exist. It is not surprising that the trade zone with the highest level of trade in the world is Western Europe. The European Union has set out to create a single market by removing trade barriers and providing for new European-wide rules to guide firms. The effect of this rule creation has been to create a market that in many ways resembles the internal American market.

One arena in which agreements have not occurred is the creation of a world market for corporate control. It is relatively difficult to engage in hostile takeovers in any society except the United States and Great Britain. Earlier I suggested that property rights were at the core of the relations between national elites and states. Most national elites have resisted having transfer property rights transferred to the highest bidder because they would lose power. States remain players in the creation of the global economy because their elites depend on them to preserve their power and guarantee entry to global markets.

The market model proposed here offers conceptual tools to help study processes of globalization. It provides a working definition of whether a particular market is globalized. This definition can be used to establish the degree to which a world market exists for a particular commodity and the level of integration of that market. It also can be used to examine over time if a particular market is becoming more or less integrated. So, for example, over time, the world automobile industry has become more integrated. There are fewer firms, and more of those firms operate in many parts of the world. What is most interesting in the recent past is that the national identities of these firms is blurring so: Daimler bought Chrysler, Renault bought Nissan, and Ford bought Jaguar. Finally, one important implication of globalization is that one would expect that globalization in a particular market would spill over through invasion into another market. So the pharmaceutical industry contains a small number of large firms that operate on a global basis. An industry like biotechnology can be changed dramatically by the entry of these firms onto their turf. This implies that there are a great many empirical projects that can be done to study states, markets, and changes in the nature of the market due to entry of firms from other societies.

The response to globalization by governments is also explicable from this perspective. They strive to protect local industries not focused on the global market under threat by non–home country firms, and they strive to open the markets of the competitors of their own global firms. Governments remain central to these processes because workers, entrepreneurs, and managers depend upon them to protect them and expand their opportunities.

Conclusion

Markets are social constructions that reflect the unique political-cultural construction of their firms and nations. The creation of markets implies societal solutions to the problems of property rights, governance structures, conceptions of control, and rules of exchange. There are many paths to those solutions, each of which may promote the survival of firms. I have sketched the interconnections between states and markets and the outcomes produced by various actions. I have extracted general principles by which these outcomes can be understood.

I have argued that stable markets reflect status hierarchies that define incumbents and challengers, and that market leaders enforce the market social order and signal how crises are to be handled. These complex role structures in markets operate through the social relations between actors (which are generically called *networks*). My view of markets takes seriously the problem of how states interact with markets to produce general rules by which social structures can be formed. It also makes market structures easier to observe, takes into account the role of actors' intentions in the production of market structures, and makes more sense of how firms are likely to behave under different market conditions.

I have tried to give a political reading to the process of market dynamics. The liability of newness of firms results, at least partially, from the lack of social structure in a market and the social movement–like search for such a structure. Legitimacy is bestowed by states on markets. A "stable" market for a population ecologist resembles one in which a conception of control is shared. Similarly, as in population ecology, the transformation of markets results from external sources of change.

The metaphor of "markets as politics" unites these ideas. I have shown that this view makes possible a unified approach to the study of markets—an approach that focuses on the political processes that underlie market interactions. Ultimately, however, the usefulness of any metaphor is in the research it generates and the intuitive and counterintuitive insights it creates.

I motivated this section by suggesting that one reason national capitalisms persist is the unique development of market institutions in each capitalist society. I have argued that this unique development hinges on the relative power of capitalists, workers, politicians, and state bureaucrats to lay down and enforce market institutions (property rights, governance structures, conceptions of control, and rules of exchange) at the entry into modern development. This political alliance and the rules that support it have huge effects on the subsequent development of a society's economy.

These effects work in two ways. First, these groups define the status quo and try to get the state to support their position. States are the focus of firms' attention during market crises, and state actors intervene along predictable lines. Societal transformation of rules occurs only during great crises, such as war or depression. Second, if one has knowledge about how institutions are organized in a given society, one can predict that new industries will emerge with the existing societal templates. Thus, one expects that there are both institutional and organizational forces at work to prevent societies from converging in form. National elites do not willingly give up their power, and states are committed to defending it by the nature of the market institutions that are created.

PART II

5

The Logic of Employment Systems

IT HAS NOW BEEN about 20 years since sociologists began to take the problem of the structure of work seriously in empirical work on stratification. The so-called new structuralism has tried to embed the employment relation in larger units of analysis, such as organizations, sectors, classes, labor market segments, and even nation-states.[1] Theoretical work (Hodson 1986; Kalleberg 1988; Fligstein and Fernandez 1988) has tried to view the production of labor relations as the interaction between groups of laborers and employers with varying amount of resources. This latter approach has the positive effect of introducing dynamics into the formation of labor markets. But it still fails to locate these dynamics in the context of creating institutions or rules that govern these dynamics.

My purpose in this chapter is to situate the study of labor market processes in the context of the political-cultural approach. In chapter 3, I discussed how labor markets were structured by the constitution of conceptions of property rights, governance structures, and rules of exchange. I want to explore in a more explicit way how to think about the structuring of work in a society as the outcome of the political conflict between workers, government officials, and capitalists and the labor market institutions they create. I want to explain how this balance of power affects the conception of work and who gets to organize it. I also want to consider how the educational system of a society is shaped by these conflicts and plays a role in reproducing a particular set of labor market institutions.

The central object to explain is the emergence of employment systems. These can be defined as the rules governing relations between groups of workers and employers that concern the general logic of how "careers" are defined and how groups organize to maintain these conceptions. These general logics inform more concrete sets of rules that help explain the organization of particular labor markets, the mobility of labor and managers, and the ways in which employers and workers organize. My approach is that proposed in chapters 2 and 3. The goal is to identify ideal-typical arrangements that reflect the dominance of various groups and to consider the hybrid possibilities that might occur in real societies. I want to view the types of employment systems as conceptions of control when they are implicated in the way that work is organized in firms in particular markets.

If the system of employment relations is thought of as a large-scale institutional project, one can ask a different set of questions than are typically considered in stratification research. How does such a system come into existence in the first place? What is its internal logic? Is it possible to tell if it is in some form of fundamental crisis that might bring about a reorganization of employment relations? How do states intervene in employment relations at different times of their transformation? What is the impact of the increased internationalization of the economy on employment systems?

The central argument is that, at the origins of industrialization, actors reach a political understanding on the structure of employment relations. This understanding structures concrete labor market practices and helps form educational institutions that are organized around these principles. This understanding also becomes a set of cultural practices that function as a template or worldview that helps actors make sense of labor markets and careers. These common understandings structure subsequent interaction across industries as new industries emerge.

I identify three employment systems that have emerged historically in advanced capitalist industrial countries: vocationalism, professionalism, and managerialism. Vocationalism is a conception of work and career that emphasizes occupational communities, industrial unions, and vocational training (either formal or on the job) for new personnel. The typical career is marked by a commitment to one industry. Professionalism is a conception of work that references a professional peer group, uses associations to maintain collegiality, and relies on universities for the training of personnel. Careers are centered on professions, not firms or industries, and once in a system of professions, an individual tends to stay for life.[2] Managerialism reflects a commitment to a particular work organization, is characterized by company unions, and relies on general schooling as a filter for admittance to the organization and firm-specific job training over the life cycle. The typical career is with one corporation. These three models of organizing careers and work come to structure labor market interactions and the organization of schooling.

In the sections that follow, I will first consider the problem of creating institutions such as employment systems by emphasizing the role of states, firms, and other organized groups. I will then specify the unique types of dynamics from which real employment systems emerge, allowing us to answer the questions posed above about the emergence, logic, and transformation of employment systems. Finally, I will sketch how this view helps us make sense of the dominant systems of employment relations that have emerged in Western Europe, the United States, and Japan.

There are a number of interesting implications of the view proposed here. One can use this approach to identify and examine crucial historical moments in employment systems. One can see that, once in existence, the organization of labor markets is difficult to change. Workers, employers, governments, and those who run the education system have a stake in the current structure. This limits the possibility for transformation of employment systems across sectors. So, for instance, discussions in the United States about reforming the educational system to promote vocationalism (e.g. Reich 1991) go on without regard to existing employment relations in large firms, which promote managerialism or professionalism. Such reforms are likely to have little effect because a shift to a vocational educational system ignores the operation of labor markets that are structured by managerialism and professionalism.

Once employment systems are in place, conflict in employment relations is dynamic, but limited by larger arrangements. The unique systems of employment relations that have evolved across modern capitalist societies are deeply rooted in the unique development of each society and the mutual interaction of sectors. This history creates a kind of path dependence such that institutions are not easily borrowed or transplanted except under the most dire circumstances. Systems of employment relations can be most easily displaced as new parts of the economy emerge and as organized actors, either workers or firms, change the terms of exchange. Of course, even in these cases, the old system of power and organization provides templates for new organization. One also expects some workers to find themselves subject to "managerialist" systems, while others are subject to professional systems, depending on the firms they work for.

Employment Systems as Institutional Projects

In this section, I would like to abstractly discuss the relevant groups that make up the organizational field of employment systems in industrial societies. Then I discuss how these groups might align themselves in an ideal-typical set of situations to produce the dominance of one of three conceptions of employment systems: managerialism, vocationalism, and professionalism. I view these outcomes as the result of the different strengths among the competing groups. In capitalist economies, the means of production are primarily held in private hands. As part of these property rights, the owners and managers of capital claim the right to control employment relations. Most of the focus of the attention of employers and their representative groups is on getting states to guarantee their rights to control employment systems. Most Marxist theories assume that the state comes down on the side of the owners of capital (Miliband 1969).

If the most powerful forces in society are owners and managers of capital, then they will be able to organize the field of employment relations and get their institutional project. But to do so generally in society, they need the state and either the professions or workers' representatives as active partners in the process. The power of workers and professionals has two sources: skill and status differences, and the ability to control the supply of labor and skills. They build associations and unions in order to gain power. Potentially, a large number of groups can form around these various tactics. But, practically, groups use two major conceptions of control to control employment relations: those associated with "blue collar" ("vocationalism") and those associated with "white collar" work ("professionalism").

Larson (1977) has argued that there are no major differences in the strategies of these groups. Both focus on controlling occupational skills or labor supply as their primary source of power. Abbott (1988) argues in his "regional" theory of the division of labor, however, that strategies differ. "White collar" workers focus on professionalization as their major tactic of control. Professional projects try to use the abstract expertise of a group as grounds for self-governance. The new literature on professions also notes that they employ universities in their struggle for governance, focus their control projects on the state, and constantly try to invade other groups' professional territory. Professions, then, may use different organizational tactics and seek allies among educators, states, and other professions in order to promote their interests. The professionalism strategy can be analytically separated from the vocational strategy as different outcomes of strong worker power. Strong organization of blue-collar labor results in vocational systems. Professionalization depends on expertise, and, not surprisingly, projects to professionalize markets are frequently undertaken with the help of the state and the educational system.

A question increasingly discussed in the professionalization literature is the possibility of another type of alliance: between professions and managers. In a number of societies, the management function itself has become increasingly professionalized. The management function may either be conceived of as a generalist position attached to organizations in general or be defined as a specialized activity attached to a function performed in the organization. One example of a professional and generalist view of management is encapsulated in the masters in business administration (M.B.A.) degree. The degree signifies that its recipient has general skills in all aspects of business, marketing, production, finance and accounting, and business strategy. The popularity of the degree in the United States demonstrates that a professional, but generalist, conception of management dominates thinking in some business circles. Another conception of management that is professional, but not generalist, concerns functional specialization in the firm. Here, managers have specific skills, such as finance or marketing skills. They spend their careers in specific functional departments in firms and approach the problems of the firm from the perspective of their specialization. These functional specializations are worldviews that cause managers to interpret the situation of their firm from their point of view. It is likely that a high degree of professionalization or

TABLE 5.1
The Logic of Employment Systems

Attribute	Vocationalism	Professionalism	Managerialism
Affiliative unit	Industrial trade union	Professional association	Firm (or company union)
Training	"On the job"	Postgraduate education	University
Intragenerational mobility (career)	Intraoccupational	Intraoccupational	Intrafirm

functional orientation of the management function will lead managers to a preference for professionals as allies in the struggle with workers (Abbott 1988, 1989, Burrage 1990; Byrkjeflot 1993). This is because managers will view professionals as people with expertise that will support and implement a particular strategic vision for the firm.

The constitution of rules regarding employment relations turns on the organizational and entrepreneurial capacities of these various parties, the general political and economic environment, and the particular historical period in which employment systems come into existence. It is possible to abstract away from historical particularism to identify several ideal-typical outcomes of this struggle for the creation of employment systems.

Earlier, I asserted that three ideal-typical institutional sets of arrangements dominated the existing types of employment systems: managerialism, vocationalism, and professionalism. Table 5.1 summarizes our characterization of these employment systems. I think these types reflect very much the relative power of the capitalists, workers, professionals, the state, and educators. If firms have the upper hand, they tend to institutionalize *managerialism* as the model of employment relations. Here, managers control who enters the firms, and they use internal labor markets as devices to create primary and secondary labor markets. Firms and societies dominated by managerialism tend to have company unions, use status credentials as the primary filter for admittance into the organization, and engage in firm-specific training over the life cycle to create careers for valued employees. The typical career is with one corporation. This model is similar to what Burawoy (1985) calls hegemonic despotism, to Edwards's (1979) bureaucratic control, or to Williamson's (1975, 1985) view of the employment relation.

Opposition to firms' control over labor markets can come from two main sources. Strong workers' organizations produce vocationalism. These groups focus on producing occupational career tracks. I call this conception of control *vocationalism* because it relies on vocational training, either on the job or in certified programs where the training is done both at work and in classrooms. The distinction between management and workers is not as strong in such systems, since the management function is less professionalized and since lower management often is recruited from the rank of workers. Those hiring new workers and lower supervisors are influenced by a worker perspective, because they have the same vocational training as those they recruit. The typical career is marked by a commitment to one occupation or a field of occupations within an industry (Streeck 1996, 142–44).

White-collar workers are inclined toward *professionalism*, in which privilege is exerted because of expert knowledge (Stinchcombe 1959). Professionalism is a conception of work that references a professional expert peer group, uses associations to maintain collegiality, and relies on universities for training of personnel. There are at least two variants of professionalism, however, depending on the extent to which professions rely on the state or on private associations. In state professionalism, the state takes a direct role in the construction of a professional system. It creates a system of schools and accreditation. It often sets up a system of exams for entry into these schools and thereby creates a hierarchy of professionals. Finally, it is often the leading employer of professionals. State professionalism creates experts that can help governments take political problems and submit them to professional expertise, thereby working to depoliticize them. Professional systems that rely on private associations for credentialing tend to have more autonomy from state and corporate actors. Here, boards of experts credential new professionals either through exam systems or by governing training programs. Such systems rely on governments, of course, to legitimate their right for a monopoly over the credentialing process. But they maintain their autonomy by declaring that they are the only ones with sufficient knowledge to certify other professionals. Careers in both these variants are centered on expertise or fields of knowledge and are therefore not specific to a firm or industry.

The challenge, when speaking about employment systems, is to bring the education system into the analysis. Abbott argues that "the 12 years spent in school by most citizens . . . clearly provide the implicit model for later industrial relations . . . education is the main girder supporting modern staffing structures" (Abbott 1989, 287–88). The extent to which a society develops vocationalist, managerial, or professional systems is both a cause and an effect of the structure of the whole system from kindergarten to graduate studies.

Marxist scholars (Bowles and Gintis 1976) have tended to see the educational system as a source of reproduction and legitimation of capitalist inequalities. While schools function to reproduce employment systems once they are formed, they can have pivotal effects in two sorts of ways. First, at critical moments where the possibility exists for employment systems to emerge, actors in the educational system allied with managers, professionals, workers, or the state can weigh in to institutionalize some system of employment relations. This is particularly important for groups trying to establish themselves as professionals. Universities serve as bases of power to legitimate the claims of these groups to control certification.

Second, once in place, educational elites can affect the supply of different types of groups. In this way, there can be feedback into employment systems that can tend to reproduce or undermine them. The massive production of lawyers in the United States in the 1970s and 1980s has altered many features of the employment relation, including the propensity of workers to use the court system to exert control. Another example is the attempt of medical schools to control the labor supply of physicians in the United States, thereby increasing the relative incomes and autonomy of physicians (Starr 1982).

To the degree that educators form a distinct group within societies, they are divided along lines reflecting the relative size and power of their potential client populations. Primary and secondary schools compete with community colleges and universities for funding and influence. The conception of control embedded in vocationalism tends to be supported by secondary schools and community colleges, while professionalism tends to garner support from the universities. This is because secondary schools and community colleges will see their mission as preparing students for specific jobs. Universities stress that students are prepared to think analytically about problems. Their students possess many kinds of abstract knowledge by majoring in particular fields. Universities are gateways to more advanced professional training. They are staffed by academics who view themselves as possessors of expert knowledge. The huge post-Second World War expansion of higher education in the U.S. fuelled an expansion in the knowledge base of the population. About 25% of the population now has college degrees. Not surprisingly, the number of professional and managerial workers has increased over this time as well. This has reinforced the power of universities.

Variations and Transformations in Employment Systems

These ideal-typical accounts can be usefully modified in three ways, in order to make them more useful for analysis. First, it is important to consider how mixes of these pure types can produce stable institutional outcomes. Second, it is also important to consider how one may use the analysis of institutional change that was described in the last section to specify the conditions under which one may identify the trajectory of a given set of institutions governing employment relations. In other words, how can one tell if a system is coming into existence, is stable and perhaps spreading, or is open to transformation? Finally, it is useful to suggest how one uses this perspective to ask and answer questions about historical systems of employment relations.

It is the case that "mixed" types of employment relations can come into existence. This can happen in a number of ways. First, since different sectors of the economy have emerged at different historical moments, one system of employment relations may dominate certain sectors of the economy, while another dominate others. Thus, the dominance of one system of employment relations depends on the relative power of organized groups at the moment of the founding of the industry.

There is another way in which the industrial structure of a country can affect the mix of employment systems. It may be that firms located in large-scale industries (what have been called core firms; see Averitt 1968) are dominated by managerialism, while firms in the periphery may have a more mixed mode of employment relations, such as vocationalism (as in the U.S. construction sector) or professionalism (business services) in combination with managerialism. This is because some smaller firms that employ skilled labor have fewer abilities to resist workers' attempts at organization, particularly professionals.

Finally, political compromises between organized groups might produce mixed outcomes that embed features of several of the systems. One can easily imagine an alliance between managerialism and professionalism (Brint 1994). Here, managers would claim to control their firms, but would grant professionals independent status in certain expert occupations and rely on expert advice for the structuring of their organizations. Societal variations in the trend toward externalization of professional business services in modern economies might symbolize the degree to which professionals have been able to reach a compromise with their employers.[3] Similarly, one can imagine a situation where managerialism and vocationalism coexisted side by side. In certain large firms, managers and workers might negotiate internal labor markets such that workers controled work rules and seniority and managers and professionals controlled the organization of work (as in the U.S. automobile industry).

The Dynamics of Systems of Employment Relations

The purpose of this section is to consider where employment systems come from and how they become institutionalized. Employment systems reflect the construction of interests produced by the structural positions of groups.

But they are also, to some degree, political and social constructions that reflect reactions to other groups and the experiences of similarly placed groups in other countries and other times. This suggests that the initial timing and conditions of employment relations have important effects for the formation of institutions around the employment relations in a given society. At crucial points in time, power constellations in society and differentiated patterns in education have crystallized and been "frozen" into institutions that have continued to shape employment systems even after those initial conditions have changed.

Every society comprises a huge number of fields connected in a great many ways. A given field may be both dependent on some fields and, at the same time, dominant over others. States connect directly and indirectly to every existing organizational field. Thus, organizations and various organized groups often find themselves as participants in a multitude of fields. The large-scale institutional project described here, that is, the making of a society-wide employment system, requires interaction between participants in a wide variety of fields. At the early stages of rapid capitalist development, a large number of organizational fields (those organized around large-scale product markets) faced the problem of developing stable employment relations. The process by which these relations emerged should be the focus of sustained study. One would need to identify key organizations and actors and how they tried to resolve their problems in the context of their organizational fields. One would want to be sensitive to which solutions proved more general and spread to other fields. Finally, my perspective suggests that states had to be involved in the ratification, if not the creation, of stable employment relations. Thus the constitution of the policy domain of employment relations needs to be a constant arena of focus.

Using the language developed earlier, the problem is how the various organized forces come together to establish a stable employment system at the level of organizational fields. One expects that this problem is most acute for rapidly growing sectors of the economy where well-known employment relations do not exist. Initial conditions are important in several ways. First, some states developed interventionist strategies in their economies at an early historical junction, whereas others were less developed and remained regulatory (Dobbin 1994). States provided social insurance schemes, and the character of state regulation of labor relations in some instances created important advantages for workers and professions in their different bargaining positions vis-à-vis employers (Burawoy 1985, 126). Second, the relative power of workers and firms depended on the importance of skill level in the production system and the supply of skilled labor.

The extreme cases are useful to describe. If there is a plentiful supply of skilled labor and a government that does not intervene in labor market processes, then the most likely outcome is for managers and owners to organize systems of employment relations. They will choose to create firm internal labor markets that give some workers careers in the organizations and isolate others in secondary labor markets. If labor is well organized, skills are not plentiful in society, and governments intervene on the side of workers, one would expect vocationalism. Workers will control labor markets and will work to provide training and opportunities for workers in a particular industry. If workers and managers were in a stalemate and government intervention is possible, then one expects state professionalism to predominate. In this situation, the government can produce experts who help guide workers and managers toward "rational" solutions to employment relation problems. Associational professionalism results under several conditions. If managers have the upper hand and the state follows management's lead, one strategy for some workers is to try to form professions. This legitimates their claim on their abstract knowledge and brings in the state to buttress a private group's claim on credentialing people with this knowledge. Associational professionalism forces managers to recognize this claim and pay more for their expertise. Another way for associational professionalism to come about is if neither workers nor managers are well organized. Here, associational groups use their claim on abstract knowledge to forward their group interest.

If employment systems are conceptions of control certified by the state and institutionalized at crucial junctures in history, it is relevant to find out what industries were dominant at those junctures. One expects that the most rapidly growing industries were the site for new experiments in institutions surrounding the employment relation (Stinchcombe 1965). Once these took hold and were ratified or legalized by the state, they spread to organizational fields where similar conditions held sway. Once a system of employment relations was institutionalized more generally, it would greatly shape the possibilities for new systems of employment to come into existence. It would do so in a number of ways. First, the emergence or rapid growth of an industrial or technical educational system would be influenced by the set of employment relations in the most important industries at the time. The system would be producing individuals who would take up positions also in the new industries and in the policy domain of employment relations. Second, as new industrial fields opened up, the first place that managers and workers would look for models of employment relations would be nearby industries.

New systems of employment relations are likely to have two sources. As already mentioned, new industries emerge with different balances of power between important groups. More interesting is the case where employment relations are transformed in existing industries. From my perspective, changes in employment relations in existing industries depend on the failure of existing conceptions of employment relations in supporting economic growth (economic crisis) or the failure of the education system to produce motivated and adequately skilled workers (motivation crisis).

The balance of power within employment relations would have to be perceived to be creating negative conditions for dominant groups in order to convince these groups to shift their tactics. This could occur in several ways. First, in a general economic downturn (e.g., the Great Depression of the 1930s), one expects systems of employment relations to come under pressure from all of the groups involved. If the largest firms begin to go bankrupt or if the skills supply situation changes dramatically, then existing systems are threatened. Second, crises generated by states (wars and political upheaval) can easily undermine employment systems (Baron, Dobbin, and Jennings 1986). These can be direct, whereby states intervene to alter the functioning of labor markets, or indirect, through the passage of what appears to be unrelated legislation. Finally, invasion of the major industries of a given society by other firms utilizing different employment relations can force reorganization of remaining firms' employment relations.

Insights into Comparative Employment Systems

This is not the place to undertake a substantial comparison of the voluminous historical and sociological histories of the employment relations in the industrialized societies. It is useful, however, to try to bring this theoretical apparatus to bear on what is known about the employment systems and institutional history of the United States, Germany, Japan, and France.

Since the approach here is "ideal typical," one wants to view the tendencies of these societies as they are currently configured. Some of what follows is speculative, precisely because the research on many of the points made here has not been done. From my perspective, Germany most clearly conforms to the vocational model, France seems to best fit the state professional model, Japan the managerialist model, whereas the United States reflects a compromise between the managerial and professional models. It is probably the case that in each society there are examples of industries organized according to each of the models. But since states are arguably the units that legitimate employment systems, it is plausible to begin with the hypothesis that a single system can emerge. An ambitious research agenda would ask whether or not societies could be characterized in this way, and if so, how the system was modified across sectors over time.

Germany: Vocationalism

The story of the deal struck in the 1870s between Bismarck and the state, on the one hand, and heavy industry, on the other, is well known. Germany was a late industrializer that developed cartels and a high degree of integration in the economy by the involvement of states and banks. Germany was particularly strong in producer goods and export industries, and the explicit aim was to "catch up" with Britain and other more advanced industrialized countries, and develop strong military power. However, the employment system that developed was most influenced by the strength of German workers' associations. I argue that this relative strength led to key concessions granted by the state and firms in their search for rapid industrial development and led to the eventual accession of a vocationalist system.

What is particularly interesting is the way the state developed an advanced system of welfare provision early on, and how the education system was structured to create differentiated skills (Muller, Ringer, and Simon 1987; Ziegler 1997). The welfare system facilitated the emergence of unions by granting them independence from their employers. The functionally differentiated technical education system made it difficult for potential professional groups and managers to appropriate workers' skills (Caplan 1990; Streeck 1984).

This combination gave unions the impetus to organize across firms and within industries. The state intervened in labor relations, but was in the long run unable to stop the union buildup and the growth of the Social Democratic Party. The state was more successful in establishing a distinction between white- and blue-collar workers. The social insurance law granted white-collar workers and civil servants privileges, and this made an alliance between these groups and workers more unlikely. There were, however, no legal restrictions that restrained discontented white-collar workers from unionizing, and strong labor unions were established among engineers as well as other white-collar groups in the twentieth century. Craft workers, however, appear to have been successful in matching skills supply with demand. The German economy was very skill-intensive because of its emphasis on producer goods, and this tended to favor the organization of workers.

In the post–World War II era, the revival of the German economy turned on preserving the "social compact" between German workers and employers. The very idea that workers should have control over firms represented the long history of cooperation between employers and workers, and the relative political and economic strength of workers. Many authors have characterized the German work system as less hierarchical with less differentiation between workers and managers (Streeck 1984; Maurice, Sellior, and Silveste 1984; Jurgens et al. 1993; Thelen 1991). Skilled workers often rose to become managers because of their knowledge of production processes.

During the 1990s, some scholars argued that the system was breaking down under the pressures of global competition (Streeck 1996). But the evidence for this remains difficult to assemble (for evidence on a counterinterpretation, see Jurgens, Malsch, and Dohse 1993). Even Streeck (1996, 156–70) suggests that there is more accommodation than transformation of the core system. It is clear that as Germany becomes less dependent on manufacturing, more professional or managerial systems may emerge in new industries.

United States: Managerialism-Professionalism

The U.S. case shows very clearly a mix of employment systems. It also shows a diversified education system and a system of social insurance provision less directed by the state than in most other industrialized countries. Working-class organization in the United States has been weak, and the link between workers and professionals, which could theoretically lead to vocationalist employment relations, did not emerge. It is for this reason that we say that managerialist employment relations predominated early in the century, and that they increasingly were joined by professionalist ones. Professionalist employment relations appeared in newer sectors of the economy and therefore did not supplant the managerialist system. In the core of the American economy, there appears to have been some compromise between managerialist and vocationalist models, beginning in the 1930s.

In the late nineteenth century, it appeared as if the United States was developing a strong labor movement. But, in a series of labor struggles, established unions such as the Knights of Labor were systematically defeated and destroyed by the employers' associations. The federal and state governments in the United States either did nothing or were openly hostile toward union organizing efforts (Voss 1993). By 1920, managerialist tendencies in American employment relations came into strong play (Jacoby 1997). It is no surprise that "Taylorism" and "Fordism" dominated the structuring of the employment system.

The U.S. labor movement continued to resist this development, however, and the Wagner Act (1937) made it easier for unions to organize. After bloody struggles in a number of core industries, unions and firms agreed to a mix of managerialism and vocationalism in those industries.

The employment system that developed in the automobile, steel, and other core industries reflected the relatively greater organized power of workers in those industries. Managerialism continued to dominate firms, but elements of vocationalism began to creep into American labor market practices. Formal rules, careers and job ladders, and benefits began to enter into these negotiations.

Jacoby (1997) has argued that managerialist conceptions of firms resulted in workers being provided with corporate welfare (i.e., pensions, health care, other benefits) as a result of the conflicts between labor and management. He views these developments in mostly negative terms and does not reflect upon how workers gained by their relative power to push employers to worry about their concerns. The real expansion of professionals came in the United States after World War II. I speculate that this expansion was fueled by the great increase in the size of the college-educated population after the war. The G.I. Bill enrolled millions of returning veterans in universities, and their advanced training produced a "market" for professionals in the postwar era. A large number of professionalization projects have been undertaken in the postwar era. One important research field is to document the number of groups that have attempted to professionalize and to gauge how successful they have been.

By and large, the owners and managers of firms have not resisted the professionalization of various classes of their employees. The expertise of these groups, be they consultants, specialists, engineers, or academic groups, has been sought out and employed in both large and medium-sized businesses. The role of the state in this process has been relatively reactive. The certification of professionals has been left to professional associations. The educational elites located in universities have promoted this process precisely because it has strengthened their claim over scarce societal resources.

France: State Professionalism

In comparison with Germany and the United States, France displays a third variant of industrial development. France developed a diversified consumer industry early on and did not develop the high level of bank involvement, concentration, and emphasis on producer goods characterizing late developers. Lash and Urry (1987) have argued that this was because France was really quite industrially advanced. Like Britain, France got to experience the "penalty of taking the lead" (Veblen 1939). The state was, however, much more interventionist than in the case of Britain. The French government had a long history of intervention in employment relations and the education system. The state, thus, promoted the agenda of state professionalist employment relations.

The key feature that led to state domination of the employment system was the inability of employer or worker organizations to dominate industrial relations. In different historical periods, the battle between workers and employers often turned violent and potentially revolutionary. The organizational apparatuses that could be brought to bear on this conflict were found in the state and among the professions attached to it. Credentials became the coin of the realm, and the development of elite educational institutions worked to create an elite that viewed its role as the direction of society through the government, not through the private economy. The present employment system, then, is the result of state intervention in the economy and the gradual penetration of the economy by "cadres" and professionals with state credentials. Bourdieu (1996) analyzes the close linkages between elite schools (*grandes écoles*) and the training of managers and professionals for both the state and industry.

Boltanski's study (1987) of the making of this group, the emergence of which he traces to the economic crisis in the 1930s, might be interpreted as a study of the institutionalization of a state professionalist conception of control in the French economy. Exactly how this conception of control is institutionalized as an employment system, however, is more difficult to detect from this study. In order to do this we need more information about how the state has certified the relationship between white-collar and blue-collar groups in French society, and what kind of institutionalized division of labor has emerged among the major groups (Boltanski 1987; Lash and Urry 1987; Ziegler 1997).

Japan: Managerialism

Burawoy characterizes Japan as a society "in which the state offers little or no social insurance and abstains from the regulation of factory apparatuses" (1985, 144). From my perspective, the purest example of managerialism exists in that society. Japan is also, along with Germany, the classic case of a late-developing nation displaying the "advantages of backwardness" (Veblen 1939). The timing of industrialization was later in Japan than in any of the other cases. The emphasis was put on production of producer goods and export as in Germany, but the task structure, the degree of internationalization, and the organizational models in these industries were different. Generally, Japanese labor was not well organized, but Japanese firms were. The Japanese state led industrialization before World War II, but the economy remained in the private hands of a small number of families, who were given wide latitude in their handling of labor relations.

After World War II, labor laws and antitrust laws similar to those in the United States were established in Japan in a "top down" approach. There was an intensified period of class struggle before the Korean War, but this ended in the early 1950s. The result of these struggles produced the institutions of enterprise unions, a much less interventionist state in labor affairs than even in the case of the United States, and the establishment of a new type of business group (the keiretsu). The major victory for workers was the permanent employment system. This is the major compromise in the Japanese system that makes it less than a pure case of managerialism.

This last aspect is particularly relevant here. It is important to note that the high degree of job security granted to Japanese workers who were part of this system was limited to the core firms in Japanese industry. In recessions, core firms would force their peripheral suppliers and customers to accept extra workers. This shift would continue down the chain until the smallest firms would be forced to lay off their workers (Kalleberg and Lincoln 1988). This combined a "hegemonic" system in the core with a "despotic" system with insecure jobs in the peripheral industries. As Whitehill argues, however, "life-time employment, whether actually experienced or not, remains an ideal norm to which all companies, large and small, aspire" (Whitehill 1991, 131; Aoki 1988).

Rohlen has argued that the Japanese school system represents a particularly strong legitimation of the prevailing organizational structures, and that the uniformity at the lower levels combined with an intensely status-stratified system at higher levels creates dedicated and docile workers (Rohlen 1983). Competition is intense among students at the lower level because they need to be accepted at a high-status university in order to be granted entry into the permanent employment system. Because of this strong expectation of lifetime employment within a single company among the highest educated, Japanese firms continue to develop extensive in-house educational programs. Once the university graduates are part of this system, however, they have to accept the notion of a broad career. Job rotation, usually every three to five years, is an expected part of every manager's career advancement.

Japanese managers are neither pure generalists, as are American managers, nor more narrowly specialized in one occupation, as are the Germans; rather they are "multispecialists." The major distinction in the core firms in Japan is between top executives and employees. The line separating blue-collar workers from white-collar workers is much more blurred in Japan than in any of the other cases (Koike and Inoki 1990; Kuwahara 1989; Whitehill 1991; Dore 1973). Japanese skills are generated in the firm, for the firm, and by the firm (Dore and Sako 1989). Firm-specific skills increase loyalty to the firm and a sense of community.

Research Agendas

The approach outlined here has two important implications. It suggests that systems of employment relations have a unique social origin that can only be studied historically. But I have also provided an ideal-typical analysis that specifies what sort of power arrangements are consistent with different outcomes. The cases illustrate that historical processes in each society that reflected the path into industrialization had profound effects on the system of employment that emerged. Where firms were strong, more managerialist systems emerged (Japan); where workers were strong, more vocationalist systems emerged (Germany). Where the two sides were forced to compromise, mixtures of systems came into being (France, United States). Once general arrangements emerged in the societies, educational systems came to buttress them.

It is useful to consider some of the implications of the perspective developed here for existing and future research. The thrust of the theoretical perspective put forward here is that the time is ripe for the opening of the field of stratification and organizations to more historical, more comparative, and more political and institutional approaches. The political-cultural approach encourages scholars to take up the issues of the formation, crisis, and transformation of employment systems. A set of conceptual distinctions has been offered for the important features of employment systems. I have also provided rudimentary hypotheses about how pure cases might turn out. Taken together, these arguments can inform more sustained analyses of employment systems and untangle the compromises systems reflect and the changes current assaults on them are likely to yield.

One of the most pressing research projects this suggests is to think about whether the general view we have of the types of employment systems in advanced industrial countries is historically accurate. Are there single systems of employment relations in modern industrial societies? Do our ideal types capture the most important distinctions among systems of employment relations? If societies contain multiple systems, is that explained by sectoral differences (i.e., core/periphery effects), path dependence (i.e., the moment of emergence), or compromises within sectors, or perhaps combinations of all three? It may be possible to synthesize what is known from disparate literatures (labor history, the history and study of professions, managerial history) to fill in the some of the gaps, but certainly much research remains to be done.

It is useful to study systems of employment relations beyond their originating moments in the entry into industrialization. Severe external crises have beset advanced industrial societies (two world wars, the depression of the 1930s), and huge institutional reorganizations have resulted. It is important to study these events and their aftermath more closely to see how the terms of employment were altered as a consequence. So, for instance, World War II did not appear to change the employment system in Germany, but it may have in Japan.

The framework developed can be applied to examine how the current organization of employment relations accounts for patterns of stratification we currently observe. It is useful to develop an example. The research on sex segregation of occupations has produced two somewhat anomalous results. First, we know that the vast majority of women continue to be segregated into a small number of occupations (Reskin and Roos 1990). But we also know that at the higher end of the occupational structure, women have entered certain professions, such as lawyers, doctors, managers, and professors, but not others, such as engineers (Reskin and Roos 1990; Wright and Jacobs 1994; Jacobs 1989, 1992). How would the political-cultural approach explain such patterns of change? The main mechanism of change must be focused on the relative power of women to force educational organizations, professional associations, and firms to change their training and hiring practices. One would expect men and managers who have benefited from the traditional division of labor to continue to support their privilege and resist women's entry into male-dominated occupations.

This would lead one to hypothesize that changes in sex segregation would be uneven because in different institutional spheres women and men would be able to draw on different resources. So, for example, given that men control training programs for craft occupations such as plumbers and construction workers, one should not be surprised that women have had a difficult time breaking into these occupations. These programs are organized on a local basis and are difficult to monitor. Moreover, men make life difficult for individual women who try to enter such programs. It is difficult to get credentials for women under these conditions, and if they obtain them, they will likely face harassment on the job.

On the other hand, since the 1970s, women have attended and graduated from universities at relatively high rates. This means that they have been increasingly likely to have credentials to enter managerial jobs and gain admission into professional schools. Not surprisingly, it is in these kinds of occupations that sex segregation has been weakened. This has been helped along by the women's movement (mainly organized by educated women), the use of equal opportunity law against universities and large corporations, and the relative success of women professionals and managers. These factors have worked over time to undermine the power of men to keep women from some more valued occupations (Dobbin et al. 1993; Sutton et al. 1994).

The political-cultural approach implies that it is the changing resources such as education, political and legal activism, and taking positions of power and authority that have given women more opportunities in some of the occupations in American societies. The converse is true as well. Women were less likely to make advances in fields where authority for credentialing was decentralized (allowing men and employers to keep women out), where the use of law was made difficult because firms were small and less likely to embrace equal opportunity laws, and where obtaining credentials was difficult or impossible. This is a testable hypothesis.

It is also possible to study the evolution of employment systems within or across industries as they emerge. One would argue that employment practices in a given newly emerging industry would owe greatly to existing practices from "nearby" industries. A succession of practices would reflect the ongoing political struggle to define these practices and the relative resources of various groups of workers and managers. So, for example, at their origin in new industries, such as computers and biotechnology, one expects professional models of employment relations to dominate. The initial balance of power may be with engineers and other professionals. This balance may "lock in," but one can also see that, as technologies settle down, the balance may shift back to managers, who may try to impose more orderly labor markets. One interesting feature of high-technology industries is that technology does change, and that fact makes it difficult for managers to control the situation, implying that professionalism may dominate.

I have argued that existing employment systems, once in place, prove to be stable. Such systems serve the interests of important groups and are usually transformed only when they are in severe crisis. One source of crisis that may affect stable employment systems in advanced capitalist countries is the internationalization of the world's economy. The nature and trajectory of the Japanese and German employment systems is a matter of some academic and political attention. The critical question posed is whether or not these distinctive systems of employment relations can weather the increase in international competition in general and the change toward a more information-and service-oriented economy.

My argument is that these current institutional arrangements provide managers in these societies with ways to react to short-term economic crises. So, while the lifetime employment system in Japan is under duress, its survival depends on firms being able to shift workers across organizations. How long and how far this can go will determine if the conditions for institutional transformation exist. Similarly, the economic crisis in Germany has started to force employers to rethink their employment systems. One strategy has been to shorten workweeks temporarily. This is a measure that reflects an adjustment within the existing system of employment relations. But if these adjustments fail, then the wholesale transformation of the system is possible. The German education system appears to be in crisis as the vocational system declines. This is mainly due to the shift away from manufacturing. As industry is more focused on services and high-valued-added products, the demand for skilled machine workers has declined. This has put pressure on the universities to expand, particularly as business has greater demands for people with advanced technical training in engineering and information technology. This will fuel a shift away from a vocational system, perhaps, toward a professionalization model. In the United States, the employment system appears to be, for the time being, the most stable. The managerial-professional model allows firms to shed workers in downturns and contract to keep workers they favor and need.

Finally, it is important to more closely link the development of educational institutions in a society to the system of employment relations. Once systems of education have expanded, they can have unintended effects on employment relations. I have argued that the "professionalization" projects of the postwar era in the United States have been fueled to a large degree by the expansion of higher education and its supporters in state and federal governments. It would be useful to explore this process more institutionally and seek out evidence to solidify this argument.

Conclusion

The theoretical arguments proposed have drawn their inspiration from three literatures: the political-cultural approach, the "old" institutional economics, and Marxism. The argument about the "new" institutionalism was made most explicit. It is useful to briefly link our project to these other traditions. There were two strands of the "old" institutional economics. The first focused on how noneconomic institutions shaped economic action (Veblen 1932; Commons 1934). This literature took for granted that political processes were at the core of the construction of institutions. A later version of this tradition informed analyses of labor markets (Kerr 1954; Dunlop 1957; Doeringer and Piore 1971). Here, the view was that groups would try to exercise control over atomistic labor market processes by constructing labor market segments, characterized by bargaining arrangements that invoked credentials, constrained labor supply, and tried to raise wages. The basic insight in the literature was that labor markets could be negotiated, and that this would affect a large number of outcomes. My institutional analysis begins with a bargaining view of the players involved in the formation of employment systems.

Marxism, of course, has a great deal to say about the employment system (Edwards 1979; Burawoy 1985; Braverman 1974). The basic insight is that capitalists and workers face off over issues of control in the labor force and that capitalists generally have the upper hand. I concur with this argument as well. If one limits oneself to just the advanced industrial societies, managerialism and, to a lesser degree, professionalism dominate employment relations. In few societies is vocationalism the core model, Germany being the purest case. This results from the fact that capitalists tend to be much better organized, have more resources, and can frequently call on states to intervene in their favor.

But I think that Marxism and the "old" institutional economics share several problems which are somewhat resolved by the political-cultural approach. First, states should be treated as both exogenous to, and part of, the process by which employment relations are negotiated. States do not only intervene on the side of capitalists (as in Marxism) or merely provide protection for privileged groups of workers (as in institutional economics). They must be seen as partners to bargains. Second, workers sometimes are able to organize alternative institutions within the framework of capitalism. Therefore, the class struggle approach needs to allow for more possible outcomes, such as professionalism, vocationalism, and the various political compromises discussed.

Third, neither the old institutionalism nor Marxism theory has a theory of institutions. This means they cannot make sense of how institutions become stable. Once institutions are in place, they are difficult to dislodge for two reasons: they are templates for action, and they organize existing interests and reward certain groups who then have a great deal at stake in defending them. The process of institutionalization suggests why systems of employment relations can last for long periods of time. Both institutional economics and Marxism focus narrowly on the relation between workers and capitalists. Our perspective broadens that relation and embeds it in larger societal arrangements, including states, educational systems, and existing models of employment relations, and the previous history of those arrangements.

A final difference of opinion follows from the political-cultural framework as well. Changes in employment relations are not likely to be endogenous to the bargaining process, as Marxism or institutional economics suggests, but exogenous. To change an employment system requires a crisis in the existing system, one usually caused by exogenous shocks. If a given bargain is held in place by a given distribution of resources, new bargains require those distributions to change. This most frequently occurs during major events and their aftermath, such as war or depressions, or the force of international competition. But it can also result from secular changes such as shifts in the skills of groups in society and changes from a manufacturing to a service economy.

The political-cultural approach to studying employment systems gives scholars a great deal of leverage on making sense of what has happened, what is possible, and what strategies make the most sense given current institutional arrangements. The purpose of this theorizing is to suggest that projects couched in these more historical, political, and institutional terms are likely to prove fruitful in understanding how stratification and organizational processes intertwine.

6

The Dynamics of U.S. Firms and the Issue of Ownership and Control in the 1970s

THE QUESTION of who controls the large modern corporation in the United States is one of the most enduring in modern social science.[1] Sociologists who have studied the issue have gone in two directions: they have either been interested in detecting a capitalist class and discovering the nature of its cohesion (Zeitlin 1974; Useem 1984), or else they have tried to use organizational theory to account for the structure of the relations among large-scale business organizations (Burt 1983; Mintz and Schwartz 1985; White 1981; Fligstein 1990; Baker 1984, 1990). Economists have approached the question by being concerned about the possible negative effects of the separation of ownership from control in producing maximum profits (Williamson 1964, 1985; Marris 1964; Jensen and Meckling 1976; Fama and Jensen 1983a, 1983b; Holmstrom 1982; MacNeil 1985). What is at stake in this debate is our understanding of how large corporations operate and the nature of the worlds that are constructed around them.

Much of the evidence for the effects of owner versus management versus bank control and the composition of boards of directors on the financial performance of corporations in the United States is mixed or negative (Burt 1983; Herman 1981; for evidence that supports some effect, see Pennings 1980; see Scherer 1980 for a review). These analyses have a number of problems. They use different measures of control and generally use only one measure of performance (profits) with a cross-sectional research design. Even more important, there are almost no attempts to model the effects of the various forms of control on important strategic decisions, such as product mix, mergers, and which subunit dominates firms (for an exception, see Palmer et al. 1987, 1995).

The major empirical contribution of this chapter is to expand these analyses in a number of ways. First, several measures of forms of control are tested simultaneously in order to assess if any has particular advantages. Second, in addition to a cross-sectional design, a panel design is utilized to assess whether or not forms of control affect outcomes over time. Third, a larger number of important organizational outcomes is modeled, thereby extending attempts to test versions of control theory to other variables. Finally, theories that emphasize the importance of bank versus owner versus managerial control are contrasted with the political-cultural view that focuses on interorganizational factors as predictors of outcomes.

The major substantive conclusion is that ownership and the presence of bank interlocks are not very important determinants of the strategic and financial outcomes of large firms. A far more plausible model is that the actors who control corporations are all interested in generating profits and, as such, pay attention to what is occurring in their organizations and organizational fields as cues to guide their behavior. Family owners, bank owners, managers, and bank directors behave according to the dictates of the market field in which the firm is embedded and the internal dynamics of their organizations.

The empirical results support the view that American capitalism is organized as a set of markets where firms meet to compete and try to produce self-reproducing role structures. The social relations that exist among people who are owners, members of boards, and top managers are not consequential for making sense of how the managers and owners of the largest firms operate in the United States. I am not arguing that economic elites do not exist. While there is an elite, the elite is linked through its common conception of what produces successful outcomes for firms. This imagery of the world of top managers and owners focuses on their common cultural understandings and the forms of social relations they establish to create stable relationships with their principal competitors.

Economic sociologists have been debating the nature of the sociological embeddedness of markets in the United States for almost 20 years. Much of the work has focused on network analyses (Burt 1983; Granovetter 1985; Baker 1984), and a fair amount of that work has used boards of directors and bank interlocks as the basis of the network data (Burt 1983; Mintz and Schwartz 1985). The results of this study suggest that American firms are neither constrained nor enabled by this form of network embeddedness (a result discussed more generally in this literature by Stinchcombe 1990).

Therefore, the social structure of American firms may be studied more adequately by targeting the existing distribution of power in the firm, the behavior of competitors in the firm's main markets (White 1981), and the relations of the firm to the government (Fligstein 1990). Further, it is the substantive content of those relations (i.e., the background of CEOs and the existing conceptions of action that dominate competitors) that best predicts any given firm's actions—not the mere existence of social relations among them.

Review of the Literature

In this section, relevant literature from three perspectives, the literature on management versus family or individual control, the literature on the potential for bank control, and the recent organizational literature, is considered. Much of the sociological research has tried to establish the existence of an economic elite or capitalist class and has therefore been uninterested in differences in the economic behavior of corporations (Zeitlin 1974; Allen 1974; Useem 1984). This chapter does not address the concern of that research, nor does it focus on the translation of elites' interests into political action (Mizruchi 1989). The purpose of this chapter is to examine the determinants of the strategic behavior of large firms and their relation to the control debate.

Corporate control will be defined as the power to determine the broad policies guiding the corporation, including decisions regarding capital structure (such as equity, debt, profits, and cash flow), geographic expansion, product diversification, corporate structure, and mergers (see Herman 1981 for a similar definition). The question this chapter seeks to answer is whether differences in ownership patterns and bank interlocks actually affect actions that firms undertake in the United States. The review asks why the groups have varying interests that cause them to make strategic decisions differently.

Management versus Owner Control

Economists have been interested in the control debate ever since Berle and Means (1933) asserted that there was an increasing separation between the ownership and control of the largest firms (theoretical arguments for the relation are presented in Marris 1964; Williamson 1964). Their concern is the degree to which managerial discretion causes firms to fail to pursue profit maximization. The theory suggests that managers try to protect their jobs and therefore avoid courses of action that could threaten their positions, while owners act in a more entrepreneurial fashion. The alternative tactics managers could pursue include settling for lower, but more stable, profits by aiming for growth in sales and assets over profits, acting for the public interest instead of shareholder interests, increasing their salaries and perquisites, and implementing strategies that are low risk. Managers would thus be more likely than owners to diversify in their efforts to spread risk across product lines. They would also use mergers for corporate growth because buying an existing company is less risky than entering a new business.

Several advances in economic theory have altered this debate. Williamson (1985, 311–22), extending a transaction cost perspective, has argued that the governance structure of joint stock corporations has been set up to minimize opportunism on the part of managers. This opportunism arises from information asymmetries between boards of directors and top managers. Boards of directors act to control this asymmetry by writing contracts for top managers that bond their interests to those of the shareholders. The multidivisional form is also a control mechanism that makes managerial opportunism more difficult (Williamson 1985, 320–22). While Williamson thinks these devices align interests, he also argues that managerial discretion and opportunism are always possible.

Agency theorists make a similar case.[2] The basis of their analysis is the principal-agent model, which emphasizes that one common feature of economic life is that individuals (principals) engage others (agents) to perform some service. The interests of the two do not always coincide, and so the principal must establish appropriate incentives for the agent and monitor the behavior of the agent to ensure that the agent acts in the principal's interests (Jensen and Meckling 1976, 308). Agency theory seeks to explain why the joint stock corporation exists, how the principal-agent relation between owners and managers is structured, and how that relation can go astray.

Fama and Jensen (1983b) argue that the joint stock corporation comes into existence in situations where technology requires a large amount of capital, a demand exists for specialized agents to utilize economies of scale, and a large pool of capital is needed to bond contracts and organization-specific assets. As they put it, "The benefits of unrestricted common stock residual claims in activities where optimal organizations are large and complex offset the agency costs resulting from separation of decision functions and residual risk-bearing" (Fama and Jensen 1983b, 346).

The principal-agent relation between boards of directors and managers can go awry when boards lack the will or the information to enforce discipline on managers. This occurs most frequently when stock ownership is diffused or institutional investors dominate (Jensen 1989; for an analysis of other dependent variables that use a similar argument, see Graves 1988; Fombrun and Stanley 1990). An oft-used measure of managerial discretion is free cash flow, which indicates whether managers are holding capital instead of distributing it to shareholders. Other strategies that reflect managerial control include diversification and growth in sales and assets with little growth in profits. Diversification can represent a tactic to hold onto free cash flow and enter less profitable businesses (for a dissenting view, see Amit and Wernerfelt 1990). Managerial salaries tend to be tied to the firm's growth, and examining the determinants of variables such as the ratio of profits to sales and assets suggests whether or not managers are sacrificing profits for growth.

Bank Control

The issue of financial control over the largest firms has lurked in the social science literature since the turn of the last century. The role of financiers in the merger movement of 1895–1905 is well known (Lamoreaux 1985; Mizruchi 1982). The literature on bank control has recently focused on the extent of that control and its effects on the behavior of large firms. Banks, insurance companies, mutual funds, and pension funds have all increased their holdings in large industrial firms (Herman 1981). The interesting question is whether they extended their involvement to active control over strategic decisions and, if so, in what direction. Those who argue for bank control can be divided into three camps: bank control through ownership, bank hegemony achieved by banks' key position in the financial system, and the potential for bank influence due to financial dependence. The strongest advocate of direct bank control is Kotz (1978). He argues that finance-controlled firms are more likely to take on external debt than non-finance-controlled firms and that thus their debt/equity ratio should be higher. This propensity to assume debt also makes them more likely to engage in mergers than non-finance-controlled firms. The presence of finance control over an entire industry should lower competition and raise profits, which can be indexed by the degree of bank interlocks. Hence, finance control leads to higher profitability for firms.

Mintz and Schwartz's (1985) approach is to argue that banks exert hegemony over the industrial system by virtue of their key control over the capital markets. This structural position has two effects. First, bankers intervene in corporations under conditions of crisis and replace managements who fail to provide profitable returns. Second, bankers are at the center of corporate interlocks, and they can use this influence to help firms collude or cooperate.

Unfortunately, it is usually difficult to ascertain the direction of influence between bankers and internal corporate representatives. Indeed, there is evidence that bankers are invited onto the board to co-opt them into making loans to the firm (Burt 1983; for a debate on this question, see the Herman-Kotz exchange [Herman 1979, 1980; Kotz 1980]). Bankers may also be brought onto boards of directors when firms are in financial trouble (Mizruchi and Stearns 1983). This evidence suggests that bankers themselves are being used as much as they are influencing the course of the organization.

These problems have led to a third position that posits a more complex relation between banks and firms. Because bankers often play a number of roles, one expects their influence to depend on the situation and their relative power. Bankers who are brought onto boards because of the financial dependence of firms are the most likely to have influence over the firm's financial structure and choice of debt instruments (Hirsch 1987). But bankers could be brought onto the board for a number of reasons, including co-optation, prestige, or social and political connections (Herman 1981). This explains why historically banks have been at the center of firm interlocks, but different banks have occupied these positions over time (Mizruchi 1982) and why board of directors interlocks are notoriously unstable and renewed less than 15% of the time (Palmer 1983).

Market Dynamics and Management Control

The organizational literature has increasingly focused on the construction of organizational fields (DiMaggio 1985). The actions of organizations are thought to be shaped by the links between any given organization and the organizations surrounding it.[3] Two literatures are relevant: the external control of organizations approach (Pfeffer and Salancik 1978; Burt 1983) and the political-cultural approach. Each has a different perspective on important mechanisms governing organizational embeddedness.

Firms exist in markets, within which they are dependent on other organizations for inputs and the consumption of outputs. The external control of organizations perspective suggests that actors who can make claims on delivering inputs or outputs are likely to have a disproportionate say in the internal allocation of resources (Pfeffer and Salancik 1978). Burt (1983) used this perspective to argue that boards of directors are used by firms as mechanisms to co-opt organizations in the environment. His analysis shows that outside directors are often representatives of firms that are important customers or suppliers. The presence of bankers on boards of directors can be explained by the need to generate capital. Unfortunately, Burt is unable to show that these ties actually produce additional profits for the firm, which seems to undermine the claim that this co-optation has positive effects.

The political-cultural approach expands on the insights suggested by institutional theory (Meyer and Rowan 1977; DiMaggio and Powell 1983, 1991) and the work of White (1981) on the structuring of markets by focusing on how the intraorganizational power struggle is structured in large firms and how it is affected by, and affects, its principal markets (Perrow 1970; Fligstein 1987, 1990). This sociological view offers explicit hypotheses about the links between firms, their markets, and the structuring of their behavior.

The issue for any firm is what courses of action to pursue. Since a priori the actual effect of any given strategy may be difficult to assess, there may be conflict over the goals of the firm. There are two bases for control: ownership and authority. To the degree that owners are in control of large firms, they are able to direct the course of those firms, but even ownership groups have to formulate a view of the world in order to take action.

The basic problem for managers and owners is to create a stable world so their firms continue to exist. This necessitates the construction of a stable market where actors come to take one another's actions into account in the framing of their actions. Two problems are involved in creating a stable market: a set of general and enforceable understandings is required, and those understandings must be legitimated by the government.

Where do conceptions of control come from? Since conceptions of control require a perspective on the world, these perspectives can have two sources: they can be borrowed from other firms or markets, or they can be embedded in how the different subunits of the firm conceptualize the problems and solutions for that firm. Subunit background provides actors with a way of seeing the world. A conception of control dictates a filter that actors apply to view their internal and external problems and to define how to solve those problems. Effective conceptions of control diffuse and come to dominate and define the firm's behavior in markets. In this way they operate both as a cultural template structuring new actions (i.e., what behaviors make sense) and as a set of structures limiting the possibilities for action (i.e., what others are doing, thereby structuring what reactions are possible).

Groups within firms gain and maintain power as a function of their ability to promote organizational survival and create stable markets. From this perspective, markets are more than socially constructed meanings, they are systems of power. The largest organizations generally control the markets and dictate their rules. Smaller organizations benefit from this system as long as they fall in line with the organizations setting the rules. All participants of the market come to see the world in a similar way and react to one another's moves from this perspective. I have termed this theoretical approach "political-cultural" because it focuses on the intra- and inter-organizational power struggles and suggests that the goal of such struggles is to create shared meanings, that is, local cultures that operate to produce stable interactions. The approach is also political in the sense that the state can enter into and regulate actions in any given market.

In the 1970s, most large American corporations were dominated by the finance conception of control, which viewed the firm as a bundle of assets deployed in order to maximize short-term earnings (Fligstein 1990, chap. 6). The finance conception of control originated with executives who were trained in finance methods and were primarily financial officers. Their balance sheet approach implies that the firm is no longer in the business of producing commodities, but instead operates as a set of assets. In such circumstances, divisions of the firm that do not perform up to expectations are sold off and new ones purchased. A central tactic is the use of mergers (and divestitures), often for diversification, to achieve growth.

The finance conception of control displaced the sales-and-marketing conception of control beginning in the late 1950s. Sales-and-marketing executives favor policies that boost sales by increasing marketing, differentiating products, and engaging in diversification of product lines. The finance conception emerged in the postwar era as a function of the increasingly diversified nature of the firm and the aggressive antitrust policies of the Truman and Eisenhower administrations (Fligstein 1990, chap. 6). Subsequently, many of the largest firms have become dominated by finance personnel espousing a finance conception of control (Fligstein 1987). Their claim on expertise is based on their ability to evaluate different product lines by their profitability and hence manage the large firm as an investment portfolio. Their claim on power is derived from the relative success of such a point of view in generating growth in the firm. One of the key hypotheses that this implies is that those acting with a finance conception are able to produce growth in sales, assets, or profits, mainly through mergers and diversification.

During the merger movement of the 1960s, two of every five firms that were larger than $10 million in assets were merger targets (Fligstein 1990, chap. 7). If one's field was invaded by firms using the finance conception of control, one could either adopt a similar view or risk becoming a target for merger. In this way, the markets of many of the largest corporations were reorganized by the finance conception of the corporation.

Hypotheses

The critical issue in the literatures I have outlined is how the agents who control the largest corporations affect the actions of these corporations. The political-cultural approach stresses the current structure of the situation, both internal and external to the organization, as the wellspring of action. The owner/management/bank debate suggests that the goals of specific interest groups, such as owners and creditors, differ and cause the organization to act differently, net of its internal configuration and its links to its field. These are very different images of the field of the largest corporations in the United States circa 1970. The one stresses the organization of property rights as pivotal to the stability of large firms, while the other stresses the nature of firms' interactions with their principal competitors.

The dependent variables studied here are of two types: financial and strategic. Financial outcomes are to some extent strategic choices. For instance, the amount of free cash flow is determined by decisions to retain or disburse earnings. Three other types of strategic decisions are modeled: whether firms undertake mergers, whether firms have diversified their products, and the subunit background of the corporate CEO. These actions reflect strategic policies of the organization. The use of mergers is an important decision regarding the allocation of capital. The decision to diversify the product mix reflects the actual definition of the organization in terms of its goals. The background of the incumbent CEO is an indication of which organizational subunit is responsible for determining the firm's strategy (Pfeffer 1981).

The management versus owner control literature predicts that manager-controlled firms are more likely to increase equity over debt, decrease the ratios of returns to assets and sales, and have relatively low returns on equity, relatively high price-to-earnings ratios (because of low payouts), and relatively high levels of free cash flow. The return-on-assets and return-on-sales variables reflect the degree to which managers are trading off earnings for assets or sales. Manager-controlled firms also favor mergers and diversification. All of these actions reflect management propensity to retain or reinvest earnings rather than disburse them to shareholders.

There are a number of indicators of management control, including a low percentage of stock held by a single family, individual, or bank, or a high percentage of stock held by institutional investors, a gauge of shareholder passivity (Jensen 1989). Product diversification is another indicator of management control, as managers tend to diversify rather than disburse earnings. From the transaction costs perspective, the presence of a multidivisional form suggests that managers are more constrained in their actions.

Bank control is indexed by the percentage of voting shares held by the largest bank and the number of bank interlocks on the board of directors. The bank control literature predicts that firms controlled by banks are more likely to pursue merger strategies in order to increase the power of the banks. They should also be more likely to have higher returns on equity and higher debt-to-equity ratios. The predictions of the financial hegemony perspective are indeterminate, although interlocks could be associated with higher returns on equity and higher debt-to-equity ratios. The financial dependence perspective suggests that the presence of bank control makes firms more likely to engage in mergers and have high debt-to-equity ratios. Network views that see boards of directors as co-optive devices to lessen resource dependence predict that bankers on the board and bank interlocks should enhance financial performance.

The political-cultural perspective stresses three types of factors that govern the financial and strategic choices of firms: the behavior of the firm's principal competitors, defined here in terms of the other large firms that occupy the same industry (specified by the two-digit Standard Industrial Classification, hereafter, SIC), the already existing strategies and structures, and which subunit controls the organization. The major hypotheses of the political-cultural perspective focus on the degree to which an organization and its organizational field are dominated by the finance conception of control. If other firms in one's field are diversifying or merging, indicating the dominance of the finance conception of control, one is more likely to engage in those activities as well.

Existing strategy of the firm is a powerful determinant of many outcomes, including growth and mergers, and reflects entrenched systems of power. Finance-controlled firms will be diversified and should be more likely to engage in mergers and show higher growth rates and returns than firms that are not diversified. This prediction runs counter to that of agency theory, which views diversification as lowering returns on assets and sales. The multidivisional form is the favorite structural vehicle for finance-oriented diversification and mergers, and its presence should positively affect growth in sales, assets, and profits.

The subunit that controls the CEO of the firm operates as an indicator of which conception of control dominates the firm as well (Fligstein 1987). Sales-and-marketing and finance CEOs will be more likely to lead firms that are diversified than manufacturing CEOs and be more likely to engage in mergers. Sales-and-marketing CEOs tend to lead firms with lower returns on assets and sales, reflecting their preference for sales growth over asset and profit growth. They are also less likely to engage in product-unrelated diversification and more likely to engage in product-related diversification. Finance CEOs are expected to be adept at producing profits for all measures, including returns on assets, sales, and equity.

The growth of large firms is determined, to some degree, by the rise or fall of the specific industry in which the firm resides. If the industry is expanding, then one expects sales, assets, and profits of a given firm to increase. This is not, of course, an effect of the social organization of a given field, but a purely economic variable.

It should be noted that a number of the variables index items for multiple theories, but the theories predict different effects (for instance, the measures of diversification). Additionally, agency theory and transaction cost theory are probably impossible to falsify. If it turns out that management-controlled firms do not use managerial discretion to lower profits, the result implies that the mechanisms to control managerial opportunism work. On the other hand, if evidence exists that managers do not favor profit maximization, then the mechanisms have failed. Therefore, the theory cannot be proven incorrect and can only be used to suggest the existence of opportunism.

Data and Methods

The selection of a data set and a time frame is hampered by a number of problems, largely stemming from the character of the existing measures of control. First, many of the control measures refer to different time periods, ranging from the mid-1960s to the early 1970s. Second, almost all of the control measures have taken the largest industrial corporations as the focus of their attention. This is understandable given the important role of large corporations in the U.S. economy. However, it means that no data exist on control forms over a large number of firms for a given industry.

Given these limitations, the one hundred largest industrial corporations in the United States in 1969 and the firms that entered the list of the one hundred largest industrial corporations between 1969 and 1979 are the focus of study. These data were obtained from *Fortune* magazine (1970, 1980). This design was chosen to create a panel study of large firms (in essence, the population of the largest). The panel design allows one to test how the initial conditions, which include the control types and the organizational factors, affect the behavior of the firm over a subsequent period of time. The decade-long time frame allows for the fact that strategic changes and effects of control accumulate slowly in the largest corporations. By modeling such change over long periods, one is more likely to observe such effects. For the financial measures, 10 years stabilizes the effects of year-to-year fluctuations. The initial year was chosen as 1969 because a number of the control and organizational variables had available measures for this year. One problem created by this choice is that financial data refer to 1969 and 1970, years when the economy and stock market were depressed.

The measures of forms of control are not straightforward to operationalize. Indeed, proponents have not been able to agree on how to measure them, and there is substantial disagreement on which firms fall into the bank, owner, or management control categories. The approach followed is to operationalize measures of control that might be general to all theories.[4] The percentage of stock held by the largest family or individual (Herman 1981), the largest percentage of stock with voting rights held by a bank (U.S. House of Representatives 1971; U.S. Senate 1973), and the percentage of the stock held by institutional investors in 1969 (U.S. House of Representatives 1971) were measured. The number of bank interlocks through boards of directors (U.S. House of Representatives 1969) was operationalized as well. Substantial data were missing for the bank control (25%) and the interlock measures (37%).

In order to maximize the number of cases in the analysis, two dummy variables were created. They were coded 0 if data was missing for the case, and 1 if it was available. The observations with missing data for the bank and interlock variables were then recoded 0. If there is some systematic bias in the way in which the data on control are related to the outcomes, the dummy variables will be statistically significant. Thirty-two separate coefficients for these dummy variables were estimated, and only two are statistically significant. By chance, one would expect one or two of the coefficients to be statistically significantly related to the outcomes, and therefore one can conclude that selectivity of missing data on these two variables is not a serious problem.

The measures of forms of control suffer from two sorts of problems. First, they may or may not tap into control. Since these are the only measures we have of stock ownership patterns, one must accept them as face valid. Second, we measure control at only one point in time. Since the analysis used the control variable to predict change over a substantial period (10 years), it may be the case that control shifted over the period. Little is known about the stability of the control variables because they have not been systematically measured over time. In order to maximize the possibility of discovering control effects, models for each of the dependent variables are run at the first time point (i.e., the cross section) as well as look for effects of control over time. It should be noted that most of the organizational variables are also being measured only at the first time point as well, and they may have similar problems. One advantage to this situation is that one does not confuse the causal order of important relationships. Since the exogenous variables are measured at the first time point, they are clearly causes of outcomes over the decade.

A large number of dependent variables was used in this analysis. First, free cash flow, market value, price-to-earnings ratio, return on assets, after-tax profit margin (return on sales), return on equity, and debt-to-equity ratio in 1970 were analyzed (Compustat 1989).[5] These variables were taken from corporate reports and 10-K forms and coded by Compustat, which is produced by Standard and Poor's. Free cash flow could not be adequately constructed using its standard definition for the first time period (1970) due to the unavailability of requisite data. Consequently, it was approximated by subtracting current liabilities from current assets for both time periods. The calculations for all variables appear in the appendix to this chapter. The 1980 levels of these variables plus the 1980 value of assets and sales were also analyzed. Dollar amounts were adjusted to 1967 levels. In the panel analysis the level of each of the dependent variables at the first point in time was included as a regressor.[6]

Corporate strategy was coded into three categories: product-dominant, product-related, product-unrelated. These categories were coded using Rumelt (1974) and Moody's manuals. Product-dominant implies that firms produce more than 70% of their revenues in a single product line. Product-related implies that firms produce multiple products that were related or market extensions (for example: chemical companies producing paint and explosives), with no single line accounting for more than 70% of output. Product-unrelated strategies imply that firms are engaged in unrelated businesses for a substantial portion of their revenue (no product could account for more than 70% of revenue). Two dummy variables were coded indicating whether or not a firm had a product-related strategy (coded 1 on one of the dummy variables) or a product-unrelated strategy (coded 1 on the other dummy variable). They refer to 1969.

Corporate structure refers to the existence of a multidivisional form. A dummy variable was coded 1 if a firm had a multidivisional form as its structure in 1969. This data was coded from Rumelt (1974) and Moody's (1980).

Mergers were coded using the Federal Trade Commission's *Report on Mergers* (1981). The total number of mergers engaged in from 1969 to 1979 was summed for each firm. On examination of the variable, it was found that a distinction between firms that engaged in mergers and those that did not best captured the skewed distribution. Therefore, this variable was coded 0 if firms did not engage in mergers and 1 if they did. The variable indicating firms' previous merger behavior is the total number of mergers engaged in during 1959 to 1969. This variable did not require dichotomization.

The subunit background of the corporate chief executive officer was coded in 1969 and 1979. Once the name of the CEO was collected from Moody's manuals, their entry was pursued in *Who's Who in America, Who's Who in Finance and Industry*, and other sources. From the description of each CEO's career, a decision was made as to how the person came up through the firm on the basis of previous job titles. If the person switched firms, the subunit background was decided on the basis of job titles across the career. The following categories were coded: manufacturing, sales and marketing, finance, entrepreneur, lawyer, general management, other, and unable to ascertain. The general management category reflects whether a person held different titles in different parts of the firm (for example, plant manager and vice president in charge of finance). In the data analysis presented here, the measure has been collapsed into three dummy variables: if the CEO was a manufacturing person, a finance person, or a sales-and-marketing person. The omitted category is all others.

The organizational field variables all refer to the year 1969 and were based on the characteristics of the major industry of the firm (two-digit SIC). The change in the growth in assets from 1969 to 1979 in the industry was used as a measure of industry growth, with the change in assets for each firm in the analysis subtracted from the industry's change in order to remove any spurious relation between the measures. This variable serves as a rough measure of increase in demand. The percentages of other large firms that had product-related and product-unrelated strategies in the industry were coded to predict whether or not a given firm also had a product-related or product-unrelated strategy. Similarly, the percentages of the other large firms in the industry that had finance, sales-and-marketing, and manufacturing CEOs in 1969 were used to predict the CEO in 1979.

These measures have a number of potential problems. They assume that the relevant organizational field comprises direct competitors, which are also large firms. If these measures do predict outcomes, then one can assert they have predictive validity. One could argue that these measures tap into what is economically efficient for firms of a given type and that any association is merely due to the correlation between what is efficient and what others are doing. This criticism is less easy to answer and implies that one needs to be cautious in accepting the organizational field interpretation of these variables.

Two techniques were used to analyze the data. A least squares regression was used to analyze the level and change in the financial measures. Logit analysis was used to analyze whether or not a firm engaged in a merger, whether or not a firm had a product-dominant, -related, or -unrelated strategy (product-dominant was the left-out category), and the background of the CEO in 1979 (the "other" category was the left-out category). This procedure is appropriate because these are qualitative dependent variables. All calculations were performed using the software package Statistical Analysis System (SAS).

Results

The hypotheses will be considered first by first examining the effects of the control, industry, and organizational variables on the financial performance measures in 1970. Then the panel results are discussed. Finally, changes in the qualitative variables will be discussed. The means and standard deviations for the variables used in the analyses are presented in table 6.1.

Table 6.2 contains the results for the regression analyses of the various measures of financial performance in 1970. My models do not explain a lot of the variation in financial performance in 1970, and the measures of forms of control fare poorly. It is useful to consider the specific hypotheses more closely. There is no evidence that bank or family shareholding affects any of the measures of financial performance. The lack of these effects suggests that managers unconstrained by owners, in the cross section, do not generate excesses of free cash flow, reduce the firm's market value, increase equity over debt, or favor assets and sales to profits. Further, bank ownership did not make firms more profitable (by any measure of profits), nor did it make firms more likely to favor debt over equity.

Firms that were highly interlocked were actually less profitable in terms of returns on assets, sales, and equity, contradicting the bank control hypothesis that firms with interlocks would be more profitable. There is also no effect of the multidivisional form on the financial performance of firms, undermining transaction costs arguments. An agency or transaction cost

TABLE 6.1
Means and Standard Deviations for Variables Used in the Analysis

Variable	Label	Mean	Std. Dev.
MERGER1	Merger activity, 1959–69	1.69	2.17
MERGER2	Merger activity, 1969–79	0.56	0.76
INDGROW	Growth of industry	4.94	4.98
RELN	Product-related strategy, 1969	0.55	0.49
UNRELN	Product-unrelated strategy, 1969	0.20	0.40
MDF1	Multidivisional form, 1969	0.73	0.44
SALEPR	Sales president, 1969	0.19	0.39
MANPRES	Manufacturing president, 1969	0.24	0.42
FINPR	Finance president, 1969	0.22	0.41
PERREL	% of firms related strategy	47.43	26.58
PERUNREL	% of firms unrelated strategy	18.16	16.12
FINDPER	% of firms finance president	17.08	8.34
SINDPER	% of firms manufacturing president	19.26	16.90
MINDPER	% of firms sales president	25.13	20.51
FCF80	Free cash flow, 1980	437.79	568.19
MV80	Market value, 1980	0.21	0.31
PE80	Price/earnings ratio, 1980	3.76	2.94
ROA80	After-tax return assets, 1980	2.02	1.79
PM80	After-tax profit margin, 1980	2.12	1.93

Note: N = 120. Data sources and coding are discussed in the text.

theorist can conclude that managers were sufficiently constrained during 1970 so as to not act against the interests of shareholders. For a bank or family control theorist there is no evidence to support the view that these groups affected the financial performance of firms.

What effects did predict financial performance? Generally, the more shares held by institutional investors, the more poorly the firm performed

TABLE 6.1 (*continued*)
Means and Standard Deviations for Variables Used in the Analysis

Variable	Label	Mean	Std. Dev.
ROE80	After-tax return equity, 1980	12.75	70.95
DE80	Debt/equity ratio, 1980	0.18	1.18
ASSETS80	Assets, 1980	5137.83	7961.98
SALES80	Sales, 1980	4926.26	6699.99
FCF70	Free cash flow, 1970	403.85	454.63
MV70	Market value, 1970	2615.13	4701.90
PE70	Price/earnings ratio, 1970	13.57	24.60
ROA70	After-tax return assets, 1970	3.52	2.63
PM70	After-tax profit margin, 1970	4.97	3.34
ROE70	After-tax return equity, 1970	8.35	7.24
DE70	Debt/equity ratio, 1970	0.54	0.80
ASSETS70	Assets, 1970	3987.13	6301.19
SALES70	Sales, 1970	2573.81	2928.85
ILOCK	Bank interlocks, 1969	2.71	2.81
BANK	Largest bank shareholder, 1969	3.05	3.78
FAMILY	Largest family shareholder, 1970	4.95	10.46
ILOCK_D	Missing data, interlocks	0.25	0.43
BANK_D	Missing data, bank shareholder	0.36	0.48
INSTIPER	% shares held by institutions	0.11	0.06

Note: $N = 120$. Data sources coding are discussed in the text.

in terms of returns on assets, sales, equity, and market value. One can interpret this result in two ways. First, this is evidence that there was a problem with separation of ownership from control. Alternatively, 1970 was a bad year for the stock market, and many stocks lost value. It is possible that firms held by institutional investors fared more poorly during the downturn because these investors had overbought certain stocks during the boom from 1967 to 1969. If these results hold up in the panel analysis,

TABLE 6.2

Regression Analysis of the Determinants of Various Measures of Financial Performance, 1970

| | Dependent Variables | | | | | | | | | | | | |
| | Free Cash Flow | | Market Value | | Price/Earnings | | After-Tax Return on Assets | | Profit Margin | | Return on Equity | | Debt./Equity Ratio | |
Independent Variable	b	SE(b)	b	SE(b)	b	SE(b)	b	SE(b)	b	SE(b)	b	SE(b)	b	SE(b)
MERGER1	24.35	23.12	6.24	233.21	-0.01	1.27	0.02	0.11	0.12	0.15	0.38	0.36	0.01	0.04
MDF1	101.85	110.49	1602.48	1114.43	-0.03	6.07	-0.14	0.57	0.38	0.74	-1.49	1.74	0.13	0.19
RELN	-34.93	115.22	-681.45	1162.16	16.14**	6.33	0.92	0.59	1.21	0.77	3.68*	1.82	-0.06	0.20
UNRELN	-101.62	161.86	-2673.03	1632.52	17.11*	8.89	-0.54	0.83	-1.83*	1.08	-1.08	2.56	0.70**	0.29
MANPRES	-72.73	124.40	933.30	1254.75	2.50	6.83	-0.35	0.64	1.79*	0.83	-0.58	1.97	-0.10	0.22
SALEPR	167.88	130.58	2830.78*	1317.01	-0.36	7.17	0.52	0.67	0.28	0.87	1.28	2.06	0.10	0.23
FINPR	-16.68	128.00	200.75*	91.03	-9.06	7.03	0.91*	0.36	0.49*	0.25	-1.24	2.02	-0.12	0.23
INSTIPER	-756.54	872.64	-22549.05**	8801.20	-23.53	47.95	-10.45*	4.52	-10.15*	5.85	-6.18*	3.81	-0.54	1.57
ILOCK	31.99	20.30	61.79	204.78	-2.43*	1.11	-0.27*	0.10	-0.40**	0.13	-0.53*	0.32	-0.00	0.03
BANK	-20.56	15.13	-205.41	152.66	-0.41	0.83	0.05	0.07	0.04	0.10	0.25	0.23	-0.04	0.02
FAMILY	8.62	5.88	-20.98	59.31	-0.06	0.32	0.01	0.03	-0.00	0.03	0.12	0.09	0.00	0.01
ILOCK_D	173.02	139.13	-1666.51	1403.30	-13.87	7.64	-0.65	0.72	-1.33	0.93	-0.09	2.20	0.03	0.25
BANK_D	-316.70*	122.97	-3493.67**	1240.27	1.66	6.75	-0.30	0.63	-0.57	0.82	0.17	1.94	-0.29	0.22
INTERCEPT	499.77*	217.33	6059.23**	2191.98	15.79	11.94	4.86**	1.12	5.96**	1.45	7.71*	3.44	0.66*	0.39
R²	0.08		0.14		0.16		0.05		0.16		0.05		0.07	

Note: N = 109. Variables are defined in the text.

*p < .05.   **p < .01, one-tailed t-test.

then this will be evidence for the thesis that managers control firms with a large percentage of stock held by institutional investors and are acting to increase variables other than profits.

Several of the political-cultural variables also predicted financial performance. There is evidence that diversified firms had a higher return on equity and a higher price-to-earnings ratio. This suggests that the agency theory view that diversification reflects management control and an unwise use of a firm's resources is flawed. Instead, diversification proved profitable. Firms with unrelated product mixes also held higher debt, reflecting the acquisitive conglomerates' strategy of using debt to diversify. This also undermines the view that management-controlled firms are likely to favor the issuance of equity over debt.

Finally, there is evidence that the background of the CEO affected financial performance. Finance CEOs were able to improve firms' balance sheets, as their firms had higher return on assets, return on sales, and market value than firms headed by other types of CEOs. Sales-and-marketing CEOs also were able to increase the market value of their firms. We interpret these effects as the operation of the special expertise of these types of CEOs, who aimed at improving their firms' performance on exactly these measures.

The evidence for the effects of forms of control on changes in financial performance is in table 6.3. The panel results parallel the cross-sectional results. Because the previous level of performance is included as a regressor in these equations, the rest of the parameters can be interpreted as predictors of change in the dependent variables (Kessler and Greenberg 1981, chap. 2). Firms that were linked by bank interlocks generally underperformed other firms. They had lower returns on assets, sales, equity, and price-to-earnings ratio. Thus, being networked in the financial system did not prove to be a benefit. Further, firms that were interlocked had lower debt-to-equity ratios, suggesting that these firms favored equity over debt. None of these predictions supports a view that bank control directed profits over the decade toward banks. There was no direct effect of banks being significant shareholders on the financial performance of firms. Firms that had large bank shareholders did no better or worse than anyone else.

There are several effects of family holdings on performance. Family-controlled firms had lower returns on assets and sales and a lower price-to-earnings ratio. They also experienced less growth in sales over the decade. The higher the share of family holdings, the less well firms performed. This contradicts all of the theories of managerial control and suggests that family control during the turbulent economic times of the 1970s was not a good way to increase shareholder value.

The percentage of shares held by the institutional investors did not affect the change in the financial performance of firms. This shows that the re-

TABLE 6.3

Regression Analysis of the Determinants of Various Measures of Financial Performance, 1970–1980

| | Dependent Variables | | | | | | | | | | | | | | | | |
| Independent Variables | Free Cash Flow | | Market Value | | Price/Earnings | | Debt./Equity Ratio | | Assets 1980 | | Sales 1980 | | Return on Assets | | Profit Margin | | Return on Equity | |
	b	SE(b)	b	SE(b)	b	SE(b)	b	SE(b)	b	SE(b)	b	SE(b)	b	SE(b)	b	SE(b)	b	SE(b)
LAG-DEP-VAR1	0.97**	0.10	0.52**	0.03	-0.00	0.01	0.42**	0.15	1.20**	0.04	1.86**	0.13	0.30**	0.06	0.31**	0.05	0.00	1.11
MERGER1	-6.62	22.30	-129.11	83.35	-0.01	0.14	0.01	0.06	-85.40	102.40	-190.02	165.01	0.00	0.07	0.03	0.07	-1.68	4.06
MDF1	-22.29	107.04	63.74	402.23	-0.31	0.69	-0.33	0.30	-68.51	487.28	29.56	86.99	-0.15	0.34	-0.22	0.36	26.48	19.36
INDGROW	15.07	9.64	252.34**	35.53	-0.03	0.06	0.00	0.02	171.12**	44.87	531.80**	72.02	0.07**	0.03	-0.01	0.03	-0.08	1.72
RELN	18.91	106.78	-175.68	398.92	-0.19	0.71	0.49*	0.20	290.15*	144.28	-112.46	202.63	0.17	0.34	0.40	0.36	35.78*	19.79
UNRELN	4.91	156.10	109.38	586.58	-0.27	1.03	0.68*	0.35	-71.23	112.41	-54.56	155.22	0.68	0.50	0.70	0.53	-38.80	28.36
MANPRES	188.54	121.95	10.44	456.85	0.50	0.79	0.25	0.34	-48.53	62.23	94.04	92.90	-0.03	0.39	-0.13	0.42	-7.39	22.12
SALEPR	34.83	126.35	-111.05	478.13	-1.15	0.80	0.35	0.35	569.53*	274.53	502.82*	234.28	-0.39	0.39	-0.62	0.42	-8.47	22.54
FINPR	23.54	118.99	129.34**	44.38	0.17	0.78	-0.49	0.34	413.74**	172.63	476.66**	187.26	0.72*	0.38	0.72*	0.40	42.27*	21.63
INSTIPER	276.32	816.04	63.18	3145.90	3.67	5.31	1.32	2.32	-5103.50	3842.90	1074.97	2331.62	1.60	2.70	1.68	2.79	22.52	148.04
ILOCK	-33.32	19.72	-3.82	73.25	-0.26*	0.13	-0.15**	0.05	-71.43	88.84	-266.92	147.62	-0.23*	0.06	-0.19*	0.06	-10.80*	3.63
BANK	-20.11	14.27	-2.88	53.40	-0.05	0.09	0.01	0.04	-53.43	65.10	-61.61	106.28	-0.00	0.04	0.01	0.04	-0.24	2.58
FAMILY	-9.28	5.52	-31.62	20.36	-0.06*	0.03	-0.00	0.01	-7.22	25.35	-73.98*	41.51	-0.05*	0.01	-0.04*	0.01	0.38	0.99
ILOCK_D	-65.88	132.98	-397.35	494.75	0.06	0.86	-0.19	0.37	-431.11	605.71	-296.48	278.34	-0.60	0.42	-0.13	0.45	35.85	23.77
BANK_D	-97.49	121.05	-115.83	454.77	0.36	0.75	0.18	0.33	-372.44	546.71	-519.57	620.54	0.16	0.37	0.23	0.39	2.44	21.14
INTERCEPT	164.09	210.44	115.60	798.03	4.85**	1.35	-0.08	0.60	634.81	558.58	-566.42	1602.26	1.56*	0.72	1.23	0.75	-21.63	38.38
R2	0.52		0.78		0.03		0.14		0.94		0.80		0.41		0.43		0.15	

Note: $N = 106$ Each dependent variable was lagged to its 1970 value.

$* p < .05.$ $** p < .01.$ one-tailed t-test.

sults for 1970 were probably an artifact of the poor performance of firms whose stock was disproportionately held by institutional investors during the 1970s and not an effect of managerial control.

The most systematic predictor of change in financial outcomes during the 1970s was the asset growth of the industry. This variable positively affects growth in return on assets, growth in assets, sales, and market value of the firm. From an investor's point of view, the best type of firm to own stock in was one that was located in a growing industry.

The political-cultural variables also predict changes in outcomes in the 1970s. Sales-and-marketing CEOs produced growth in assets and sales for their firms. Finance CEOs produced growth in assets, and returns on assets, sales, and equity, as well as market value. Firms with product-related strategies were likely to increase their return on equity, while firms with product-unrelated strategies did no worse or better than firms with product-dominant strategies. Firms with product-related and product-unrelated strategies were also likely to carry higher debts than product-dominant firms, reflecting their merger growth strategies of the 1960s and 1970s.

Taken together, the results suggest that forms of control generally were not important predictors of the financial performance of large corporations either in the cross section or over time. Instead, the growth of the industry and the product strategy and background of the CEO were the most important predictors of performance. Managerial firms were not underperforming either bank- or family-controlled firms and, indeed, were outperforming such firms.

One interesting question to ask is what determined the strategies of firms. Table 6.4 presents results to see if there is evidence that control types affected strategic decisions beyond financial performance. None of the control measures predicts whether or not a firm engaged in a merger in the 1970s. Similarly, bank interlocks did not make firms more likely to engage in mergers. The only measures that predict mergers are the political-cultural ones. If a firm had engaged in mergers in the 1960s, it was more likely to engage in mergers in the 1970s. Firms with product-related and -unrelated strategies were more likely than firms with a product-dominant strategy to participate in mergers. Finally, firms with a finance CEO were more likely to have a merger in the 1970s. These results suggest that mergers as a strategy were entirely the product of organizational factors and unaffected by the measures of forms of control.

The equation predicting firm product mix in 1980 is also shown in table 6.4. None of the control measures predicts whether or not firms are diversified. Thus there is no evidence that diversification is undertaken by managers who are acting on their own behalf against the interests of owners. Instead the evidence suggests that diversified firms performed better than

TABLE 6.4
Logistic Regression Analysis of the Determinants of Various Organizational Characteristics

Independent Variables	Merger, 1970–80		Strategy, 1980 — Related		Strategy, 1980 — Unrelated		President's Origins, 1980 — MANPRES		President's Origins, 1980 — SALEPR		President's Origins, 1980 — FINPR	
	b	SE(b)	b	SE(b)	b	SE(b)	b	SE(b)	b	SE(b)	b	SE(b)
MERGER1	0.23*	0.12	1.59**	0.48	0.27*	0.13	0.27	0.17	0.42*	0.23	0.05	0.18
RELN	1.38*	0.65			0.04	0.39	0.24*	0.12	0.05	0.39		
UNRELN	1.97*	0.86			0.53	0.53	1.65*	0.87	0.60*	0.24		
MANPRES	0.72	0.61	0.20	0.54	0.20	0.43						
SALEPR	0.73	0.64	0.02	0.57	0.02	0.37						
FINPR	1.21*	0.65	0.18	0.53	0.31*	0.14	1.57**	0.61	0.68*	0.33		0.79
MDF1	-0.79	0.57			-0.04	0.36	0.63	0.37	0.50	0.75	0.75	0.13
INSTIPER	-0.66	4.29	3.81	7.25	1.43	5.61	0.02	0.08	-0.27	0.17	-0.28*	0.03
BANK	0.05	0.08	0.03	0.13	0.04	0.12	0.03	0.03	-0.04	0.06	-0.03	0.13
FAMILY	-0.03	0.03	0.09	0.06	0.04	0.06	-0.14	0.15	0.08	0.17	-0.08	0.43
I-LOCK	0.4	0.10	0.03	0.16	-0.03	0.13	0.14	0.40	0.42	0.60	0.94	0.48
BANK-D	0.80	0.61	-0.05	0.53	-0.09	0.40	0.03	0.47	0.60	0.66	0.51	
I-LOCK-D	0.73	0.70	0.34	0.61	0.30	0.43						
PERREL		0.03**	0.01	0.00	0.01							
PERRUNREL		-0.07**	0.02	0.06**	0.02							
FINDPER				0.01	0.05	0.02	0.05	0.04*	0.01			
SINDPER					-0.01	-0.01	0.03	0.06*	0.02	0.01	0.03	
MINDPER	0.05*	0.02	-0.04	0.03	-0.01	0.021						
INTERCEPT	-2.29**	1.18	3.60**	1.67	2.03*	1.14	-0.34	1.52	-3.27	2.47	-0.82	0.57
	$\chi^2 = 22.65$, df = 13		$\chi^2 = 56.72$, df = 29				$\chi^2 = 47.70$, df = 54					

Note: N = 110.

* $p < 0.05$.   ** $p < 0.01$, one-tailed test.

nondiversified firms (see tables 6.2 and 6.3) and that these firms undertook these tactics for organizational, not control, reasons. Three sorts of political-cultural variables affected whether or not a firm was diversified in 1980: if a firm had engaged in a merger during the 1960s, if a firm had a finance CEO in 1969, and if a firm was in an industry where there were high percentages of firms with product-related and product-unrelated strategies.

Finally, the determinants of what types of CEOs were in place in 1980 are presented. Some of the control variables have interesting effects. For instance, family-controlled firms were less likely to have finance CEOs. Given that finance CEO–led firms outperformed other firms in the 1970s, this proved to be a mistake. Second, firms with a high percentage of stock held by institutional investors tended to have sales-and-marketing or finance CEOs. This can be interpreted as an effect of manager control; that is, managers tended to control these types of firms, and they selected CEOs from power bases that were in ascendance.

There are clear organizational effects on who gets to be CEO. Firms that had mergers or product-diversified strategies were more likely to have sales-and-marketing or finance CEOs, consistent with the argument made earlier. Further, industries with high percentages of finance or sales-and-marketing CEOs tended to affect the firm's propensity to have finance or sales-and-marketing CEOs. This clearly reflects an isomorphic process (DiMaggio and Powell 1983).

Discussion and Conclusions

Overall, the agency theorists and the sociological theorists who focus on forms of control, either family, management, bank, or resource dependence through bank interlocks, do not do a good job of explaining how large corporations perform or how they behave strategically. Bankers, owners, and managers live in organizations that are systems of power and located in organizational fields that help define successful behavior. If they attempt to construct their actions outside that context, then they threaten to undermine the organization that is producing wealth for them. The controlling force that determines courses of successful action is thus emergent in organizational interaction. The theory that accounts for these patterns most effectively is the political-cultural approach.

One might be tempted to argue that the political-cultural approach is consistent with a standard economic view that the market sends signals to managers about what works, and they follow suit. The problem with the economic view is that it cannot specify strategies except after the fact. The political-cultural approach evaluates the relative efficacy of competing perspectives in producing outcomes. Economic theory could not theorize these variables precisely because it is not concerned with capturing differences in conceptions of control among firms and markets. It is also the case that these effects exist net of the growth of the industry (a rough indicator of the demand for the product), and, therefore, they cannot have a purely economic interpretation.

An agency or transaction costs theorist can interpret these results as evidence that managers were sufficiently constrained by boards of directors, contracts, and financial markets. Indeed, there is evidence that professional managers actually outperformed their counterparts in family-owned firms. But, to the degree that these perspectives are testable, there is little evidence in their favor. First, it is clear that managers do not favor free cash flow. Diversification, which was supposed to be bad, generally had positive effects. The data analysis shows that the conventional wisdom about the 1970s was wrong as well: financially oriented executives who ran diversified firms and engaged in mergers outperformed their counterparts on average.

There has been a lot of interest in creating a sociology of markets in the recent literature, and much of that discussion has focused, and I believe rightly so, on the problem of social embeddedness (Granovetter 1985). The theoretical difficulty is deciding what that embeddedness consists of. The results presented here suggest two things. First, organizational and not financial or ownership embeddedness is likely to be a more important cause of actions of firms than anything else in the case of the United States. This means efforts should concentrate on specifying models of the relations between firms that focus on intra- and interorganizational processes, such as the construction of strategic action and the cultural frames by which such a construction makes sense.

Second, the type of embeddedness we choose should be relevant to the problem. The connections between firms, banks, owners, and managers just does not significantly predict much that is interesting in the strategic choices of firms; and therefore we should theoretically focus on what does. The concentration upon the board of directors as a source of network data in general and financial linkages across boards of directors in particular should be abandoned unless one can theoretically specify why they might be relevant (for an example that explicitly concerns investment banks, see Baker 1990). More relevant network data would focus on how firms obtain knowledge of competitors (trade publications, associations, meetings, and market research) and how they filter their use of that information.

This does not imply that elites do not exist or that they do not organize to achieve collective political ends. Instead, it implies that the substantive content of economic actions taken by elites who control the large corporation will not be uncovered by a narrow view of their interests. Those interests are determined by the context of their actions, that is, the organizational situations in which they find themselves. Organizational theory provides an alternative sociological view that forces one to take seriously the nature of the relations among large-scale corporations, the internal structuring of those organizations, and the problem of constructing courses of action. In short, I think that a real sociology of markets needs to focus on some of the elements that have proved to be important here: inter- and intraorganizational politics and the specification of cultural frames that define the social relations between actors.

Appendix A

The financial measures listed below were constructed from Compustat II data as follows:

Market Value = Stock Price (Close) × Common Shares Outstanding

Price-Earnings Ratio = Stock Price (Close) / Earnings per Share Excluding Extraordinary Items

Return on Assets = 100 × Income before Extraordinary Items / (Total Assets + Total Gross Property, Plant, and Equipment – Total Net Property, Plant, and Equipment)

Profit Margin = 100 × Income before Extraordinary Items / Net Sales

Return on Equity = 100 × Income before Extraordinary Items Adjusted for Common Stock Equivalents / Total Common Equity

Debt-Equity Ratio = Total Long-Term Debt / Total Common Equity

Assets = Total Assets + Total Gross Property, Plant, and Equipment – Total Net Property, Plant, and Equipment

Sales = Net Sales

Free Cash Flow = Current Assets – Current Liabilities

7

The Rise of the Shareholder Value Conception of the Firm and the Merger Movement in the 1980s

MERGER MOVEMENTS involve a reorganization of corporate assets across the population of the largest firms in the economy.[1] As such, they signal a crisis of the old conception of control for the largest firms and the rise of a new one (Stearns and Allan 1996; Davis and Stout 1992; Ocasio and Kim 1999). The merger movement at the turn of the twentieth century was an attempt by the largest corporations to control competition by directly absorbing their principal competitors (Fligstein 1990, chap. 3). During the nineteenth century, firms confronted by cutthroat competition tried to produce cartels with their major competitors. Cartels were illegal, and failed to stabilize firms. The Sherman Act inadvertently provided firms with a legal way to combine to try to control competition: merger between competitors. Between 1895 and 1905, this conception of control spread, and there was an enormous consolidation of firms that resulted in increased concentration of production in a few firms in many industries. The merger movement of the 1920s produced the manufacturing conception of control and oligopolies, and the 1960s produced the finance conception of control and highly diversified firms in the core of the American economy.

The 1980s witnessed the largest of the four merger movements in this century (Stearns and Allan 1996; Davis, Diekmann, and Tinsley 1994; Davis and Thompson 1994). If I am correct in my observation that merger movements herald the crisis or death of the existing conception of control and the emergence of a new conception of control, then it follows that the 1980s merger movement must signal a new way to conceive of the large corporation. My central argument in this chapter is that the finance conception of the firm that dominated large American corporations from the mid-1960s onward suffered a crisis in the 1970s. The cultural definition of this crisis became the perception that firms were not profitable enough for their shareholders (what a Marxist would call an accumulation crisis): that is, managers were not managing assets to maximize what came to be called "shareholder value."

The objective causes of this crisis were twofold: (1) competition from foreign firms, primarily Japanese, that were cutting into the market shares of U.S. electronics and automobile producers, and (2) the general economic conditions in the United States during the 1970s, with slow economic growth, high inflation, and low corporate profits. These exogenous shocks to the finance conception of the large corporation caused actors to doubt that the finance conception could continue to be profitable for the largest firms in the economy. The alternative that emerged to the finance conception of the firm was what can be called the *shareholder value conception of the firm*.

To understand an organizational change like the change in a dominant conception of control, it is necessary to consider the role of culture in framing the possibility for strategic action. For actors to undertake new forms of action, they must decide to rethink their interests, develop a plan to operationalize those interests, and have the power to enforce that view. Culture comes into play to provide actors with a cognitive frame that offers solutions to the problem of strategic action.

In the context of profit-making firms, the question can be put in a different way: the issue is not that managers seek out profit, but how they do so. It is to this issue that the political-cultural approach can add to economic views of how firms operate. Managerial actions are embedded, constrained, and shaped by the cultural frames of actors and the structure of interorganizational relations. The ways managers attempt to make profit reflect these frames and their relations to relevant fields of action.

From this perspective one can view the financial reorganization of the largest American corporations in the 1980s. The shareholder value conception of the firm uses rhetoric that diagnoses the problems of firms in terms of ideas imported from agency theory. The key idea in the shareholder value conception of the firm is that the only legitimate purpose of firms is to maximize shareholder value (see Jensen 1989 for a rhetorical development of this argument). The main indicator of whether or not management teams are maximizing shareholder value is the share price of the firm on the stock market. Managers who fail to maximize shareholder value fail to raise the share price of the firm. They deserve to be ousted by boards of directors. From this point of view, if bad managers co-opt boards of directors, then alternative teams of managers can use the market for corporate control to get the most out of a given firm's assets.

To raise share prices in the 1980s, managers were told that they needed to divest unproductive product lines, make investments in core businesses in which they were dominant (often through mergers), repurchase their stock to reduce its supply and therefore increase demand for it, and take on debt to force managers to cut costs (Davis and Stout 1992; Davis, Diekmann, and Tinsley 1994). This chapter provides quantitative models to examine the conditions under which corporations were most likely to engage in these forms of financial reorganization and adopt the shareholder value conception of the firm.

The shift from the finance conception of control to the shareholder value conception of control is a subtle one. The finance conception of the firm viewed the firm as a bundle of assets that managers deployed and redeployed by the buying and selling of firms. Diversified portfolios of product lines were manipulated to maximize profits (Fligstein 1990, chap. 7). The finance conception of control therefore already viewed the firm in primarily financial terms. The shareholder value conception of control is also a financial set of strategies, but it had a particular critique of the finance conception of firms. The shareholder value perspective viewed the principal failure of the finance conception of control as the failure to maximize shareholder value by raising share prices. There are two interesting questions to ask: where did this new financial conception of the firm come from, and which actors used it to define and promote their interests?

The theory of fields offers a great deal of insight into the dynamics of what happened. Incumbent firms using the finance conception of control should have defended themselves by reasserting their power in the face of an economic crisis. The definition of the crisis and its solution, however, were pushed forward by powerful outsiders. The shareholder value conception of the firm obviously privileges those who own stock. It is not surprising that these outsiders who claimed to represent the interests of shareholders were investment bankers or institutional investors such as mutual funds. The representatives of these organizations were able to define the crisis, formalize the solutions, and push the shareholder value conception of the firm on managers who were resistant. Since the shareholder value conception was based on financial reasoning, it was possible for financial executives to become convinced of its virtue. One might expect that in order to stay in power in firms, they embraced the new financial strategies and helped spread the new conception of control.

Davis and Thompson (1994) have described the shareholder value conception of control and the merger movement it built as a kind of social movement, consistent with the political-cultural approach. Their argument supports the view that existing management teams recognized that a new form of financial analysis was sweeping across firms. If managers wanted to keep their independence, they needed to go along with the strategies consistent with that analysis.[2] Actors came to adopt the shareholder value perspective, and it spread across the population of the largest firms. Managers either picked up the mantra and strategies of shareholder value or found themselves without jobs (Useem 1993).

The version of the story I have told is a blend of stories available from the business press, the scholarly literature, and a political-cultural analysis of how these events fit together. Three approaches can be drawn on to make sense of how these historical events evolved. Finance economics considers the conditions under which firms would issue equity and debt and why the market for corporate control promotes the overall efficiency of firms by forcing them to deploy their assets properly (Fama and Jensen 1983a, 1983b; Fama 1980; for a review see Lorie et al. 1985). Sociological theories of the merger movement suggest two approaches. First, the extension of control over firms by banks and institutional investors makes firms more vulnerable to financial manipulation (Mintz and Schwartz 1985; Kotz 1978; Brancato and Gaughan 1988). Second, the dominance of finance CEOs in large firms, the spread of the shareholder value conception of the firm as indexed by competitors' behavior, and the product mix of the firm may have affected who was going to adopt the shareholder value conception of the firm. The role of the state was important as well. In particular, lax antitrust policies and the tax cuts of the Reagan administration produced the conditions that have led to the financial reorganization of firms.

What Is to Be Explained?

Hirsch has argued that the 1980s merger movement legitimated the hostile takeover as a "a normal event rather than a deviant innovation" (1986, 821). His account of the process by which hostile takeovers became commonplace and his discussion of the colorful language invented to describe them forms the starting point for discussion. The finance conception of the corporation was the "normal" way to think about corporations during the 1970s (Fligstein 1990, chap. 7). This conception of the corporation viewed the firm as a bundle of assets to be deployed or redeployed depending on the short-run rates of return that could be earned by buying and selling firms. The theory of such mergers during the 1960s was that firms held a portfolio of diversified assets that grew at different rates and had different rates of profits. The idea was to insure the survival of the firm by balancing off product lines in a way that controlled for the effects of the business cycle and the relative growth rates of different industries.

The American corporation in the early 1980s was under siege from two exogenous forces: the high inflation and slow economic growth of the 1970s, and increased foreign competition. The inflation of the 1970s had a perverse effect on large corporations. Their real assets (i.e., land, buildings, machines) were increasing in value. High interest rates pushed investors toward fixed-income securities such as government bonds. This left many large American firms undervalued in the stock market (Friedman 1985a). Simultaneously, foreign competition, particularly with the Japanese, heated up, and American firms lost market shares and, in some cases, entire markets in automobiles and electronics. This presented a "crisis" of profitability to the managers of large firms.

In the context of the response to these exogenous shocks, three important facts must be explained. First, why was the response to the crisis narrowly framed in terms of maximizing shareholder value by concentrating on raising stock prices? Second, how can one explain the timing of the merger movement? Finally, why did some managers embrace the shareholder value conception of control, while some did not? Those who resisted its spread were targets in the market for corporate control. The theories reviewed propose quite different answers to these questions.

Finance Economics

Finance economics has been concerned with the issue of what determines the capital structure of firms, and how financial markets come to place value on those structures. The key imagery is that firms can be conceived of in terms of their capital structures (Modigliani and Miller 1958; Myers 1984). These structures consist of equity (the value of shareholders' stake in the firm, i.e., the stock price multiplied by the number of shares), assets, and debt (what the firm owes its creditors, in particular, banks and bondholders). The decision to hold some mix of equity and debt has been the focus of continuous analysis (Modigliani and Miller 1958; Myers 1984; Ross 1977; Marsh 1982; Miller 1977; Friedman 1985a, 1985b). Since both equity and debt are claims on the firm's cash flow and assets, they are alternative ways for managers to fund firms' capital structures. The issue is what that capital structure should look like from the point of view of optimizing returns.

A related issue is the mode of governance for the corporation and its relation to the mix of equity and debt (Jensen and Meckling 1976). Large firms often separate ownership from control. In this case, the owners of the capital and the managers are not the same persons, and this produces a principal-agent problem (Fama 1980; Jensen and Meckling 1976). The principals' concern is the behavior of agents (i.e., managers) and how they can be monitored to ensure that they act to maximize the gains of the principals (i.e., the owners). In the context of the capital structure of the firm, the two sides may have different interests in the relative mix of debt and equity and in how the mix affects dividends and stock prices.

Owners may prefer debt to equity, as debt tends to maintain the value of their holdings by not lowering stock prices or diluting earnings. On the other hand, managers gain by issuing equity, which diffuses potential control of owners. Managers, however, also have an interest in keeping the stock price up and dividends stable because they can lose control of the corporation if the firm's performance deteriorates. Indeed, one of the most potent arguments for the unimportance of the supposed principal-agent problem is that firms with ineffective managers have low stock prices and become merger targets (Fama and Jensen 1983a). There is evidence to support this view: managers first pay for expansion of the firm through retained earnings, then use short-term or long-term debt, and only in the last resort do they issue equity (Myers 1984).

The important factors thought to determine the relative mix of the capital structure are the bond and stock markets (Jensen and Meckling 1976; Fama and Jensen 1983a). The markets operate to control the behavior of both managers and owners by properly evaluating the relative value of the firm, its riskiness, and its future prospects (Lorie, Dodd, and Kimpton 1985, especially chaps. 4, 5). To the degree that both markets operate efficiently (i.e., change their evaluations quickly in response to news about the firm's current and future prospects), managers of firms are forced to act to maximize assets or face losing control over firms. The most important model of stock market evaluation, the capital assets price model (CAPM), assumes that the firm's price reflects its riskiness as an investment (Sharpe 1964).

The merger movement of the 1980s can be explained from this perspective in the following way. The stock market declined significantly in the 1970s, as high inflation meant that investors sought out higher rates of return to protect their money and left the uncertain stock market for high fixed yields in the corporate and government bond markets. Stock prices were low, and the market value of firms (the stock price multiplied by the number of outstanding shares) was low. High inflation and slow economic growth also meant that profits were low, but that the assets of large corporations (i.e., land, buildings, plants, product lines) were increasing in value. Managers also tended to hold onto cash to use for internal investment and to avoid taking on expensive debt. Prudent managers found themselves holding lots of cash and keeping their debt low. In spite of this financial prudence, the value of their firms on the stock market and profits were low relative to assets that were inflated (Fama and Schwert 1977; Fama 1981; Taggart 1985; Hendershott and Huang 1985).

From the point of view of finance economics, efficient managers realized their predicament and engaged in actions to increase profitability and equity, while inefficient managers did not recognize their situation and act quickly enough to remedy it. In the late 1970s and early 1980s, financially oriented analysts began to buy undervalued corporations by paying a premium to current stockholders and then selling the pieces of the firm at high enough profits to make money. The decision to liquidate firms depended on whether the buyer intended to turn a quick profit or to attempt to run the firm more profitably. The market for corporate control over assets heated up and created the 1980s merger movement.

Efficient managers who wanted to maintain control over their firms had to engage in actions to increase stock price and hence bring their equity in line with their real net worth. They used a number of tactics. First, many purchased shares of their own stocks either with retained earnings or by borrowing funds. This had the effect of reducing the amount of stock in circulation and driving up the stock price. If the money was borrowed, increased indebtedness also lowered net worth. Taken together, these effects lowered the odds of takeover. Managers could use debt to finance the buyout or purchase of stock of other firms, which could increase their indebtedness as well and make them less attractive candidates for mergers. Presumably, such buyouts would raise profits and increase assets without diluting equity. Finally, they could divest themselves of divisions that were underperforming and use profits to repurchase stock shares, distribute extra dividends to shareholders, or engage in mergers with, or stock purchases of, other firms.

Manager, Owner, and Bank Control

As I noted in the previous chapter, organizational and political sociologists have long been fascinated by the issue of who controls the large corporations. Much of the original interest in this field was sparked by the potential for the concentration of power in the hands of owners of the large corporations. Sociologists have generally attempted to refute the Berle and Means hypothesis (1933) that managers were coming to control large corporations. The central claim of political sociologists was that the amount of managerial control of the largest corporations was greatly overstated (Zeitlin 1974; Burch 1972; Kotz 1978).

Scholars interested in this debate have recently suggested why and how ownership forms might produce different results. Most of these attempts use some form of resource dependence theory as the mechanism of control (Pfeffer and Salancik 1978). The argument is that organizations are dependent on their environments for resources. Hence, the greatest leverage on a firm is potentially from organizations that have important resources a firm needs. For instance, Burt (1983) argues that firms systematically seek to co-opt these dependencies, mainly by putting important suppliers or customers on boards of directors, in order to secure their support.

Using organizational interdependence as a theoretical starting point, a number of authors have proposed some advancements to the control debate. Mintz and Schwartz (1985) have tried to show the centrality of banks, insurance companies, and other institutional investors in controlling the large corporations by examining two forms of data: corporate interlock data and selected cases of organizational intervention by banks. Network methods reveal that banks and insurance companies are the central links between firms (Mintz and Schwartz 1985; Mizruchi 1982; Pennings 1980). It is also the case that when corporations are in crisis, large debt-holders, often banks or insurance companies, supervise financial reorganization. Mintz and Schwartz argue that this produces financial hegemony, which implies that the dependence of firms on outside financing opens them up to the potential of being controlled, or at least limited in their actions, by banks.

Burt (1983) argues that the capture of financial investors or suppliers of boards of directors allows firms to co-opt their important dependencies. This is an alternative perspective to the one developed by Mintz and Schwartz because it has managers actively controlling their environment and potentially reducing the prospects for external control. Burt, however, was unable to show the effects of such interdependencies on profits.

The strongest statement of the potential of bank control comes from Kotz (1978). He argues that management-controlled (and presumably family-controlled) firms avoid debt in order to lessen financial control. Conversely, financial institutions use their control over firms to increase their business. Firms already under the control of large financial institutions are more likely to go into debt. Finance-controlled firms are more likely to engage in mergers for similar reasons. Mizruchi and Stearns (1988) have provided evidence that a firm's debt is correlated with the presence of bankers on the board of directors.

Brancato and Gaughan (1988) argue that large institutional investors increasingly control the stock of large firms. They suggest that this might have another unwelcome effect on firms. Since institutional investors generally work with short profit horizons, finance-controlled firms (or any firm controlled by a large institutional investor) are likely to be under considerable pressure to generate short-term profits. Failure to do so may result in management turnover or the prospect of having the firm sold off.

These literatures can be combined to suggest an account of the financial reorganization of the large corporation in the 1980s. The finance control literature would argue that banks and institutional investors have increased their power over firms in the past 20 years (Kotz 1978; Mizruchi and Stearns 1988; Mintz and Schwartz 1985). The basis of this control is direct ownership of equity or large holdings of corporate bonds. Boards of directors function to give banks monitoring power over firms. The increases that have occurred in financial manipulations, such as stock repurchases, higher levels of indebtedness, and mergers and divestments in the 1980s, can be explained by the increase of bank and institutional investor control. In the cross section, one would expect that bank- and institutional investor–controlled firms would be more likely than manager- or family-owned firms to undertake such actions. It is the rise of finance-controlled firms that accounts for the rise of financially oriented maneuvers.

The Crisis of the Finance Conception of Control and the Rise of the Shareholder Value Conception of Control

The final perspective is based on the political-cultural approach to firms, which combines elements of both stories. Firms' strategic actions are shaped by two primary forces: the behavior of their competitors and the actions of the government to define what is competitive and anticompetitive behavior between firms. The key argument is that managers and owners in firms search for stable patterns of interaction with their largest competitors. Once stable patterns prove to be both legal and profitable, firms set up organizational fields that tend to produce and reproduce those patterns. The principles that guide interaction in those fields can be termed a conception of control. Managers across firms develop expectations of one another's behavior, and that increases the reproducibility of a given set of rules. The managers who come to control firms are selected on the basis of their allegiance to a given conception of control (Fligstein 1987).

Two conditions produced the finance conception of control. First, large firms in the postwar era were already fairly diversified in their product lines. The problem of internally controlling a large number of products opened an opportunity for executives who could claim to evaluate the profit potential of each product line. Finance executives reduced the information problem to the rate of return earned by product lines and thereby made the large diversified corporation manageable. Second, the federal government was strictly enforcing the antitrust laws in the early postwar era and had passed an antimerger law that made it difficult to merge with direct competitors or suppliers. This encouraged product-diversified mergers. The financial executives who could evaluate products outside of a firm's expertise were invaluable in such efforts (Fligstein 1990, chap. 6).

The most spectacular organizational examples of the new finance conception came from firms outside the mainstream of American corporate life. The men who pioneered the acquisitive conglomerate (Tex Thornton at Textron, Jim Ling at L-T-V, and Harold Geneen at ITT) showed how financial machinations involving debt could be used to produce rapid growth with little investment of capital. Many of the financial forms of reorganization, including mergers, divestitures, leveraged buyouts, the accumulation of debt, and stock repurchasing, were invented or perfected in this period. The 1960s witnessed a large-scale merger movement in which many of the largest corporations substantially increased their size and diversification. As a result of this success, finance executives increasingly became CEOs of large corporations (Fligstein 1987).

By 1969, the finance conception of control had come to dominate the world of the largest corporations. The merger movement of the 1960s was ended by two phenomena. The Nixon administration's Antitrust Division filed lawsuits against some of the largest acquisitive conglomerates and thereby put a chill on the stock market. The decline of the stock market beginning in 1969 and the increase in interest rates, which pushed that decline along, made it less profitable to engage in merger activity. The 1970s were not kind to large corporations. High inflation and slow economic growth combined to give large firms undervalued assets, low stock prices, and low profitability. The most acquisitive of the 1960s conglomerates performed less well during the 1970s. But the finance conception of control remained dominant in the corporate world.

From this perspective, the conditions were right for some form of change in the conception of control governing large corporations. There was a crisis of profitability for the largest corporations. There were two problems: first, what would a new analysis of problems look like and what new way of doing things would it propose; and second, what would the government do in response to the production of a new conception of control? It turned out that the presidential election of 1980 provided two positive sparks to the financial reorganization of firms.

William Baxter, Reagan's attorney general in charge of antitrust, announced new merger guidelines in 1981. These guidelines committed the government to approving almost all mergers except those that lead to concentration ratios within a product line greater than 80%. This gave the green light to all forms of mergers, large and small, vertical and horizontal. The Reagan administration also substantially reduced corporate income taxes, thereby providing capital for the merger movement. From this perspective, the 1980s market for corporate control was driven by the already existing finance conception of the firm and the changes in the regulatory environment.

Who came up with the shareholder value conception of the firm, and how did those who adhered to it relate to those who were working with the finance conception of control? Given what is now known about the merger movement, it is possible to suggest that institutional investors, including investment banks, insurance companies, and mutual funds, provided some of the stimulus for the shareholder value conception of the firm.

It was less clear what strategies would help increase profitability and maximize shareholder value. It is here that some of the ideas of agency theory and financial economics came into play. If firms had market values that were larger than the value of their salable assets (often caused by the high inflation and low stock prices), money could be made by breaking them up. These breakups focused on the amount of cash a firm had and how much such assets as land and buildings were actually worth. Many firms were purchased by issuing bonds based on projections about how much debt could be serviced by the firm. Borrowed money (what became high-yield, or junk bonds) was used to gain control over a firm's assets. Then debt service would force internal reorganization of the firm, which resulted in a sell-off of parts of the firm and a reduction of the number of employees in other parts of the firm.

Hypotheses

All of the perspectives point to financial conceptions of the corporation before 1980 as being pivotal to understanding what happened after 1980. Yet they point to radically different actors, interests, and power bases as causally significant. While the theories can be reconciled at some level, there are distinct differences between them that suggest different mechanisms by which the financial reorganization of large corporations can be explained. It is possible, of course, that a number of these mechanisms are in operation and their effects could have been complementary (and indeed, the empirical results will show that this is the case).

It would be difficult to distinguish between these three explanations in terms of their ability to explain the timing of the merger wave because all offer reasons as to why the late 1970s and early 1980s were pivotal. But they can be distinguished as explanations of which firms were likely to be reorganized or targets of mergers. To the degree that the mechanisms they propose to explain which firms were involved actually do so, one can offer more or less support for their general view of the timing of that event. For instance, if firms that had more undervalued assets were more likely to be merger candidates, then one can infer that the general undervaluing of assets was important as a precipitating factor for the merger movement.

The differences between the theories, however, are quite real and deeply rooted. For agency theory and finance economics, all managers have to pay attention to is their stock price and its relation to debt, equity, earnings, and the value of assets. Therefore, manager-, bank-, and family-controlled firms would all behave in terms of these underlying calculations. This means that the mechanism that would predict action was centered in the underlying financial fundamentals of firms. For firms whose stock price fell too low, we would expect financial reorganization such as stock repurchases, divestitures, or increased debt independent of who controlled the firm. Similarly, for those firms that did not reorganize, we would expect them to be more likely to be takeover targets.

The bank control thesis predicts that financial reorganization is more likely to occur in firms with bankers and large institutional investors on their boards of directors as holders of both equity and debt. Mergers and divestitures and increased indebtedness should follow from the presence of bank and institutional investors. This view stresses the role of powerful actors and the dependence of firms upon those actors. In this sense, the financial perspectives of these actors and their base of power as holders of equity and debt force managers toward forms of financial reorganization beneficial to bankers and institutional investors interested in short-run gain.

The finance conception of control focuses on three mechanisms as leading to increased likelihood of financial reorganization. First, the presence of a finance-oriented CEO increases the likelihood of financial reorganization because the logical course of action for those executives is to use those tools to attempt to increase profitability. Second, in firms that do not have finance-oriented executives as CEOs, we may still see a propensity to engage in financial reorganization if other firms in their organizational field are doing so. This is because the field may be dominated by the finance conception of control. Hence, appropriate behavior is suggested by competitors, independent of the background of the CEO.

Finally, the product mix of a firm signifies the presence of a finance conception of control as well. This could work in two ways. Firms that are diversified into related or unrelated products have managers who are more likely to evaluate product lines by their relative profitability. These managers are more likely to be operating with a shareholder value conception of control and engage in forms of financial reorganization as a result. It may also be that managers trying to raise their share prices would note that diversified firms were unpopular and, in order to signal that they were on board with the shareholder value conception of the firm, sell off diversified product lines.

Data and Methods

The sample used to test the hypotheses include the one hundred largest industrial corporations in the United States in 1979. Data was coded for each year for the period 1979 to 1987. The beginning and end of any merger movement cannot be dated precisely. The most recent merger wave arguably began in 1981, and the selection of 1979 as the starting year allows us to obtain data for years before the beginning of the real upturn in mergers. The list was obtained from *Fortune* magazine (1980). Nine observations existed per case for each company, unless that company was bought out. After a firm was merged into another, no further information was collected.

The selection of the largest firms can be justified on a number of grounds. The largest corporations are the most important business organizations in American society. They have been the focus of most of the theorizing and empirical work just discussed, partly because there is a great deal of data publicly available for these organizations. Further, the actions of their managers operate as a role model for other firms. One could argue that the largest firms are a restricted sample and therefore our parameter estimates suffer from sample selection bias. This is only a problem if one is asserting that the parameter estimates obtained here apply to a larger sample of firms, say for all publicly held corporations. I make no such claims here. Indeed, the focus of this study is the population of the largest firms, and therefore we are not sampling, but instead providing population parameters.

There were two dependent variables in the analysis: whether or not the firm was merged and whether or not the firm engaged in the various forms of financial reorganization. The variable indicating whether or not the firm was merged in a given year was coded as a dummy variable with the code of 1 signifying that the firm was merged. Information about merger activity was collected from Moody's *Manual* (1980–88). Out of the one hundred largest corporations coded in 1979, one-fifth had been bought out by 1987. Those companies were as follows:

American Can	Signal Co.
Cities Service	Sperry Rand
Continental Oil	General Foods
Getty Oil	Continental Can
Gulf Oil	Beatrice Foods
Kennecott Copper	Superior Oil
Marathon Oil	Federated Department Stores
RCA	Safeway
Republic Steel	Owens-Illinois Glass
Shell Oil	Standard Oil–Ohio

Four forms of financial reorganization were selected based on the theoretical considerations discussed earlier: mergers, divestitures, acquiring one's own stock, and acquiring stock of other firms. Information about acquiring one's own stock was collected from the Wall Street Journal Index (1980–88). The other data were coded from Moody's *Manual* (1980–88). The four types of reorganization were coded in several ways: (1) as dummy variables indicating whether or not the firm had evidence of taking that form of reorganization in a given year, (2) as a simple scale in which was summed, in a given year, whether the company engaged in any of the reorganization activities, and (3) as a factor scale.

TABLE 7.1
Results of Factor Analysis of Forms of Financial Reorganization

Variable[a]	Factor Weight
Mergers	0.56
Divestitures	0.40
Stock Purchases	0.49
Stock of others purchased	0.39
Eigenvalue	1.84
Percentage of Variation Explained	0.54

Note: [a] Variables are defined in the text

The factor scale was obtained using an oblique rotation in the statistical package SPSS. The results are presented in table 7.1. It is useful to consider them in some detail. The four forms of financial reorganization do form one unique factor with an eigenvalue greater than 1. The factor weights are relatively similar, implying that each of the forms of financial reorganization is equally important for the underlying construct. Together, these results give credence to our notion that the forms of financial reorganization reflect a set of behaviors that is undertaken by managers with the goal of increasing the financial value of the firm; that is, they reflect a shareholder value conception of the corporation. Managers were likely to undertake more than one of the actions in a given year and thereby were either dominated in their behavior by a finance conception of action or not. Both the factor scores and the simple additive scale were used in the analysis.

We created three independent variables to test the finance conception of control hypothesis. The first is a dummy variable coding whether or not the chief executive officer of the company has a finance background (1 = finance CEO). The name of the CEO in 1979 was found using Moody's *Manual* (1980). Other sources, such as *Who's Who in America* and *Who's Who in Business*, were then used to decipher the CEO's job background. If the CEO had held a number of jobs that were not in finance functions, then the person was not coded as a finance CEO.

The second independent variable concerns the percentage of other firms in an organizational field with finance CEOs. The argument was that while a company might not have a finance CEO, other firms in their field might be dominated by the finance conception of control. If the company believes the other firms with finance CEOs have a competitive edge, then it is likely to engage in activities similar to its competition. To capture this mimetic effect, the percentage of finance CEOs among the one hundred largest firms in 1979 was calculated in each industry (measured at the two-digit SIC code level). Each firm's CEO was excluded from that calculation in order to make the measure orthogonal from the measure of the background of the CEO of a given firm.

The last independent variable has to do with the product mix of the firm. Firms with related or unrelated product mixes were more likely to be controlled by the finance conception of control than firms with production concentrated in one dominant line. A product-dominant strategy entails a firm that produces more than 70% of its revenues in a single product line. A product-related strategy entails a firm that produces many related products or market extensions (e.g., a chemical company producing paints and explosives). However, no single line accounts for more than 70% of the output. A product-unrelated strategy entails a firm that involves itself in unrelated businesses for a substantial portion of its revenue (for instance, L-T-V, at one point in time, produced guided missiles and steel and owned a rental car company). Information for this data was collected from Rumelt (1974) and Moody's *Manual* (1980). Two dummy variables were coded to reflect this distinction. The left-out category for the measure was product-dominant. Each of the other variables was coded 1 if the product mix was related or unrelated.

The second hypothesis being tested concerns how corporate activity is a function of who controls the company. There are three independent variables used to index control. The first measures how owners' activity differs from managers' activity in terms of engaging in reorganization tactics. A dummy variable was created in which a company controlled by an owner was coded as 1. I used Herman's (1981) coding scheme, as his data referred to the period closest to 1979.

The second and third independent variables concern the composition of the board of directors. It has been argued that individuals on the board of directors have a potential to control activities of the company (Burt 1983). Thus, the second independent variable measures the percentage of bankers on the board of directors for each given year, and the third independent variable measures the percentage of nonbank financial institutions (e.g., insurance companies, pension funds) on the board of directors for each given year. Information for these measures was collected from Moody's *Manual* (1980–88), Standard and Poor's Register of Corporations, Directors and Executives (1979–86), and The Corporate 1000 (1985, 1987).

The last hypothesis being tested concerns the finance economics argument. This view stresses the importance of maintaining a balance between equity and debt so that a company is not in a position to be merged. The prediction is that a company's actions are a function of its financial position. The variable measuring this is calculated as follows:

(Assets – Debts)/ (# Of Outstanding Shares × Price of Shares)

The numerator of this measure contains the net worth of the firm, while the denominator reflects the firm's equity. The argument is that when this ratio is less than one, the equity is worth more than the net assets and financial reorganization is unlikely. As the ratio grows greater than one, the net worth is greater than the equity and the firm is more likely to be a reorganized or a target of takeovers. The value of the debts and assets was collected from Moody's *Manual* (1980–88). The stock price and number of shares was collected from Moody's *Manual* and the Daily Stock Price Record (Dow Jones 1979–88). All measures refer to conditions at the end of the year.

The analysis proceeds in the following way. First, I look for a causal relationship between all of the independent variables and the first dependent variable, reorganization activity. Then the reorganization variable is used and the other independent variables are used to predict whether or not the company has been the object of a merger. There ought to be a negative relationship between having undertaken forms of financial reorganization and being bought out.

The data is structured such that some of the independent variables are constants throughout the nine years investigated (i.e., finance presidents, owner- or manager-controlled), and some are variable throughout the investigation (i.e., composition of the board of directors, assets/stock value). Because the goal of the analysis is to use the data yearly to predict the dependent variables, the independent variables that changed yearly are lagged by one year, thereby reducing the number of observations from nine to eight years.

Two methods were used to analyze the data. When the continuous dependent variables were analyzed, an error components model with fixed effects was used to specify the error structure. This is because there are multiple observations on the same units of analysis over time. When the dependent variable was discrete, in the case of whether or not the firm was merged, a discrete time, discrete data model was used (Allison 1982). All statistical techniques were performed using the software package LIMDEP.

Results

The list of the one hundred largest companies that were objects of a merger during the years 1979–87 shows that the merger movement greatly affected the population of the largest firms in the American economy. A brief glance at the list shows that 7 out of 20 of those merged were oil companies.

TABLE 7.2
Means and Standard Deviations for Variables Used in the Analysis of Financial
Reorganization

Variable[a]	Mean	SD
Merged	0.03	
Reorg 1	0.50	0.43
Reorg 2	1.03	0.89
% Fin. pres.	0.32	0.20
Fin. pres.	0.32	0.46
Related Strategy	0.55	0.49
Unrelated Strategy	0.24	0.43
Owner Control	0.25	0.47
% Bank Directors	0.03	0.05
% Institution Dir.	0.04	0.05
Assets/Stock	0.81	0.98

Note: N = 753.
[a] Variables defined in the text.

There were 22 oil companies on the list in 1979, and this number is higher than would be expected. Table 7.2 presents the means and standard deviations of the variables for the eight years investigated (N = 753). All firms with missing data were removed from the analysis. The REORG1 variable is the measure of the shareholder value conception of the firm computed by factor analysis. The REORG2 variable is the additive scale for the same measure.

The variables concerning the financial conception of control hypothesis reveal that 32% of the companies had finance presidents and that in each field an average of 32% of the firms had finance presidents in their organizational fields. Most companies were likely to engage in some type of product diversification: 55% of the firms had a product-related strategy, and 24% had a product-unrelated strategy, which shows that these tactics, which reflect the finance conception of control, have become quite common.

Only 25% of the companies were controlled by the owners. The majority (75%), thus, were controlled by managers. The boards of directors were made up of 3% bankers and 4% institutional investors. The rest of the boards of directors were company insiders or outsiders with no financial institutional attachment. The net worth/value ratio variable associated with finance economics has a mean of 0.81. This means that, on average,

TABLE 7.3
Error Components Model Predicting Financial Reorganization

Variable[a]	Reorg 1		Reorg 2	
	b	SE (b)	b	SE (b)
%FINPRES.	−0.12	0.20	−0.06	0.10
FINPRES	0.06*	0.03	0.03*	0.01
RELATEDSTRATEGY	0.31**	0.08	0.15**	0.04
UNRELATEDSTRATEGY	0.30**	0.10	0.14**	0.05
OWNERCONTROL	−0.01	0.02	−0.01	0.01
%BANKDIRECTORS	0.57	0.61	0.25	0.29
%INSTITUTIONDIR	1.66**	0.60	0.78**	0.29
ASSET/STOCK	−0.03	0.03	−0.01	0.02
CONSTANT	0.74	0.36	0.37	0.19
R2	0.30		0.32	

Note: $N = 753$.
[a] Variables defined in the text.
* $p < 0.05$.   ** $p < 0.01$.

a company's net worth was less than its stock value (number of shares multiplied by the price of the stock). The average firm was thus not likely to be bought out. As the ratio increases past 1.00, we find that assets become more valuable than the stock. It is in these cases that finance economists predict a merger. Given that the standard deviation was quite large (.98), a great many firms were likely merger candidates.

Table 7.3 is an attempt to model the conditions under which firms used the shareholder value conception of control. Table 7.4 models the determinants of each of the reorganization activities separately. Because results from the factor analysis support the idea that the four reorganization activities are conceptually related, tables 7.3 and 7.4 are considered together.

Table 7.3 demonstrates that REORG1 (the factor measure) and REORG2 (the additive measure) are predicted by the same variables. The first three variables represent measures related to the finance conception of control. The percentage of finance CEOs in an organizational field had no effect on the reorganization variable. But whether or not the CEO was a finance CEO and if the company had a product-related or unrelated type of product mix had a significant, positive effect on firms engaging in forms of financial reorganization. This is strong evidence that firms that already were dominated by the finance conception of control were likely to have managers who engaged in financial reorganization of their firms.

TABLE 7.4
Logit Models Predicting Forms of Financial Reorganization

Variable[a]	Mergers		Divestitures		Stock Purchase		Stock Repurchases of Others[a]	
	b	SE (b)	b	SE (b)	b	SE (b)	b	SE (b)
%FINPRES	0.05	0.26	0.14	0.48	0.09	0.26	−0.25	0.81
FINPRES	1.30*	0.63	0.54*	0.18	1.38*	0.62	0.32*	0.14
RELATEDSTRATEGY	0.34*	0.17	0.59**	0.21	0.29*	0.12	0.34*	0.16
UNRELATEDSTRATEGY	0.33*	0.15	0.66**	0.25	0.29*	0.14	0.69	0.41
OWNERCONTROL	−0.03	0.08	0.05	0.05	−0.04	0.08	−0.03	0.10
%BANKDIRECTORS	0.40	0.80	1.12	1.47	−0.27	0.40	0.59	0.48
%INSTITUTIONDIR	1.64**	0.81	2.23**	0.74	1.16**	0.37	0.72	0.38
ASSET/STOCK	−0.01	0.32	0.21*	0.10	0.02	0.08	0.08	0.11
CONSTANT	−1.83**	0.32	−1.24**	0.25	−1.71**	0.31	−2.51**	0.40
	$\chi^2 = 10.89$, df = 8		$\chi^2 = 21.0$, df = 8		$\chi^2 = 9.15$, df = 8		$\chi^2 = 11.80$, df = 8	

Note: N = 753.
[a] Variables defined in text.
* $p < 0.05$.   ** $p < 0.01$.

Variables measuring the owner/manager/banker factors show that only the percentage of institutional investors on the board of directors had an effect on the dependent variable. Neither the types of control over the firm nor the percentage of bankers on the board of directors had a significant effect on whether or not the company reorganized. In this case, institutional investors were able to convince managers to undertake financial reorganization.

The finance economic hypothesis had no support in this analysis. The actual financial situation of the company in terms of its ratio of net to stock worth had no effect on the likelihood of managers engaging in financial reorganization. One interpretation of this, is that the balance sheets of firms were not sufficient conditions to promote the reorganization of firms. Instead, such reorganization took place only if there were actors for whom those actions made sense. The fact that firms who had institutional investors on their boards or who were already dominated by the finance conception of control were more likely to engage in forms of financial reorganization shows the importance of actors who have a perspective on the world and the power to enforce it.

Table 7.4 treats each reorganization activity as a separate measure. Generally, the results are almost identical to those from table 7.3. The differences from these results and the results from table 7.3 are small, but worth mentioning. Whether or not the firm had a finance CEO was a significant predictor of each of the four reorganization activities. However, whether or not the firm had a product-unrelated strategy had no significant effect on purchasing stock from other companies. The percentage of institutional investors on the board of directors also did not have a significant effect on the stock purchase variable. In the factor score, this variable was the weakest on the factor loading, and therefore the fact that the variables that explain it are less consistent than the variables that explain the other variables is not surprising.

The net worth/stock ratio also had an effect on divestitures. Firms with assets worth a great deal more than stock were more likely to divest themselves of divisions than firms in which assets and stocks were more evenly matched. This is consistent with the prediction that the finance economists make. It suggests that the sale of assets is undertaken to increase the stock price and make the firm less attractive to takeover.

Table 7.5 presents the results from the second part of the analysis, in which a discrete time/discrete data model is used to predict a company's being a merger target. Only two variables had a significant effect on whether or not a company was bought out. The first variable, as expected, was the reorganization variable. Reorganization had a negative effect on being merged. In other words, companies engaging in the shareholder value conception of control were less likely to be targets of a merger. The second variable predicting company merger was the percentage of bankers on the board of the directors.

In firms operating with the finance conception of control or with institutional investors convincing managers to accept the shareholder value conception of control, one can see an orientation toward using the shareholder value conception of control as a way to increase profits and not as a way to force the firm into merger with another firm. On the other hand, bankers on the board of directors do not affect reorganization activity, yet they do affect whether or not a company is likely to be a target of merger. One plausible interpretation is that bankers are brought onto the board of directors as firms are failing. In this context, in order to secure their financial investments, bankers force the sale of the company.

Conclusion

The 1980s reflected a shift in the dominant conception of control from the finance to the shareholder value conception of the corporation for large

TABLE 7.5
Logit Models Predicting Whether or Not a Firm Was Bought Out or Merged

Variable[a]	b	SE (b)	b	SE (b)
REORG 1			-0.55**	0.10
REORG 2	−0.29**	0.05		
%FINPRES	−0.29	0.57	−0.38	0.29
FINPRES	−0.43	0.76	−0.47	0.34
RELATEDSTRATEGY	−0.38	0.69	−0.11	0.10
UNRELATEDSTRATEGY	0.47	0.76	0.30	0.24
OWNERCONTROL	−0.64	0.80	−0.04	0.04
%BANKDIRECTORS	4.36**	1.71	9.56**	3.79
%INSTITUTIONDIR	−0.41	0.25	0.48	0.58
ASSET/STOCK	−0.25	0.28	−0.24	0.42
CONSTANT	−2.35**	0.42	−2.15**	0.63
	$\chi^2 = 12.5, df = 9$		$\chi^2 = 24.2, df = 9$	

Note: N = 753.
[a] Variables defined in the text.
* $p < 0.05$.   ** $p < 0.01$.

U.S. corporations. Finance CEOs were more likely to observe the new conception of control and steer their firms toward the shareholder value point of view. Firms with diversified product mix (which presumably were guided by the finance conception of control) were also likely to engage in mergers, divestitures, stock buybacks, and stock purchases of other firms. This result is consistent with the evidence from Davis, Kickmann, and Tinsley (1994) that the 1980s merger movement caused more diversified firms to become less diversified. Diversified firms engaged in mergers and divestitures more frequently than less diversified firms.

Obviously, these firms were paring product lines and buying more market shares in product lines in which they were more dominant. Where actors with the finance conception of control did not dominate, institutional institutions played a role as the agents of change forcing managers to shift toward the shareholder value conception of control. Institutional investors got managers to concentrate on the shareholder value conception of the firm, presumably to increase stock prices and prevent mergers. Banks, who probably held mostly corporate debt, often came on the scene quite late in the process. Their presence was associated with selling off the firm. Both banks and institutional investors caused non-finance-oriented managers to pay attention to issues of shareholder value.

The lack of effect of the basic financial facts of the firm in predicting either reorganization or ultimate merger could be due to one of two factors. First, it is possible that the measure used was flawed and that other measures might show such effects. Second, if the results are accepted, they show that the existence of rich assets relative to stock price may be a necessary, but not a sufficient, condition for the reorganization of firms. From my perspective, actors must come forward to perceive this situation and act.

These results suggest that the economic actions of the leaders of the largest firms have increasingly been informed by a certain perspective on what the firm is. This cultural construction has become a powerful tool of key actors to make profits. These results support the view that economic actors are embedded in a social world that shapes their interests, perceptions, and actions. The finance conception of the firm already privileged viewing the firm in primarily financial terms. The shareholder value critique of the firm was couched in those terms and proposed a somewhat different set of financial tools to inform corporate strategy. The social world provides the intellectual justification for a certain view of the corporation, and different actors use that view to justify acting in terms of that view. The results presented here reinforce the general sense that market relations are embedded in social relations and that actions make sense only when understood from the context of these social relations (Granovetter 1985).

While no direct evidence for the importance of public policy in the generation of the financial reorganization of large firms is presented, it is clear that one implication of this investigation is that these forces must have produced the intensification of the finance orientation toward firms. There are two plausible hypotheses in this regard. First, the Reagan administration's suspension of the antitrust laws and its tax policies in the early 1980s certainly provided some impetus to finance-oriented managers and institutional investors. Second, the 1970s did leave large corporations asset-rich and stock price-poor. Additional work should attempt to adjudicate between these competing explanations of the initial shocks that produced the financial reorganization of American corporations.

Now that the shareholder value conception of the large corporation has triumphed, its supporters dominate discourse about the corporation (Jensen 1989). In the world of the largest firms, corporate moves are evaluated primarily for their effect on share prices. Actions that appear to threaten share price often result in the pummeling of share prices. The power and interests that have produced this view now control the world of the largest firms in the United States.

This does not mean that the shareholder value conception of the firm has triumphed once and for all. A new crisis of profitability might push forward a new conception of control. In the 1990s, globalization and the emergence of new information technologies are both candidates for producing a crisis in the shareholder value conception of the firm. The strategies that maximized shareholder value during the 1980s and 1990s may run their course as ways of raising profits. While the economy in the 1990s in the United States was growing at a high rate, there were pressures on large firms to continue to raise profits. It is too early to tell if the so-called new economy of information technologies produces a new conception of control and a set of strategies that reorganizes the shareholder value emphasis on equity, debt, and the buying and selling of firms.

8

Corporate Control in Capitalist Societies

RECENT WORK has brought issues of corporate governance to the forefront of organization theory (Williamson 1975, 1985; Fama and Jensen 1983a, 1983b; Fligstein 1990; Campbell and Lindberg 1990; Roe 1994).[1] Here, governance is broadly defined as the internal organization of the firm and the links between the firm and its suppliers, competitors, customers, and the state. A working hypothesis across a number of disciplines is that the viability of the industrial enterprise may be intimately linked to issues of governance. There are, however, still significant theoretical differences over how to explain variations in governance structures. Economic accounts have focused on efficiency considerations, while work in sociology has tended to emphasize social, political, and cultural factors.

All of these approaches implicitly or explicitly conceptualize corporate governance as a problem of managing interdependence. To ensure continued growth and profitability, owners and managers must make sure that organizational processes are performed smoothly and predictably. Those seeking to govern the firm must gain control over the firm's internal and external environments in order to manage and stabilize these interdependencies.

The problem of internal control focuses primarily on issues of hierarchy and the motivation of boards of owners, boards of directors, managers, and workers. The basic condition of interdependence creates the principal-agent problem (Hansmann 1996). Actors responsible for the firm's performance do not carry out production and implement policies by themselves, but are dependent on others to do so. They must therefore find some means of motivating or inducing those actors to perform such tasks in consummate rather than perfunctory fashion. The literature on organizations typically identifies three different types of internal control problems: the relationship between management and workers, the separation of ownership and control (Berle and Means 1933), and the division of labor between different levels of management (Chandler 1962, 1977; Freeland 1994).

External control involves an even wider range of interdependencies, including interactions with competitors, suppliers, capital markets, and the state. It is generally assumed that corporate management must ensure stable, predictable relationships with each of these sets of actors in order to achieve profitability and growth. Relations with competitors, for example, center around explicit or implicit understandings about how business is to be carried out and the form competition will take (White 1981). In transacting with suppliers, management must ensure that quality is adequate, delivery is timely, and prices stable. Relations with the state are even more complex. Because the state defines and regulates the conditions that make transactions possible, including the limits of contract and property rights, it holds the power to legitimize various concrete institutional arrangements.

Few theories of governance attempt to examine all of the interdependencies between the firm and its environments. Instead, they tend to argue that one set of interdependencies, be it agency costs, transaction costs, population density, power, networks, information, trust, or institutional legitimacy, is critical to organizational survival. It is this focus on different interdependencies as causal mechanisms that has led to competing frameworks to explain corporate governance structures.

Not surprisingly, approaches that focus on different causal mechanisms reach divergent conclusions about the modern corporation. Efficiency analysts, for instance, often contend that, as firms face similar constraints in worldwide markets, a convergence of organizational forms is likely to occur (see, for instance, Jensen 1989). Others see governance structures as politically and culturally unique entities arising out of historically specific circumstances and conditions (Hamilton and Biggart 1988; Fligstein 1990).

In this review, I seek to assess the adequacy of existing explanations that purport to account for variations in corporate governance arrangements across societies. I am particularly interested in the extent to which existing theories can explain three types of corporate issues: the structure of property rights, the nature of competitive and cooperative arrangements across firms, and the strategies that firms use for growth and expansion, particularly with regard to vertical integration and diversification. I review economic and sociological accounts of corporate governance, showing that the two literatures posit different types of causal mechanisms to account for variations in organizational form. Drawing on recent comparative work that focuses on industrial organization across a number of societies, I then review the existing empirical literature. I conclude with a discussion of the implications of these findings for future research.

Two caveats are in order. First, most of my discussion focuses on institutions that figure prominently in economic theory and are less the focus in sociology. This means that the economic theories will seem more concerned with the issues reviewed here than the sociological ones, although the sociological theories tend to have broader objects as their focus of explanation. My approach helps focus the comparative discussion, but I recognize that it limits our ability to discuss a wide range of issues. Second, much of what is discussed concerns the largest corporations. This is because most of what is known and theorized is limited in this way. I accept this limit and suggest that my conclusions may be limited to the largest firms in developed economies.

Economic Theories and Mechanisms

Neoclassical theory paid little attention to issues of corporate governance. It conceptualized the firm as a production function, operated by rational actors who were profit maximizers who possessed perfect information about prices, and who operated in competitive product markets. In this theory, entrepreneurs were forced to deploy their capital in an efficient manner or go out of business, and the study of the firm was a case of "applied price theory" (Stigler 1968). From this perspective, the growth of oligopolies, strategies involving product diversification, and the vertical integration of production processes were all mechanisms that created barriers to entry or undermined price competition (Caves 1992).

Nowhere was the identification of the modern corporation with inefficiency clearer than in Berle and Means's (1933) thesis concerning the separation of ownership and control. In the 1950s, managerial economics began to develop formal models of how the separation of ownership and control affected the organization of the firm (Penrose 1959; Baumol 1959; Marris 1964). This literature argued that managers pursued growth in sales or assets over profits in order to increase their own salaries or status (Marris 1964). Although the empirical work did not turn up much positive evidence for this perspective (for a review, see Caves 1992), this literature reinforced the neoclassical view that the firm reflected inefficiencies in the price mechanism.

While the "new" institutional economics is a heterogeneous phenomenon, its adherents commonly share two critiques of neoclassical theory. First, such approaches contend that the firm is the dominant form of organization in capitalism, and that economics is incomplete if it cannot account for its emergence. Second, and even more important, the new institutional economics contends that firms would not be ubiquitous if they did not help create efficient outcomes. In this literature, modern property rights, the separation of ownership and control, and the building of organizational hierarchies are seen as efficiency-generating mechanisms.

One source of the new institutional economics was the work of Coase (1937), who argued that firms emerged because there were "transaction costs" involved in entering markets, negotiating for goods and services, and enforcing contracts. Coase suggested that if the cost of carrying out a transaction in the market was higher than the cost of carrying out the same transaction within the firm, firms would internalize the transaction in order to lower costs. In this scenario, firms emerge and grow precisely when they are more efficient than the market.

The second major forerunner of new economic theories of the firm was the work of the Carnegie school (Simon 1957; March and Simon 1958). Herbert Simon laid the basis for this approach by modifying the neoclassical assumption that economic decisions were made by perfectly rational actors possessing relatively complete information about the situation in which they acted. Focusing on the fact that humans have limited information-processing capabilities and that information is often imperfect or unavailable, he argued that economic actors suffered cognitive and informational constraints that made it impossible to achieve optimal decisions. Instead, actors had general goals in mind and would search for whatever solution they could find that more or less attained these goals, a process he referred to as "satisficing."

Organizational structure was shaped by attempts to reduce the effects of these cognitive and informational constraints (Simon 1957; March and Simon 1958). By breaking corporate goals down into their constituent elements and assigning them to different subunits within the firm, managers reduced the amount of information necessary to monitor organizational performance, thereby relieving cognitive strain and minimizing the chance of information overload for a given unit. This process also provided actors in the subunits with clear cognitive outcomes to attain, thus aligning individual behavior with the overall goals of the organization (Simon 1962). In addition, subunits developed "standard operating procedures" that further simplified cognitive processing by allowing for the easy reproduction of organizational competencies. Organizations that recognized the limits of human cognition and the role of information in organizational life were more efficient and able to survive.

The transaction cost economics (TCE) of Oliver Williamson (1975, 1981, 1985) focuses on the cost of devising, monitoring, and carrying out economic transactions between or within firms, arguing that governance structures—"the explicit or implicit contractual framework within which a transaction is located (markets, firms, and mixed modes)" (1981, 1544)—are shaped by such costs. Like Simon, Williamson assumes that economic actors are boundedly rational, and he further asserts that at least some actors behave opportunistically, engaging in "self-interest seeking with guile" (1975, 26). Imperfect information raises the cost of contracting by making it more difficult to predict future outcomes. Opportunism makes it necessary to monitor transactions for malfeasance, further raising the cost of governance.

TCE argues that under certain conditions of high asset specificity, market transactions become subject to higher levels of opportunism and bounded rationality, making them more costly to govern. Asset specificity refers to a situation in which resources necessary to carry out a transaction involve "durable transaction-specific investments" that cannot be used for another purpose without significant financial loss (Williamson and Ouchi 1981, 352). Once asset-specific investments have been made, neither buyer nor seller can turn to the market as a viable alternative, and it becomes particularly important to safeguard transactions involving asset specificity against the (costly) hazards of opportunism.

In Williamson's view, it is the job of the firm (or more generally, of governance structures) to economize on transaction costs. The firm's system of authority relations is crucial in this regard (Williamson 1988, 1991), for when transactions are internalized within a firm, opportunism can be reduced through the exercise of fiat. TCE uses the same general framework to explain vertical integration, the creation of the multidivisional form and other hierarchies, the emergence of conglomerates, and the separation of ownership and control in large firms (Williamson 1975, 1985). Recently, Williamson has tried to explain more complex forms of contracting such as strategic alliances, networks, and cross-ownership patterns that appear in corporations across the world, arguing that such forms of contracting economize on transaction costs where there is genuine interdependence between organizations, but not enough to merit full-scale merger (Williamson 1991).

Agency theory views all social relations in economic interaction as reducible to a set of contracts between principals and agents. Principals are individuals who select agents to do their bidding in some matter. The key problem is aligning the interests of the agents such that they do not act against the interests of the principals. This requires writing a contract (sometimes explicitly, sometimes implicitly) that provides safeguards for both the principal and the agent. Such contracts must provide principals with a way to monitor agents and must create incentives for each side to carry out its part of the bargain (Jensen and Meckling 1976).

In agency theory, the firm is seen as a fictitious entity created by a "nexus of contracts" of the principal-agent variety. In this respect the firm is no different from the market: it "has no power of fiat, no authority, no disciplinary action any different in the slightest degree from ordinary market contracting between two people" (Alchian and Demsetz 1972, 119). Instead, the firm is a system of property rights that defines a set of principal-agent relations and divides up claims to assets and residual cash flow (Fama and Jensen 1983a, 1983b). The principal, an owner, hires employees to do part of the work. They are paid a wage and in exchange usually, though not always, relinquish claims on the profits. The contract to which they agree contains specifications of their duties, their rewards, and the rights of the principal to monitor their performance.

Agency theory argues that different divisions of property rights—the joint stock company, partnerships, sole proprietorships, nonprofit organizations—arise because these forms of organization are efficient under specific conditions. Basically, depending on the severity of agency costs (i.e., the costs of structuring, bonding, and monitoring a set of contracts among agents with conflicting interests), an alternative division of property rights makes sense (Fama and Jensen 1983b). For example, the joint stock corporation under management control is likely to thrive when the cost of setting up the firm is prohibitively high, the type of knowledge necessary to manage the firm is specialized, there are large economies of scale, and there are persons who are willing to supply capital on the hope of obtaining residual claims that are already discounted for agency costs (Fama and Jensen 1983a). Under these circumstances, the classic separation of ownership and control occurs. But according to agency theory, this arrangement does not lead to inefficiency. Instead, ownership and management interests are aligned through three mechanisms. First, managerial pay is linked to firm performance; second, boards of directors monitor managerial action; third, the market for corporate control effectively sanctions managers who misuse financial assets, even if boards of directors have been co-opted. In this account, the firm is efficient, even if product markets are not. Versions of this perspective has been used extensively in a wide variety of applications, including finance economics (Ross 1977; Myers 1984; Fama 1980; Jensen and Meckling 1976).

Neoinstitutionalist accounts usually retain the assumption that observed markets are either in, or approaching, some form of equilibrium. A more radical perspective on this issue is taken by what we label "neoevolutionary" theory in economics. Brian Arthur (1988, 1989) argues that economic institutions may have random starts. Thus, history and accident play some role in the origins of economic modes of organizing. At these originating moments, there may be several ways to organize production, none of which has any obvious advantages. Arthur has argued that during the dynamic processes whereby markets are built, one or another form of organization may have some slight advantage. Over time, institutions grow up around a certain organization, and they tend to reinforce that organization's advantage.

Arthur terms this process a *lock-in*. This lock-in occurs as a set of tiny, discrete steps that over time make a given set of arrangements institutionally embedded. Once in place, they become difficult to dislodge. Economic processes are thus dynamic up to a point, but once a particular form of organization is locked in, markets become stable and less dynamic. Market processes that evolve in this fashion are termed *path dependent*. Arthur has studied a number of processes with this model, including the introduction of new technology, the location of urban agglomerations, and the creation of technological centers such as Silicon Valley and Route 128 in Boston (1988, 1989).

His model helps explain why the entry into modernity has such a profound effect on the structure of a national economy. The historical entry into industrialization is characterized by the simultaneous formation of a large number of institutional arrangements. Once these arrangements are in place, they form institutional conditions that help organize how new organizations and industries emerge. This approach implies that property rights may be organized in a number of different ways, but, once organized, they tend to be stable and provide institutional structure to new industries that emerge.

A different view of economic dynamics comes from Nelson and Winter (1982). They argue that markets are continuously dynamic and never reach equilibrium points. This means that firms are constantly being confronted by unstable market conditions. In response, firms attempt to find ways of reproducing themselves over time. They do so by creating competencies that embed organizational procedures. The standard operating procedures of a firm produce products but also serve to monitor problems. They provide feedback to decision makers about changing conditions internal or external to the firm.

In this elegant way, Nelson and Winter are able to combine March and Simon's view of organizations with a dynamic view of market processes. Firms that fail to develop such competencies go out of business, while firms that do can prosper for relatively long periods of time. However, market processes can occasionally overwhelm even the most stable firms. This perspective does not explain which competencies will emerge from the formation of markets. But it does suggest that once they emerge, they tend toward reproduction precisely because they have reliably led to reproduction in the past. Nelson and Winter provide another argument for why one might expect distinct organizational styles across markets and societies. A set of arrangements, once in place, resists transformation because the owners and managers of firms stick to procedures that have brought them success in the past.

Sociological Theories of Control

Sociological approaches to the firm can be seen as a progression away from efficiency principles and toward a more diffuse set of political and cultural explanations for its form and dynamics (although this is by no means universally the case). In this section, I consider four general sociological approaches that are relevant to comparisons of corporate organization: resource dependence (Burt 1983; Pfeffer and Salancik 1978; Gerlach 1992), network approaches that focus on governance arrangements to increase organizational competitiveness (Powell and Smith-Doerr 1994; Piore and Sabel 1984; Powell and Brantley 1992; Saxenian 1994; Uzzi 1997, 1999; Stuart 1998), political approaches (Campbell and Lindberg 1990; Fligstein 1990; Hamilton and Biggart 1988; Mintz and Schwartz 1985; Mizruchi and Stearns 1988; Westney 1987), and institutional accounts (DiMaggio and Powell 1983, 1991; Meyer and Rowan 1977; Scott and Meyer 1994).

Sociologists tend to shy away from making claims that an organizational form is efficient in a neoclassical sense. Instead, organizational theory assumes only that organizational forms are effective; that is, they promote the survival of the organization. The "effectiveness" assumption suggests that while these approaches use very different rhetorics to describe their objects, there is a surprising degree of congruence on the important sociological mechanisms that structure organizational life. Power within and across firms, states, resource dependence, and the construction of institutions are the basic elements of sociological theorizing about the firm.

The strategic contingencies perspective on organizations dominated sociological accounts in the 1960s and early 1970s (Thompson 1967; Lawrence and Lorsch 1967). This approach drew heavily on the work of Herbert Simon and the Carnegie school, and it retained much of the economic focus on markets and rational adaptation to market conditions. Strategic contingencies accounts held that managers and owners of firms were constantly surveying their environments, interpreting "strategic contingencies" that would affect the chances of corporate survival. Having perceived such contingencies, they would alter the firm's internal strategies and structures in order to adapt to environmental conditions. The basic model was that rational actors could perceive the shifting tides of their external worlds and would have the power to act to preserve their organizations.

Much of the sociological work on organizations since the mid-1970s has been a response to the rational adaptation approach embedded in the strategic contingencies model. The criticisms go in several directions. Many scholars have argued that the strategic contingencies model focuses too heavily on rational adaptation. They retain the belief that environments are powerful determinants of organizational life chances, but they contend that neither the identification of environmental shifts nor subsequent organizational changes are as easy as strategic contingency theory suggests (Hannan and Freeman 1977, 1984; Pfeffer and Salancik 1978; Meyer and Rowan 1977). A second group of researchers argues that environments are themselves social and political constructions and that the processes by which they are created is itself an object of study (Fligstein 1990; DiMaggio 1985, 1988; Pfeffer 1981; Orru, Biggart, and Hamilton 1991, 361).

Scholars concerned with environments have continued to focus on organizational survival as a response to environmental change. Most of these views rely implicitly or explicitly on some form of resource dependence perspective. There are two sorts of views of resource dependence, one that focuses on the management of dependence and one that argues that environmental dependence is the key to survival.

The former variant of this theory argues that actors' power within the organization depends on their ability to control and solve internal and external resource dependencies (Pfeffer and Salancik 1978). This ability can derive from actors' position within the firm, their specialized knowledge, or their links to the outside world. If there is a shift in resource dependencies, there is the potential for a shift in the balance of power. Thus, powerful actors resist change in an attempt to protect their positions, while less powerful actors attempt to introduce only those changes that increase their power (Fligstein 1985, 1987).

Burt (1983) has used such resource dependence arguments to model network connections between firms and industrial sectors in the U.S. economy. His key point is that the network links between key suppliers and customers affect their profitability. If there are many suppliers and few customers, then the advantage shifts to the customer. If the relative numbers are reversed, the advantage is with the supplier. Such asymmetries should in theory produce higher-than-average profits for the resource-advantaged firm. They might also make the resource-disadvantaged firm unstable. Burt has argued that using boards of directors as connectors between suppliers and customers is one way to manage and index these types of resource dependence. Other analysts have used a similar approach in examining networks of connections among owners, managers, and banks, arguing that the patterns of interaction between these actors shape the possibilities for firms' behavior (Mizruchi and Schwartz 1987; Mintz and Schwartz 1985; Mizruchi and Stearns 1988).

A second branch of resource dependence theory has retained a greater emphasis on market selection and efficiency principles. This approach posits that the market selection occurs at the population level, where organizations survive due to their ability to function under given environmental conditions (Hannan and Freeman 1977, 1984, 1989). Once organizational forms appropriate to a given environment have been selected, structural inertia sets in, making further change difficult. In such accounts, resource dependencies are often so severe as to affect a given organization's odds of survival. Ecological analysis that focuses exclusively on selection processes is a form of environmental determinism that has resource dependence at its core.

Network approaches stress a number of ways in which networks are used to co-opt environments and increase the effectiveness of the organization.

Some stress that cooperation between competitors and suppliers can lead to positive outcomes for firms (Powell 1990). Implicitly, most of the network approaches adopt a kind of strategic contingencies view of networks as a response to organizational environments. These approaches posit a set of rather heterogeneous mechanisms that focus on how qualities of the environment make network forms of organization attractive (see Powell and Smith-Doerr 1994 for a review). Networks based in regions such as Silicon Valley utilize flexible specialization and are based on norms of reciprocity (Saxenian 1994). The networks here are effective because firms can easily gain access to goods and services they might need to compete for in a rapidly changing market environment.

In industries where innovation and learning are critical, such as biotechnology, there exists a common technological community, which works best by a constant exchange of ideas and persons (Powell and Brantley 1992). Business groups, such as the Japanese keiretsu, appear to be authority structures that coordinate a firm's activities based on common business ownership (Gerlach 1992; Lincoln, Gerlach, and Takahashi 1992). Finally, strategic alliances and joint ventures are formed for common gain between firms (Piore and Sabel 1984). Most relevant for the review here is the idea that competition and cooperation between firms can be structured very differently depending on the nature of the environment.

Critiques of resource dependence approaches have noted that an element of social construction is involved in what constitutes resource dependence. Pfeffer (1981) has made a compelling case that while there are certainly situations where resource dependence is pivotal for organizational life chances, it is also the fact that actors must interpret their interdependencies and have the power to act. In murky social worlds, perceiving interdependencies is not always a straightforward task. Moreover, even if this occurs, actors must be able to impose on others their interpretation of the strategic contingency at stake. Once it is acknowledged that this is the case, it becomes apparent that perceptions of interdependence may be as important as interdependencies themselves.

The political-cultural approach more systematically pursues the notion that resource dependence is socially constructed, leading the focus on technical environments to be supplemented by a focus on institutional environments (Fligstein 1990; Fligstein and Brantley 1992). The central problem facing organizational actors is to create a stable world so that the organization can continue to exist. This necessitates the construction of an organizational field in which actors come to recognize and take into account their mutual interdependence. These understandings are reached through political processes. Generally, the largest groups develop a collective way to control the organizational field, and they impose it on the smaller groups. There are two problems in creating a stable organizational field: finding a set of understandings that allows a political accommodation in the field, and the legitimation of those understandings by a government. These understandings operate to create a conception of control.

From this perspective, states are implicated in all features of organizational life. The organizations and institutions of the state make and administer the rules governing economic interaction in a given geographic area, and they are prepared to enforce those rules, in the last instance through force. The state's claims to set the rules for economic interaction is social in origin, and as such it is contestable. The process by which these rules are set up, transformed, and enforced is therefore an inherently political process. It follows from this that the local politics and existing practices of nations have profound effects on the form, content, and enforcement rules in organizational fields (for a similar approach, see Dobbin 1994). The formation of organizational fields depends on the politics in the field and the relation between the field and the state.

A similar approach is outlined by Campbell and Lindberg (1990), who argue that the state shapes the institutional organization of the economy mainly through the manipulation of property rights. It does so in response to pressures from economic actors, but also as a result of political choices made by actors in the state. Campbell and Lindberg define governance structures as "combinations of specific organizational forms, including markets, corporate hierarchies, associations, and networks (e.g. interlocking directorates, long term subcontracting agreements, bilateral and multilateral joint ventures, pools, cartels)" (1990, 3), while they see property rights as "the rules that determine the conditions of ownership and control over the means of production" (1990, 2). Their basic assertion is that state actors manipulate property rights to help ratify or select certain governance structures. Using evidence from seven major U.S. industries, they argue that the American state has actually had a very powerful role in the American economy by approving or disapproving of varying arrangements (Campbell et al. 1991).

Institutional theories (DiMaggio and Powell 1983; DiMaggio 1988; Meyer and Rowan 1977; Scott and Meyer 1994; Zucker 1977, 1987, 1988) complete the conceptual transition away from technical environments, focusing almost exclusively on "the socially constructed normative worlds in which organizations exist" (Orru, Biggart, and Hamilton 1991, 361). As firms interact with each other and with their environments, formal or informal rules emerge to govern interaction, and organizational fields are formed. Once these fields become institutionalized, however, they take on an independent status that has a powerful normative effect on subsequent interaction. Once socially defined institutional environments are in place, changes in organizational form are driven more by considerations of legitimacy than by concern for rational adaptation or efficiency.

Scott and Meyer's volume (1994) contains a set of interesting empirical studies that illustrate these points. Two sorts of processes are illustrated. First, the construction of meanings and the role of organized groups such as firms and states is usefully elucidated. Second, much of the work concerns the diffusion of shared meanings. Once institutions are invented, they spread, often with remarkable speed, across settings.

Institutional theory has not directly focused on the questions of ownership and control, cooperation and competition between firms, and firms' strategy and structure. It would suggest, however, that once a set of institutions around these issues is in place, it is very difficult to dislodge. Further, new organizational innovations would tend to spread to organizational fields that were close together, while more distant fields would be late adopters. Institutional theory tends to support other theoretical views that unique institutions evolve across societies and that they create stable patterns of difference impervious to market interactions.

Comparative Cases

In this section, I examine how firms and economic transactions are organized across a number of societies in order to assess how well various theories of corporate organization account for these differences. The attempt is to focus on evidence concerning the organization of property rights, competitive and cooperative arrangements, and firms' strategies of vertical integration and diversification. There are several problems involved in reviewing the comparative literature. First, the evidence available is often selective rather than comprehensive, since analysts have tended to look at variables that reflect their own perspective and have not tried to partition variance among a number of perspectives. In trying to get a coherent view of what is known about any national capitalism, one is left with a selective review that focuses on the variables that theorists have sought out. Second, most of the work on comparative organizations has been done in advanced industrial societies. We know quite a bit about business organization in the United States, Western Europe, and Japan, but we know less about the other countries of Asia and Eastern Europe, and much less about the rest of the world. This review will consider the United States, Japan, Germany, France, and more briefly, Taiwan, Korea, and China. This is a huge set of comparisons that will be done relatively superficially, primarily to illustrate the value of the theories.

It is useful to put the conclusions up front. Despite all of the discussion of globalization of the world economy and the so-called multinationalization of corporations, different societies continue to have distinctive organizational arrangements (Hollingsworth and Streeck 1994; Pauly and Reich

1997; Crouch and Streeck 1997; Dore and Berger 1997; Berger and Dore 1996; and Kitschelt et al. 1999 come to essentially the same conclusion). These arrangements are primarily the function of three factors: the unique history of each society's entry into industrialization and its subsequent institutional development, the unique form of state intervention in economies in terms of property rights and rules of competition and cooperation, and the social organization of elites (i.e., whether families, managers, or states own or exert control over corporations). The theories that appear to capture these dynamics most adequately are neoevolutionary perspectives in economics and political-cultural approaches in sociology.

Resource dependence theory is a plausible account for some of what is observed. Alliances, networks, family ownership patterns, and interlocking directorates among firms are phenomena that appear to a different degree across industries and societies. One could posit that these different arrangements reflect unique resource dependencies, but the evidence has not been gathered to prove that, and the assertion might be tautological. There is little support for agency theory as an explanation for variation across societies. While agency theory predicts that property rights converge around a single model, many societies with similar types of agency problems have very different arrangements of property rights. It is possible to construct transaction cost arguments for the differences across societies, but the evidence, like that for resource dependence, is difficult to assemble (see Aoki 1988, for an attempt to do so in the case of Japan).

The United States is considered first. Agency theory and its employment by finance economists have shaped the way we talk about the corporation, and the large American industrial corporation is discussed today primarily in financial terms. For financial economics, assets, debts, and free cash flow relative to the numbers of shares of stock and the current stock market evaluation of each share sum up all that is important to know about any given firm. In the previous chapter, I argued that the shareholder value conception of the firm now dominates the largest American corporations. Managers and owners of firms have come to view their organizations in the same way (Useem 1993). Operating divisions are bought and sold based on their short-term financial performance. Workers are fired to improve next quarter's profits, and those who are left are supposed to carry the burden by increasing their productivity.

How did this conception of the firm arise and come to dominate corporate organization in the United States? A resource dependence perspective would predict that powerful actors controlling critical resources constructed this conception of the firm for their own benefit. A huge amount of intellectual energy has gone into ascertaining the relationship between who owns corporations and who controls them (Kotz 1978; Larner 1970; Herman 1980; Mintz and Schwartz 1985). An equal amount of energy has gone into mapping the connections between banks, insurance companies, and cross-ownership patterns in American corporations, mainly through the use of interlocking directorships (for example, Mizruchi and Schwartz 1987). While there appears to be a fair amount of interlocking, it is unstable (Mizruchi 1982; Palmer 1983), and its effects have been inconsistent across studies (Burt 1983; for a review, see Fligstein and Brantley 1992). It is hard to argue that the shareholder value conception of the firm originated in these patterns of relations.

Another possible origin of the financial conception of control is the dominance of financial markets. While financial markets and investment houses (particularly, J. P. Morgan) played a key role in the turn-of-the-century merger movement in the United States (Mizruchi 1982), there is little systematic evidence that these financial institutions, particularly investment bankers and institutional investors (defined as pension funds, insurance companies, or mutual funds), played active roles in the shaping of corporate strategies and structures from 1905 until 1980 (Fligstein 1990; Fligstein and Brantley 1992). This was primarily because U.S. antitrust laws—in particular the Clayton Act, but also the Glass-Steagall Act—made interlocks between competing industrial firms illegal and bank ownership of firms problematic (Roe 1994). U.S. firms were not allowed to exhibit the financial linkages and ownership patterns that emerged in Europe and Asia. Instead, the proximate causes of the behavior of large American industrial corporations are better viewed in the context of the organizational fields in which they found themselves (see chapter 6).

The finance conception of control rose in the 1950s for two reasons. First, large firms in the postwar era were already fairly diversified. The problem of internally controlling a large number of products opened an opportunity for executives who could claim to evaluate the profit potential of each product. In order to make the large, diversified corporation manageable, finance executives reduced the information problem to a measurement of the rate of return earned by each product line. Second, the federal government was strictly enforcing the antitrust laws in the early postwar era and had passed an antimerger law that made it difficult to merge with direct competitors or suppliers. This encouraged firms to diversify in order to grow. The financial executives who could evaluate profit potential for product lines outside of a firm's area of expertise were invaluable in such efforts (Fligstein 1990, chap. 6).

The factor that solidified the finance conception of control was the challenge to firms in established organizational fields that came from corporate invaders. The executives who pioneered the acquisitive conglomerates showed how financial machinations involving debt could be used to produce rapid growth with little investment of capital. All of the financial forms of reorganization including mergers, divestitures, leveraged buyouts, the accumulation of debt, and stock repurchasing were invented or perfected in this period. The 1960s witnessed a large-scale merger movement in which many of the largest corporations substantially increased their size and diversification. Managers and owners of industrial corporations who were not active participants in the 1960s merger movement were likely to become targets from other industrial corporations in that movement (Palmer et al. 1995). As a result of this, finance executives increasingly became CEOs, and the finance conception of the corporation invaded most of the organizational fields of the largest American corporations (Fligstein 1987).

The finance conception of control that emerged in the 1960s was transformed by the merger movement of the 1980s (see chap. 7; Stearns and Allan 1996; Ocasio and Kim 1999). Friedman (1985a) has argued that the proximate cause of the 1980s merger movement was the state of the balance sheets of American corporations around 1980. The 1970s were an era of high inflation, high interest rates, and a poor stock market. By 1980, many firms found themselves with undervalued assets on their books—assets that had risen in value because of inflation and relatively low stock prices.

Another factor behind the merger movement of the 1980s was state intervention that created changes in the regulatory environment. The Reagan administration weakened antitrust laws in the 1980s by lifting many existing restrictions, giving the green light to all types of mergers, including vertical, horizontal, and conglomerate forms. At the same time, corporate taxes were substantially reduced thereby providing capital for the merger movement. These actions, when combined with the finance conception of control that had arisen in the 1960s and the undervalued corporate assets of the 1970s, led to an explosion of merger activity.

Although the mergers of the 1980s were sometimes implemented by finance-oriented executives, they were also pushed by institutional investors. There is evidence that firms with a finance-oriented CEO were more likely to engage in financial reorganization; conversely, firms without a finance CEO were more likely to become merger targets (Davis and Stout 1992). Nonetheless, institutional investors and investment bankers played key roles, strengthening the role of financial markets. They recognized that firms had undervalued assets that could be sold off for huge profits or leveraged for new asset purchases; they created the "junk bond" market, which provided a market to borrow huge sums of other people's money to engage in obtaining assets; and they used the finance conception of control to force managers to financially reorganize firms or risk becoming victims of the market for corporate control (Davis and Stout 1992; Davis and Thompson 1994). As a result, the 1980s witnessed an increase in shareholder activism (Useem 1993), particularly among large, institutional shareholders (Baums, Buxbaum, and Hopt 1993, part 2).

The growth of the shareholder value conception of control does not appear to have had a significant impact on corporate strategies regarding competition in product markets. There is some evidence that research and development expenses are pared when large mergers occur (Graves 1988). There is no systematic evidence that so-called active financial intervention by institutional investors or investment bankers changes strategies in any important way, although there is evidence that the number of products produced by the largest firms decreased in the 1980s (Davis, Kickmann, and Tinsley 1994). The strongest predictors of such behavior continue to be the primary markets in which firms operate and the strategies and structures of whom they perceive to be their main competitors.

American firms tend to be large, relatively diversified, and run by financial criteria. This is not surprising. An institutional investor in the semiconductor industry, for example, would not try to dictate whether or not managers produced a new generation of computer chips. To protect their investment, they have to know that the industry basically has short product cycles (two to four years). Opposing a new generation of computer chips would make their investment worthless. There is, however, an important caveat. The principal actors in financial markets have forced managers of large industrial corporations to increasingly emphasize short-term profits. It remains to be seen how this will affect corporate strategies in the future.

The shareholder value conception of control that has arisen in the United States has not emerged in many other advanced capitalist countries (perhaps with the exception of Great Britain; see Woolcock 1996), in large part because of preexisting sets of institutional arrangements between states and economic elites. For example, the European Union has decided to allow member states to continue to monitor mergers and decide if a given merger is in the interest of the member state. There will be no European market for corporate control in the Single Market (European Community 1985; Franks and Mayer 1990).

State-firm relations around Western Europe remain remarkably stable. The French government has sold off parts of many of the largest firms, although it continues to hold shares in firms it has brought to market (Anastassopoulos, Blanc, and Dussauge 1987). The basic French industrial policy after World War II has attempted to create "national champions" that could compete in world markets (Dyas and Thanheiser 1976). These champions are supposed to be large enough to attain economies of scale. The French government controlled investment in these firms and the direction of capital toward those firms (Jenny and Weber 1980). Indeed, during the 1960s and 1970s, the government induced mergers in given industries as part of its industrial policy.

French industrial policy shifted somewhat in the 1990s (Dumez and Jeunemaître 1990, 224; Boyer 1990, 1997). The government sold shares in some of the largest firms, and it freed managers to make investments the way they chose. Large French firms took advantage of the American and British markets for corporate control to purchase stakes in large firms in both of those countries. Because French industrial policy focused on creating firms that were supposed to attain scale economies, large French firms tended to be vertically integrated, relatively large, and undiversified in their products (Dyas and Thanheiser 1976; Green 1986). Government intervention in financial markets and its traditional ownership of firms has meant that alliance capitalism does not exist. During the 1990s, managers of French firms were given more degrees of freedom to raise money, engage in mergers, and enter and exit businesses. But continued government holdings of shares of large firms and political pressures that can be brought to bear on firms who seem to act against the "public interest" have prevented a significant market for hostile takeovers in France.

German firms have less direct national or federal intervention. However, the German Lander (the equivalent of states in the United States) continue to have substantial ownership stakes in important industrial firms (Boltho 1996). They use these stakes to affect investment patterns of local firms in order to preserve their industrial base (Stokman, Ziegler, and Scott 1985). Historically, cartels were legal in Germany. This led to cooperative behavior among German producers (Dyas and Thanheiser 1976; Kocka 1980). Today, while cartels are illegal, German antitrust law allows firms in the same industry to cooperate when their products are intended for exports. German firms thus have less incentive to merge to control competition and a great deal of incentive to cooperate (Dumez and Jeunemaître 1990).

The largest German firms are conglomerates, usually centered around a bank (Lane 1989). These can resemble the keiretsu structure of Japanese firms. Stock is held closely by families and banks, and investment is usually directed from banks (Kocka 1980; Stokman, Ziegler, and Scott 1985). There are very few assets for sale in Germany in the stock market, and those markets are relatively unimportant (Schneider-Lenne 1992). The core of the German economy, the so-called *Mittelstand*, are relatively small firms that specialize in a small set of products (Cable, Palfrey and Runge 1980; Albert 1991). These firms, typically with sales in the range of $80–$100 million, are generally family owned and controlled. They are often passed across the generations. These firms concentrate on upscale production markets for industrial goods. As a result of close holding of ownership and a lack of incentives to control competition through mergers, German firms are less integrated, smaller, and less diversified than their American counterparts (see Streeck on the continued survival of the German model, 1995, 1996).

The Japanese case has been widely studied (Abegglen and Stalk 1985; Aoki 1988; Gerlach 1992; Hadley 1970; Kono 1984; Whitley 1990; Lincoln, Gerlach, and Takahashi 1992; Kester 1992, 1996; Dore 1997). The general conclusion is that the core of the Japanese industrial economy is organized into enterprise groups. Most of these groups existed before World War II as family-owned federations of firms called zaibatsu. After the war, they were reorganized into looser groups that are called keiretsu (Yoshino 1968). The stock ownership patterns are such that each firm owns a small part of the stock of the other firms (Lincoln, Gerlach, and Takahashi 1992). The group is usually in a large number of industries, and at the core of the group is often a bank. Very few shares of the firm trade on open equity markets. Since investment is internally generated, it is usually oriented to long-run gains and holding market share (for a review of this literature, see Gerlach 1992, chap. 3).

The Japanese government has also played an active role in investment patterns in the economy, at least historically (Westney 1987; Johnson 1982). The Japanese government directed the original entry into industrialization during the Meiji Restoration. It explicitly borrowed Western models of institutions in order to rapidly move into industrial development (Westney 1987). During the postwar era, the Ministry of International Trade and Industry promoted Japanese industry in a variety of ways. Firms were encouraged to enter export markets, and credit was allocated to projects that would produce goods for export (Johnson 1982). The keiretsu structure was reinforced and used to support export activity.

There has been much discussion about whether or not the Japanese stock market will be effective in breaking up these arrangements (Kester 1996, 129). After nearly a decade of such discussion, one can only argue that the keiretsu structure remains in place. There is no market for corporate control in Japan, and there is not likely to be one. Gerlach (1992) shows that historical patterns of trading, credit, and ownership were stable in the keiretsu during the late 1980s.

Taiwan and South Korea exhibit alternative structures (Hamilton and Biggart 1988; Whitley 1990; Wade 1990; Li 1988; Liu 1987). In Taiwan, large industrial firms are family owned and controlled. Firms are relatively small (Biggart and Guillén 1999). When firms start to get large, families usually set up new firms to produce related products. Funding for these new firms comes from the earnings of the old firms. Control remains firmly in the hands of families, and the equity markets play little role in the generation of new firms and capital (Hamilton and Kao 1990). The Taiwanese government has also played very little role in the allocation of capital. The rapid development of the economy has been accomplished primarily by private hands without the intervention of either financial markets or government. Taiwanese firms are not typically large, vertically integrated, or diversified. The connections between firms mainly revolve around extensive kinship networks. Taiwanese business is the purest case of small-scale firms that are family controlled and densely networked.

The core of the Korean economy is dominated by a set of large conglomerate corporations. The Korean word *chaebol* is a direct translation of the Japanese word *keiretsu* (Hamilton and Biggart 1988). The chaebol differ from the keiretsu in two principal ways. Unlike the keiretsu, they are highly diversified family-owned firms. They are very highly integrated, and ownership and investment is centrally directed (Whitley 1990; Amsden 1989; Biggart and Guillén 1999).

The Korean government also plays a large and active role in the investment patterns of the chaebol (Amsden 1989; Wade 1990; see Biggart and Guillén 1999 for a discussion of this role in the case of the automobile industry). This intervention is a direct result of the Korean War and has continued throughout the postwar era. Indeed, government control is stronger in Korea than in any of the emerging capitalist countries in Asia. As a result, private financial markets play almost no role in the growth of the economy (Hamilton and Biggart 1988; Whitley 1992; Wade 1990). As already suggested, Korean firms are large, integrated, and diversified, yet under the control of a small number of families with strong ties to government.

There has also been some recent empirical study of mainland China. Everyone is agreed that the Chinese government continues to play an important role in the economy (Guthrie 1998; Wank 1999). There is some disagreement as to the direction of change in governance. While a small stock market has emerged, most of the stock for the largest firms continues to be held by the government (Guthrie 1999). Keister (1998) suggests that business groups with interlocking directorates have formed in China around banks to resemble keiretsu structures in Japan. She argues that firms do not integrate their structures but remain loosely connected. Guthrie (1997) studies firms in Shanghai and shows that in response to weaker ties to the governments, managers have responded by diversifying the activities of their firms. His firms appear to have divisionalized their structures. Wank (1999) emphasizes that the ownership of assets in China is now being intentionally left vague. Former state managers who now run firms are able to direct investment as if they owned the firms. They are embedded in networks with other actors, including state officials, to insure that they obtain needed resources, including capital to expand. The situation in China is sufficiently fluid that all three scholars could be right for the set of firms they studied. None of these scholars sees more convergence with American-style governance.

Conclusion

There is no evidence that the world is converging on a single form of state–finance sector–industrial corporation relations. Families, managers, and states alternate in their domination of ownership in various societies. There is also little evidence that relations between firms are converging toward markets, hierarchies, networks, or strategic alliances as the dominant form of governance, and stable situations with different configurations abound across various societies. Large firms in different societies also differ in their product mix and integration. Finally, the types and degree of state involvement in markets vary widely within and across regions. The total effect is still one of national capitalisms (for a similar conclusion, see Biggart and Guillén 1999 on the case of the world automobile industry).

Available evidence suggests that there is, as yet, no world market for corporate control. Property rights and governance structures are under the control of nation-states and local elites. As long as states claim sovereignty, they are unlikely to undermine their control over their economies in this way. Moreover, their local elites also have a great deal to gain from current arrangements, and they will oppose actions that would force conformity to someone else's standards. Even our scant review of state-firm–financial sector relations shows that while American, Japanese, and some European corporations are dominated by managers, the core of much of the rest of the world's economy is controlled by families (see Hamilton and Kao 1990 for Taiwan; Evans 1995 for Brazil and India; Leff 1978 for a review of other Third World countries, including Mexico).

While the American industrial structure is firmly in the grasp of the shareholder value conception of control, the rest of the world has steadfastly resisted importing it, for the reasons just outlined. National economies have distinct institutional arrangements that outline the relations among investment, ownership, control, and economic growth. While they are interested in world trade, national systems are set up to preserve their national systems of property rights and governance structures. In the late 1990s, there was a pickup in merger activity, particularly in Europe. Hostile mergers are still relatively rare in Europe. Many mergers that have occurred are between firms within a particular society where regional competitors have started to merge. These mergers are often under-taken to attain sufficient size to be competitive in the European market. Cross-border mergers are most frequently undertaken to serve the European market (Fligstein 2000). As Europe becomes more economically integrated, changes may follow in the control of property rights across Europe.

These results present several interesting theoretical and empirical agendas. Theoretically, there has been a tendency for competing explanations of governance to be presented as opposed to one another. Organizational form is thus understood as a matter of, for example, efficiency versus legitimacy. My review of the literature suggests that the relationship between causal mechanisms is more complicated. Economic approaches, for instance, have implicitly assumed that social structure will change to create efficiency when exchange is carried out across societal boundaries. My review suggests that different societies define property rights and the rules of competition and cooperation in different ways. These unique specifications of the noncontractual elements of contract lead to different types of interdependencies and different way of managing or resolving those problems. Efficiency is socially constructed rather than constructed by markets (Fligstein 1990, chap. 9). And there may be many ways to organize "efficiently."

Yet this should not be taken to mean that "everything is legitimacy" or that "everything is power." Market forces, although socially constructed, continue to pose important constraints on organizations. A focus on institutional environments and states should not be used to supplant an analysis of technical environments. Rather, the point should be to investigate the ways in which social and economic imperatives reinforce and contradict one another (Orru, Biggart, and Hamilton 1991). The most fruitful approaches thus far have been those that emphasize the ways in which history and social relations shape both institutional and economic relations.

Unfortunately, these theories have tended to be weak analytically. So, for instance, we have lots of evidence about the existence of multiple organizational forms, but few theories about the reasons for the existence of the variability. It is thus important that economic sociology continue to develop testable theories that explore the relationship between technical and institutional factors (for an important attempt to begin to classify business groups, see Granovetter 1994).

Finally, my review highlights the fact that theories of organization have rarely been tested across societies. Most have arisen to explain a specific aspect of governance, and they have focused on a very narrow range of cases. This is most often a function of the academic division of labor. Scholars interested in a particular society are often not particularly knowledgeable about other societies. Moreover, empirical work usually focuses only on the variables identified by a particular theoretical approach. Consequently, it is difficult to assemble a balanced view of organizations across a number of societies, and it is difficult to state conclusions with certainty. It is thus important to carry out more systematic comparative analyses across different societies.

9

Globalization

THE POLITICAL-CULTURAL APPROACH implies that the relations between political and economic elites and the long histories of their interactions have created laws and informal practices that constitute distinct national systems of property rights and governance. In the last chapter, I concluded that there is no evidence for convergence in these features of firms and markets across advanced capitalist societies. Distinct national styles of political control persist, as the political-cultural theory implies.

This conclusion, however, should strike the reader as problematic. We hear that global competition and the globalization of production are forcing firms to select similar tactics or face extinction and that, as global capitalism expands, governments become increasingly irrelevant. Michael Jensen's version (1989) of this argument focuses on American firms as the most ruthlessly efficient in the world at maximizing shareholder value. Jensen argues that in a world of global competition, eventually all firms in advanced capitalist societies will adopt the shareholder value conception of control or perish. Manuel Castells (1996) says that we are entering the world of the "information society" where winners will be on the cutting edge of information technology and losers will live with diminishing prospects. Susan Strange (1996) believes that firms are faster than governments and so anything that governments might want to do will be thwarted. Robert Reich (1991), the former labor secretary of the U.S. government, has concluded that about all the government can do in the face of globalization is to make sure that people have the opportunity to get education.

The lack of convergence in organizational forms across societies where similar technologies and environmental constraints exist, documented in the last chapter, offers a strong puzzle: if there is so much globalization, why isn't there more convergence? Instead, we observe that national institutions produce unique social relationships within and between firms. Across societies, we observe very different ownership structures (see chapter 8), relations to competitors and capital markets (see chapter 8), and relations between workers and managers (see chapter 5). Firms vary greatly in their cultures, and more formally in the degree of vertical and horizontal integration, divisionalization, the number of products they produce, and their use of mergers.

The political-cultural approach gives us analytic tools to make sense of some of the reasons why trade can grow and yet national capitalisms persist. The key is to create working definitions of globalization. It turns out that economic "globalization" indexes a number of loosely related trends, such as the growth in world trade, the increasing international spread of production, the increase in the size and complexity of supply chains, the growth of so-called network organizations, the use of information technologies to expand and alter these various tendencies, the growth of the Internet as a sales and marketing tool, the increasing integration of world financial markets, and the remarkable industrialization of Asia. These trends are supposed to produce more inequality among workers and reduce the ability of governments to intervene in labor and product markets. The central question I want to begin to answer is, how can we tell if these phenomena are really so widespread, and if they are, to what degree do they signal a reorganization of the world economy?

The political-cultural approach can be used to make sense of what it would mean for increases in world trade, changes in information technology, or global financial markets to be reorganizing every market in the world. Think about what the strong version of the globalization thesis would have to mean from the political-cultural perspective. If there are thousands (and maybe hundreds of thousands!) of markets in the world, it is hard to imagine that all of them are suddenly overrun by participants from all capitalist societies. Moreover, to argue that the conceptions of control governing all of these markets are being undermined is a dramatic hypothesis that is yet to be tested.

For governments to become irrelevant, one would have to conclude that national economic elites were either being crushed or absorbed into world capitalist expansion. It is difficult to find evidence that either of these things is happening. The principal supporters of current arrangements, national economic elites, continue to thrive. Indeed, governments are the principal actors in the various trade negotiations that open markets (GATT, NAFTA, the EU). It follows that markets are opened because it is in the interest of powerful political and economic elites to do so and that, once in place, these agreements must be monitored and enforced. It is certainly possible that states are experiencing new constraints as a result of market openings, but this has not been adequately demonstrated in the advanced industrial societies. There is no evidence that state provision of stable legal and institutional conditions for market actors is diminishing. There is little evidence that national economic elites are prepared to throw in with other international elites and jettison the nation-state.

This chapter begins by constructing the main lines of the globalization argument as it affects the organization of firms, stratification in advanced industrial societies, and the policy options of welfare states. Then I present a review of evidence that confirms the view that the changes posed by the proponents of globalization have just not occurred in the dramatic way that people have argued.

This does not mean that more and more markets are not experiencing global trade. It only means that the connections between increases in trade and the supposed outcomes (the destruction of national firm identities and existing conceptions of control) are tenuous. If the evidence for globalization causing the total reorganization of the world economy is not strong, then how can we begin to understand what features of societies global market processes might actually affect? I argued in chapter 4 that the political-cultural approach can be used to propose a conceptual understanding of globalization. The research agenda implied by the political-cultural approach has barely been started. This is because, so far, much of the observation of world economic activity is at a relatively abstract level of analysis (such as trade flows) or focuses on a particular firm, market, or event. There has been very little theorizing and even less empirical work at the field level, a task that this chapter begins to clarify.

Definitions of Globalization

Globalization generally refers to three economic processes.[1] First, there has been an increase in the amount of world trade such that firms do not just compete in their own economy, but against firms from economies around the world. A corollary of this increase is that the nature of world competition has changed. Firms use information technologies to distribute their productive activities to wherever in the world factor prices are low (Castells 1996). First World jobs can be transferred to Third World countries because factories can be controlled, skills can be transferred, and wages are sufficiently low that they make up for additional transactions costs and lower productivity (Shaiken 1993). Information technologies imply that longer and longer supply chains can be created and coordinated.

The second meaning of globalization is that the rise of the so-called Asian tigers has come at the expense of First World jobs in Europe and North America.[2] U.S., Japanese, and, to a lesser degree, European firms have transferred productive activities to Asia's inexpensive, but relatively highly skilled, labor forces. The fast growth of these economies is attributed to a number of factors: state-led development processes that produced infrastructures, ease of investment, high investment in human capital, and political stability and openness to foreign capital (Wade 1990; Akyuz and Gore 1996; Campos and Root 1996; Evans 1995; World Bank 1993).

The final meaning of globalization is that the world financial markets for debt, equity, and particularly currency have grown substantially. Analysts critical of these markets (Harvey 1995; Block 1996; Castells 1996, 435–36; Strange 1986) see the huge amount of currency being traded daily as a sign that central banks cannot control currency flows. Moreover, speculators in these markets can cause runs on currencies of a given country if they perceive that the current economic policies are likely to result in high inflation or high interest rates (McNamara 1998 reviews the arguments and evidence surrounding this assertion). World debt markets also limit governments' fiscal policy options by pricing credit at a high level. Together, world financial markets operate to force governments to pursue monetary and fiscal policies that promote low inflation, slow down economic growth, and curb deficit spending (Frieden 1991).

The growth of the world economy and its shift to a reliance on information technology is viewed as having several negative effects on developed countries. First, deindustrialization (i.e., the hollowing out of manufacturing by the closing of plants) means that high-wage blue-collar jobs disappear (Bluestone and Harrison 1982). Since these workers often have few transferable skills, they have a hard time finding new jobs. A larger pool of unskilled labor further depresses wages for low-skill jobs. Second, the new jobs being created by the global economy in the developed societies are for people with a high level of skill, what Robert Reich (1991) has called "knowledge workers." These workers get paid more because they have the ideas and skills that make economic integration possible. Since their productivity is high, their pay is going up. Taken together, these two forces produce a perverse set of outcomes. Returns to human capital are increasing for those at the top of the skill distribution, while they are decreasing for those at the bottom. This creates more societal income and wage inequality.

These stratification outcomes have a negative effect on governments (Strange, 1996; Sassen 1996; Cable 1995). The demand for government services increases because of layoffs and the increased wage pressure on low-income families. Governments try to care for these workers by running expansionary fiscal policies. Unfortunately, if they do so, they face a number of problems. If governments raise taxes on corporations, they only encourage firms to move offshore (Garrett 1995; Strange 1996). This accelerates the impact of globalization on deindustrialization by discouraging capital formation. Governments have to be careful about running large budget deficits because world currency markets will force down the value of their currency. This will increase the costs of financing deficits by world debt markets, which will demand higher interest rates. High interest rates will translate into slower economic activity.

Governments are therefore trapped, unable to respond to the negative effects of globalization. Virtuous governments can only run economic policies that promote low inflation and low tariff barriers and cut back on protection for workers and their families in the hopes of attracting foreign investment to stimulate economic growth. The only positive thing governments can do is invest in education.

Critique of Globalization Arguments

I want to begin by pointing out that this basic story is shared by many in the economics profession and their principal opposition, scholars who start from Marxist premises. For the economists, this analysis of global trade and its effects on economic growth is a good thing because it eventually results in more wealth even if it produces short-run problems of increased inequality (Stopford and Strange 1991). For the Marxists, it is a bad thing because workers lose more and more control over their lives, and thus the new phase of capitalism is even more virulent than the last (Arrighi 1998; Harvey 1995).[3] For different theoretical and political reasons, both economics and Marxism want economic forces to be structural, inevitable, and everywhere dominating action.

Readers familiar with these arguments will think that they have been proven beyond dispute and that my skepticism must be based on no more than fancy. But I want to suggest that the evidence is more ambiguous and that we should be skeptical of globalization claims for logical, theoretical, and empirical reasons. My logical argument is that it is a strong claim to assert that any one structural shift is causing everything we observe in the whole world's political economy. Given what we know—that social outcomes reflect complex causes working together in different ways across time and space—it should take a lot of evidence to convince us that the globalization story is true.

Some who trumpet globalization have a mercantilist view of trade, that is, take it to be a zero-sum game in which one society gains because another loses. This, of course, is economically naive. Societies do not compete, firms do. While there are going to be winners and losers in every society, economic growth depends on which industries are growing (i.e., finding customers for their products), which ones are not, and how much (Krugman 1994a, 1994b, 1995). Moreover, trade does produce economic growth and new jobs in all countries. At the very least, we would expect the effects of globalization on the fiscal and monetary policy of a particular state to be a function of the degree to which a given society is trade-dependent and the degree to which it is a winner or loser overall.

Finally, there are theoretical arguments about the causes of inequality, its link to trade, and the causes of competitive advantage for firms in a particular market. There are also alternative views of what states do, emphasizing that many aspects of the state are important to economic growth.

These theoretical arguments have quite a bit of empirical support that undermines strong views about the effects of globalization. It is useful to consider both theory and evidence more carefully in considering what is true and not true about the globalization story.

The Slow Expansion and Unevenness of Global Trade

It is well known that world trade has been increasing in the post–World War II era. World trade has increased almost 1,200% since 1950, while world GDP has increased 600% (OECD 1996). During the 1990s, it appeared as if world trade was growing at an alarming rate. For instance, in 1994 world trade grew by 14%, and in 1995 it grew by an astounding 20% (OECD 1996). But these numbers are misleading in two ways. First, world trade as a percentage of world economic activity stood at 16.9% in 1996. This means that about 83% of the world economy did not involve world trade (Wade 1996). While trade was growing fast in the mid-1990s, it has hardly overwhelmed the world economy.

Second, this trend toward world trade should be considered from a longer historical perspective. Numerous scholars have noted that the previous peak of world trade occurred in 1914, when it was about 14% of the world economy (Bairoch 1996; Bairoch and Kozul-Wright 1996; Kenwood and Lougheed 1992). The two world wars and the depression of the 1930s so greatly disrupted world trade, that, in 1953, it stood at only 6 percent of world GDP, only one-third of its previous high level in 1914. These events meant that it took almost 70 years to return trade to its pre–World War I level.

Figure 9.1 presents evidence on the patterns of world trade since 1953 as a percentage of world GDP. From 1953 until 1969, world trade grew gradually as a percentage of world economic activity from 6% to about 9%. Between 1969 and 1981, world trade grew dramatically and peaked in 1981 at about 16% of world GDP. Trade as a percentage of world GDP declined to about 11% in 1991. From there, it has increased in a short period of time to 14.9%. This graph shows that in the postwar era, trade has been increasing faster than world GDP. But it has done so in starts and stops. Trade began to grow dramatically in the 1990s, but it slowed in the late 1990s, mostly due to slower growth in the Asian economies (WTO 2000, 3). World trade has increased, but in a context of long-term world economic growth, and in that context the level of world trade does not suggest that national economies are being overwhelmed (for the long view, see Kenwood and Lougheed 1992). Indeed, if one looks at the world's experience in the postwar era, 1969–81 is the period of most dramatic change.

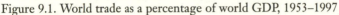

Figure 9.1. World trade as a percentage of world GDP, 1953–1997

Another claim of globalization is that the mix of products traded has changed. The story is that developed countries used to trade commodities with developing countries, while trade between advanced industrial societies was primarily in finished manufacturing goods. Now, globalization means that Third World countries engage in First World manufacturing. Bairoch (1996) summarizes a great deal of this evidence for the long run. He concludes that most world trade has historically been between advanced industrial countries and that this has changed little (it was about 65% in 1914) in the past 90 years. He also concludes that the mix of raw materials and finished goods in this trade has roughly remained the same over the century.

Figure 9.2 presents evidence on trade patterns since 1953. This graph shows more continuity than change in the relative shares of trade than the globalization argument implies. The developed world's share of trade increased, not decreased, during the decades of the 1950s and 1960s. During the oil crisis of the 1970s, the share of the developed world dropped to 64%. In the past 20 years that share ran up to peak at 72% in 1991 and has drifted down to 67%. While the developed world's percentage of trade has gone up and down, it has not trended downward.

Moreover, developed countries' percentage of manufacturing exports has actually increased from 1980 to 1995. Figure 9.2 shows that developed countries are trading with one another at higher levels, while developing countries have focused on trading more with developing countries over time. Contrary to globalization arguments, the main pattern of trade is a stable share for developed countries, developed countries trading more

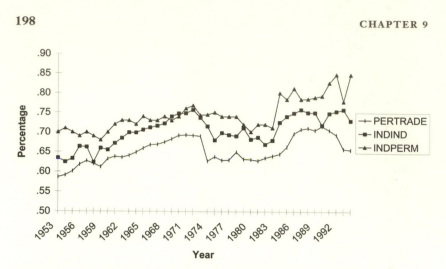

Figure 9.2. The role of developed countries in world trade. *Pertrade:* percentage of world trade by developed countries; *Indind:* percentage of world trade by developed countries with other developed countries; *Indperm:* percentage of manufacturing exports by developed countries.

with each other, and more of that trade in manufactured goods. This is not a picture of a world where jobs and economic activities are being shifted to low-wage areas. Global competition is not between the First World and the rest of the world, but instead is about an intensification of competition in the First World. U.S. firms are not competing with firms from India, but with firms from Japan and Western Europe.

How can this be, given the great economic growth in Asia? Table 9.1 presents results on the shares of world imports and exports in the regions of the world. There has been a great deal of stability in the shares of world trade for North America, Europe, Latin America, and Japan. Africa, the Middle East, Eastern Europe, and the countries of the former Soviet Union have all seen decreases in their shares. The greatest increase has been in Asia. While this evidence corroborates the view that the Asian societies have seen a great increase in their exports, the share of trade going to developed countries (North America, Europe, and Japan) has not decreased as a result of the growth. Instead, it is the share of the rest of the developing economies and the socialist world that has decreased.

Table 9.1 also presents information about imports. While Asian societies have seen a great increase in exports, their imports exceed their exports. This reflects their importation of raw materials and equipment to produce economic growth. The EU and Japan have been running trade surpluses with the rest of the world, suggesting that their goods are competitive in the world. The United States has run a persistent and large trade deficit.

TABLE 9.1
Percentage of World Merchandise Imports and Exports by Region, 1980–1995

	1980	1985	1990	1995
North America				
Exports	14.4	16.0	15.4	15.9
Imports	15.5	21.7	18.4	18.7
Latin America (with Mexico)				
Exports	5.4	5.6	4.3	4.6
Imports	5.9	4.2	3.6	4.9
Western Europe				
Exports	40.2	40.1	48.3	44.8
Imports	44.8	39.6	44.7	43.5
Eastern Europe (with C.I.S)				
Exports	7.8	8.1	3.1	3.1
Imports	7.5	7.4	3.3	2.9
Africa				
Exports	5.9	4.2	3.0	2.1
Imports	4.7	3.5	2.7	2.4
Middle East				
Exports	10.6	5.3	4.0	2.9
Imports	5.0	4.5	2.8	2.6
Japan				
Exports	6.4	9.1	8.5	9.1
Imports	6.8	6.5	6.8	6.7
Asia				
Exports	9.2	11.7	13.3	17.5
Imports	9.9	12.3	14.5	18.3

Source: WTO, 1996, table 3.1, 3.2.

TABLE 9.2
Regional Structure of World Merchandise Trade in Exports (percentage of regional exports shipped to each region, 1993)

Origins of Trade	Destination of Trade				
	North America	Western Europe	Asia	Rest of World	Total
North America	35.6	20.2	25.0	19.2	100.0
Western Europe	8.0	68.9	8.8	14.3	100.0
Asia	26.4	17.6	46.5	14.2	100.0

Source: WTO 1996, table 2.1.

While U.S. exports have grown substantially, U.S. imports have risen even more dramatically.

It is this point that is most frequently ignored in discussions about the relative success or failure of national systems of property rights and governance. For the past 15 years, the U.S. economy dominated by the shareholder value conception of control has consistently underperformed Europe and Japan in terms of the overall attractiveness of its exports. While Europe and Japan have had slow economic growth during the 1990s, the central cause of this slow growth is unlikely to be the unattractiveness of their products or, as is often asserted, their high labor costs. If European and Japanese firms produce products that are so costly to produce, why is it that these societies run trade surpluses?

Table 9.2 examines the structure of world trade by looking at the origin and destination of trade in 1993. This table shows that the largest trading partner for West European societies is Western Europe. It also demonstrates that 46.5% of exports from Asian societies end up in Asia. North America (here defined as the United States and Canada) has the most diversified trade profile. Their exports are predominantly to one another, with the rest almost evenly divided between Asia, Europe, and the rest of the world.

The picture that emerges from these tables is a world where trade over the past 15 years is increasing in absolute terms (from almost $2 trillion to almost $5 trillion), but not dramatically in relative terms. The direction of trade remains predominantly from developed to developed societies, and the share of manufacturing trade that originates in developed societies has actually increased. While Asia has grown in exports, it has not taken trade shares away from the developed world. The societies that have not gained as much in trade have been the formerly socialist societies and the rest of the developing world. In sum, increases in trade have been gradual, and there is no evidence that the developed world has lost out.

These surprising patterns deserve to be examined more closely by disaggregating trade by products and regions. Table 9.3 presents evidence relevant to globalization arguments. It has been argued that one of the sectors where the forces of globalization are most prevalent is computer and telecommunication equipment. Table 9.3 shows that this sector produced $379.4 billion in trade in 1993, a sizable number. But it accounted for only about 10% of world exports and about 1.5% of world GDP in that year. The largest trade volumes continue to be for such commodities as grain, oil, other raw materials, and metals, chemicals, and more traditional manufactured industrial goods such as machines, electrical equipment, and automobile and other transportation equipment.

The bottom of the table presents data on the shares of each of the regions' production of exports by industrial sector. The European Union (EU) ships most of its production within its confines. This percentage has increased over time (OECD 1996). Trade between the United States and Canada is mainly for mining products and manufactured goods. The bulk of exports outside of North America end up in Asia, where the United States and Canada ship large amounts of computer and telecommunication equipment. A surprising amount of Asian exports end up in Asia, particularly for agricultural, mining, and manufactured products. Asia exports a lot of computer and telecommunications equipment to the rest of the world. Much of this ends up in the United States.

The last part of table 9.3 presents the relative shares of world exports by sectors. The EU produces about 44% of world trade. It is overrepresented in manufactured goods and underrepresented in mining and computer and telecommunications equipment. North America produces about 17% of exports and is underrepresented in mining and overrepresented in agricultural and computer goods. Most of its goods end up in North America, followed by Asia. Asia accounts for about 27% of world trade and is underrepresented in every category but computer and telecommunication equipment. The rest of the world, mostly developing countries, is overrepresented in mining and agriculture, that is, raw material production.

This table gives insight into what is true and what is not true about the globalization story. Asian societies have rapidly increased their exports, which are disproportionately computer and telecommunications equipment. This is evidence that high-technology manufacturing has located in Asia. But, while the dollar amounts of these exports are large ($193.1 billion in 1993), relative to world trade, these amounts are not as significant (about 5%). Asian manufacturing outside of this sector is below Asia's share of exports, which implies that the advantage in computer and telecommunica-

TABLE 9.3
Network of Exports by Region and Product, 1993

Origin	Total in Billions $	EU	North America	Asia	Rest of World
			Destinations		
World	3,641.0	42.7	19.4	22.8	15.1
Agriculture	437.8 (12.0)[a]	47.7	11.9	23.4	17.0
Mining	433.0 (11.9)[a]	40.1	18.1	30.2	11.6
Manufacturing	2,288.9 (62.9)[a]	43.9	20.0	20.7	15.3
Computer and telecom. equip.	379.4 (10.4)[a]	36.4	27.3	27.8	8.5
European Union					
Agriculture	196.7	76.7	4.2	5.0	14.1
Mining	110.6	78.4	8.4	4.0	9.2
Manufacturing	1,162.7	67.1	8.7	9.9	14.3
Computer and telecom. equip.	102.1	71.4	9.8	9.3	9.5
North America					
Agriculture	85.6	16.2	25.6	37.7	20.5
Mining	43.2	15.0	51.6	21.9	11.5
Manufacturing	371.3	19.0	43.4	21.0	16.3
Computer and telecom. equip.	71.2	27.2	23.6	35.8	13.1
Asia					
Agriculture	83.5	15.6	11.6	61.0	21.8
Mining	69.8	6.7	4.6	83.2	5.5
Manufacturing	589.1	18.0	28.0	44.1	9.9
Computer and telecom. equip.	193.1	21.6	37.0	36.0	5.4
% of World Exports					
Agriculture	44.9	19.5	19.1	16.5	
Mining	25.5	9.9	16.1	49.5	
Manufacturing	50.8	16.2	25.9	7.1	
Computer and telecom. equip.	26.7	19.3	50.8	3.2	

Source: WTO, 1996, table A.7.
[a] Percentage of world total.

TABLE 9.4
Exports as a Percentage of GNP for Selected Advanced Industrial Countries,
1970–1995

Country	1970	1980	1985	1990	1995
United States	4.2	7.9	5.1	6.7	8.0
Germany	18.5	23.6	29.4	25.9	21.0
Japan	9.5	12.2	13.1	9.8	8.6
France	12.4	16.7	18.5	17.5	18.5
Italy	12.3	17.4	18.5	15.5	21.2
United Kingdom	15.5	21.2	21.9	18.8	21.8
Canada	19.0	23.8	24.5	20.8	33.5
OECD average	17.7	22.8	26.0	23.3	23.1

Source: OECD 1994, table 4.1; 1996a.

tions equipment has not spread overall to manufacturing. Asian countries have failed to capture an equivalent share of world manufacturing exports.

Societies where trade dependence is low are by definition less at risk from external trade and should be less open to its negative and positive effects. Table 9.4 presents exports as a percentage of GDP from 1970 to 1995 for the core OECD countries. The U.S. economy has about 8% of its economy involved in exports, up from about 4% in 1970 (OECD 1996). This is a significant increase that came about slowly. Japan's exports as a percentage of GDP have actually decreased in the past 10 years. German exports totaled 21% of GDP in 1995.[4] In general, the Europeans are the most trade dependent and the United States and Japan the least. This implies that, if increasing world trade volumes are producing pressures for changes, Europe should be most hard hit.

Change or Continuity in the Organization of Production?

One of the central claims of globalization theorists is that, in the past fifteen years, trade has changed not only quantitatively, but qualitatively. We are now supposedly in the world of the information society where information technology is driving world trade. I reiterate that while the industry is large, it constitutes only 10% of world trade and less than 2% of world economic activity. The evidence that information technology has qualitatively changed the way capitalist firms operate in the world economy, and hence global competition more generally, is difficult to assemble.

Manuel Castells (1996) has tried to do so. Even Castells is led to admit that firms across the world have organized themselves in very different ways (1996, chap. 3). His evidence shows that Asian firms in Japan, Korea, and Taiwan are organized differently from one another and from U.S. and European firms (1996, 190). This conclusion is supported by the wider scholarship (Fligstein and Freeland 1995; Whitley 1990; Hamilton and Biggart 1988; Wade 1996; Pauly and Reich 1997; see the edited books by Crouch and Streeck 1997; Berger and Dore 1996; Boyer and Drache 1996; and chapter 8). Nonetheless, he wants to claim that all of these differences are subsumable under the rubric of "informationalism."

This debate over the spread of "informationalism" or "network" styles of organizing has several problems. First, the features of organizations that scholars focus on differ from study to study. Second, it is nearly impossible to assess whether or not these features are decisive for organizational success because success is rarely studied over time. Third, the data to evaluate multiple causes and effects of success are hard to compile. Finally, the definition of this new global form is notoriously slippery. "Informationalism" as an organizational model for Castells includes business networks of suppliers and customers, the use of information technology to redistribute the economic activities of firms, global competition, the state's participation in promoting high technology, and the emergence and consolidation of the network enterprise (1996; 196–97). Even if one is sympathetic to his argument, it is not clear that these are all one phenomenon, and it is not clear that they define something new that is transformative.

It is the case that all of these factors have been part of the world economy for the past hundred years with the exception of the recent advances in information technologies. There have been global supply networks, global competition between firms, the use of new transportation and communication technologies to engage in more trade, and governments playing a large number of roles in facilitating trade. The idea that firms only recently discovered the phenomena of outsourcing or depending on supply chains flies in the face of business history, which can track these phenomena to before World War I (see the papers in the recent volume by Chandler, Amatori, and Hikino 1997).

The largest firms in the world economy have organized themselves on a worldwide scale for at least the past hundred years (Wilkins 1970; 1974; Vernon 1971; Chandler 1990; Dunning 1983). To current globologists, it may come as a surprise that the worldwide organization of production by multinationals is a phenomenon that existed before World War II (Stopford and Wells 1972) and arguably began in the middle of the nineteenth century (Dunning 1983; Wilkins 1970, 1974). By 1919, over 90% of the one hundred largest firms in the United States were already doing substantial business overseas (Fligstein 1990, chap. 3). Stopford and Wells (1972) examine how a sample of multinational firms reorganized themselves in a step-by-step fashion to coordinate production on a world scale during the 1950s and 1960s. Raymond Vernon (1971), in the same era, thought that transnational firms had become such a world power that they were not attached to any society. Japanese business networks predate World War II (indeed their roots are in the late nineteenth century), and Korean networks were modeled on Japanese organization (Hamilton and Biggart 1988). The Japanese business system was in part copied from the German system, which was already successful in producing products for export markets in the 1890s (Westney 1987).

The "informationalism" argument assumes technology is an exogenous variable that is driving social change. This argument can be easily turned on its head. Ever since firms began to attempt to coordinate business across societies (indeed, ever since corporations became "big"), they have had a huge interest in inventing new technologies to speed communication, transportation, and to process information. The search for more effective ways to handle large quantities of data began early in the century in the United States as large firms found that they could not keep track of the mountainous numbers of orders and the continuous flow of materials in their organizations (Yates 1989).

The multinational corporation is in the business of reducing the effects of time and distance on its widespread activities. Information, transportation, and communication technologies are at the core of running the large industrial enterprise, even those within a single country. The constant search for more and faster forms of control has characterized the entire history of capitalism. The railroad was among the first large capitalist industries. The demand for computer equipment, telecommunications, and new and faster forms of transportation since World War II came about precisely because large corporations were trying to take advantage of business opportunities that could only be seized on by controlling widespread activities.

Computer companies, and later computer chip and software producers, had huge incentives to build bigger and more powerful machines. At the very least, a believer in the transformed world economy would want to argue that the desire to coordinate more effectively on a world scale stimulated the production of these technologies and that that desired helped increase worldwide production (Krugman 1995). Information technology does not reduce the advantage of giant firms but instead enhances their advantages. It makes it easier for them to grow bigger, manage more activities, and generally enforce their current advantages in given markets.

There is no systematic evidence to show that "informationalism" has produced a qualitative change in the organization of firms that has caused multinationals to change in form. (Such data is very costly and difficult to collect even if one has a definition of what one is looking for.) There is also no data to suggest that network organizations (firms that contract out most of their activities, such as Nike) have substantially taken over the population of multinationals. Indeed, most large firms have had large networks of suppliers and customers since early in the century. Vertical integration of firms has been on the wane since after World War II. Few, however, have entirely jettisoned their productive capacities over the entire product chain and adopted the posture of contracting for everything.

Firms are using more information technology than they used to, but they are doing so in order to coordinate their activities better. One implication of the "network" and supply chain argument is that the largest firms are dinosaurs that will not survive their nimbler network colleagues (Powell 1990).[5] Unfortunately, there is no evidence for this. Indeed, information technology makes it possible for firms to get bigger. During the 1990s, merger movements across Europe and the United States have done exactly that (Fortune 1998). This suggests that it is not surprising that scholars who study organization structures across societies conclude that there are myriad forms that operate with surprisingly different logics, even in the same industries.

Does Globalization Cause Deindustrialization and Inequality?

So far, I have painted a picture of globalization as being more gradual over time, less revolutionary in its impacts on economies and firms, and more uneven in its economic effects on the organization of firms and societies than the thesis implies. This more complex picture should at least caution us to want to connect the growth of world trade more closely to its alleged negative effects, deindustrialization (the transfer of jobs from First to Third World economies) and increases in wage and income inequality. I will proceed by first considering the U.S. evidence for these changes, since many of the most careful studies have been done here. It is generally accepted amongst economists that only about 10–20% of the loss of manufacturing jobs in the United States is directly traceable to plant relocation in other countries (Krugman 1994a, 1994b, 1995; Bluestone 1995; Gottschalk and Joyce 1995; and the papers in Danziger and Gottschalk 1993). Most observers also agree that at least half of these jobs were lost to OECD countries such as Japan and not the Third World (Krugman 1994a, 1995). This makes sense, given the evidence I presented earlier, which shows that OECD countries mainly trade with one another and that the intensification of world trade is between First World competitors.

Most deindustrialization has a well-known cause: improvements in technological processes (Krugman 1994b, 1995). People have been replaced by new and more efficient technologies that increase the productivity of the remaining workers and eliminate the jobs of others. Even radical economists in the United States, such as Bluestone and Harrison (1982), believe that most deindustrialization reflects changes in technology.

It is useful to make this argument more concrete by considering an example. One place where some people try to tell a globalization story is the collapse of the U.S. steel industry. After World War II, the U.S. steel industry was the largest and most modern in the world. By 1970, it was in shambles. The conventional story is that basic steel production moved offshore, where labor was cheaper and U.S. steel producers could not compete.

But that story does not hold up. A world market for steel already existed after World War II. U.S. firms dominated that market (Hogan 1984). This dominance occurred even as wages in the United States were anywhere from 10 to 15 times higher than in its principal competitors (Hogan 1984). This is because U.S. firms enjoyed several other advantages: low capital costs, cheap raw materials, and a good transportation system. By the 1960s, the wage gap had closed between the United States and Western Europe and Japan (its principal competitors in the steel business) to a three-to-one ratio, and material costs continued to be in the U.S. favor. German firms had to rely on expensive coal, and Japanese firms had to transport both coal and iron ore from great distances. U.S. wage disadvantages were decreasing, not increasing, and the principal competitors were not Third World countries, but Germany and Japan.

What happened during the 1960s is that the leading firms in the U.S. steel industry invested in obsolete technology for complex reasons, one being that the new technologies were unproven on a large scale (Fligstein 1990; Bluestone and Harrison 1982; Hogan 1984). Both German and Japanese firms invested in the basic oxygen furnace. The technologies greatly lowered the cost of producing steel and wiped out the American cost advantages. This produced a glut of steel in the world market, and, given that the cost of replacing obsolete technology was prohibitive, American firms fell into decline (Hogan 1984). American firms lost their lead, not to Third World countries, but to Japan and Germany. They did so not because of cheap labor but because American managers invested in the wrong technology.

Another common assertion is that as trade in OECD countries has increased, wages have increased for high-skilled workers and decreased for low-skilled workers. While there is evidence that wage inequality has increased, very little of it has to do with trade dependence. The societies with the highest trade dependence in 1980 were in Europe; the one with the lowest was the United States. At the time, both wage and income inequality in America were higher by a substantial margin (Gottschalk and Smeeding 1995; Smeeding, Higgins, and Rainwater 1990).[6]

The two countries that have experienced the greatest increases in income inequality in the OECD in the past 15 years have been the United States and Britain (Gottschalk and Smeeding 1995; Rodrik 1996). The more trade-dependent societies of Germany and the rest of Western European actually experienced declines in income inequality during the 1980s and some small increases during the 1990s. The increases were small in magnitude, given that European incomes were much more equal to begin with, and the observed changes were much smaller in percentage terms than in the United States (Gottschalk and Smeeding 1995).

Most economists in the United States who have studied these changes agree that increases in trade can explain, at most, 10–20% of the change in U.S. income inequality (Krugman 1995; Bluestone 1995; Harrison and Bluestone 1988; see the papers in Danziger and Gottschalk 1993). Most economists stress that technological changes involved the entire economy, not just trade-sensitive sectors. As machines replaced people, particularly, as computers took over many manufacturing jobs, people with the skills to use these technologies were highly rewarded, while people without those skills suffered (Krugman 1994b). But a fair amount of inequality developed as a result of growing inequality within occupations. Frank and Cook (1995) argue that this reflected processes whereby "star" performers in professions commanded a great deal of the salary increases. A small subset of doctors, lawyers, professors, stock brokers, and other professionals has captured more of the rewards.

Economists have also focused attention upon the more sociological factors driving the reorganization of work in the United States. The increases in downsizing practices, the decline of unions, and the increase in part-time workers have had effects on income distribution and the growing insecurity of workers. Changes in tax laws that favored better-off people played some part as well. The careful studies in Danziger and Gottschalk conclude that many of these factors contributed to increases in income inequality. Bluestone (1995) tries to partition the effect of all of these factors and concludes that 80 to 90% of the change is not trade related.

Wage differences between skilled and unskilled workers across Western Europe have increased, but nowhere near the magnitude of the United States, and they were much lower in 1980. The data on returns to schooling are more sketchy, but do not reveal dramatic patterns showing that higher-educated people are able to cash in at much higher rates (see the papers in Smeeding, Higgins, and Rainwater 1990). Indeed, in some European societies such as Sweden, people with college degrees do not gain a huge wage premium (Smeeding, Higgins, and Rainwater 1990).

I think I have provided a quick, but sufficient, review to make the reader skeptical of globalization arguments. There is enough prima facie evidence to suggest that world trade, while growing, is not dominating the advanced industrial economies to the extent people claim. Firms across societies and industries have been organized globally for most of the postwar era, and while information technologies are useful in that endeavor, information and telecommunications technology are endogenous to the process of the continued expansion of multinational corporations.

Trade also does not appear to be driving deindustrialization or increases in wage and income inequality per se. Deindustrialization is driven primarily by technological change, not relative wage rates. Cross-national data on income inequality show there have been few changes in the societies where trade is greatest, those in Western Europe, while the greatest changes have taken place in the least trade-reliant society, the United States. Close examination of U.S. data shows that increasing inequality is not highly related to trade.

This suggests that the truth in the globalization story has more to do with what is going on in America than in Europe. America has seen a rapid rise in trade. This has been accompanied by a rapid increase in inequality exacerbated by political trends that have favored capital over labor. It is not trade that is driving these changes, but the reorganization of firms and work in the American context in such a way as to advantage capital. I will return to this argument.

Politics, Governments, and Financial Markets

The markets for currency, corporate equity, corporate debt, retail banking, government debt, insurance for corporations and individuals, individual debt, and debt for home ownership are separated by firms and nations. As Wade (1996) points out, there is very little integration in any world financial market except for currency, government bonds, and some futures markets for commodities. There is no world market for equities, nor any world market for corporate control. Most investment and savings are made within nations. Less than 10% of the capital stock in OECD countries is owned by citizens of other countries (Kapstein 1994). In the United States, Germany, and Japan (the three largest economies in the world), less than 5% of the workers are employed by foreign firms (Wade 1996).

I would like to remind readers that governments have been instrumental in the creation of financial markets since the Middle Ages. Indeed, the first financial market in the world was created by the king of England to raise money to support military activities (Carruthers 1996). In 1788, the French government found itself in a fiscal crisis such that its debt load was about

50% of its budget. Because it had exhausted its ability to borrow money, it responded by trying to tax the nobility. The nobles resisted and forced the king to take the unprecedented action of calling the estates general, a general meeting where representatives of the three estates of society would gather. The meeting was not able to resolve the issue of taxation and, in the summer of 1789, the French Revolution began.

My point is that governments have been instrumental in creating financial markets to benefit themselves and their most politically connected elites. Governments, for instance, are responsible for producing the world currency markets, as they moved from fixed exchange rates to market-determined rates since the 1960s (Dean and Pringle 1995; Kapstein 1994). After World War II, governments attempted to control exchange rates by fixing them and guaranteeing to back them up through the sale of gold. As world trade increased in the postwar era, governments found it more difficult to control exchange rates. Currency markets came into existence to determine the relative price of currencies based on the supply of, and demand for, any given currency. The creation of these markets could be taken as a failure of sovereign states to control the value of their money. But currency markets serve useful functions for governments and firms (Houthakker and Williamson 1996). One major function is to allow multinational firms to hedge their risks. Firms buy futures contracts on a given set of currencies and place bets on both sides, that is, that the price of two currencies will both go up and go down.

It has been frequently noted that huge amounts of money change hands in these markets daily and that this is the source of power for these markets. What is not well understood is that this process often stabilizes currency relationships in the short run. Most of the traders who move money try to take advantage of small differences in currency prices across markets located around the world. If dollars trade for 1.50 marks in one place and 1.51 marks in another, I can make money by buying lower and selling higher. These opportunities usually appear fleetingly because many traders leap in, and the differences disappear quickly, stabilizing the price of currencies (Houthakker and Williamson 1996). Changes in the relative value of currencies tend to be gradual, which helps trade and governments. Governments can then attempt to keep their currencies in a band by buying and selling into the market.

Central banks in the past 20 years have generally shifted their role from managing the business cycle through the control of money supply and interest rates to trying to promote price stability (Dean and Pringle 1995; Kapstein 1994). One argument sometimes made is that this is proof that currency markets rule, because exchange rates will quickly reflect the inflation expectations of currency traders and limit bankers to focusing on inflation.

The problem with this argument is that it gets the story backward. As a result of the oil shocks of the 1970s, there was low economic growth and high inflation across many OECD countries. To tame this inflation, many of the central bankers, notably Paul Volcker in the United States, forced interest rates higher and produced a deep recession. Since then, central bankers have more consistently attempted to insure price stability, as they were convinced that monetary policies that stimulated money supply or loan growth led to uncontrollable domestic price inflation. Currency traders come to recognize the potential for bad economic outcomes and tend to sell currencies when governments act in an inflationary manner.

There are two other downsides to these markets. First, many market participants are not using the markets to hedge currency fluctuations but instead to make bets for or against a given currency. This means that no useful economic function is being served and produces what Strange (1986) has called "casino capitalism." Second, if traders think that a given currency is suddenly in trouble, they can punish the holders of that currency. One way to understand this is that markets tend to overshoot the real exchange rate by over- or undervaluing a given currency. These processes are what gives rise to fears that currency markets can affect national interest rates and hence monetary policy.

The problem is that the degree to which this happens and the role governments play in these processes turn out to be complex. Almost all of the recent crises are the result of intended or unintended governmental policy that was framed around the politics of domestic constituencies. While currency markets may have punished currencies, the penalty usually came after long time lags and extensive policy errors.

A good case in point is Mexico, where, a recent dissertation argued, domestic politics was behind all of the changes in financial policy in the past 20 years (Kessler 1997). The peso devaluation in 1994 is often viewed as a causal outcome of the financial markets, but the events implicate governments and politics in a more ambiguous way (McKinnon 1996). At least two years before the devaluation, it was well known that the Mexican currency was overvalued (McKinnon 1996). One estimate is that six months before the devaluation, the currency was overvalued by at least 25% and maybe as much as 50%.

The Mexican government, with the consent and approval of the American government, tried to prop up the peso. Why? Because an election was coming up, and the leaders of the governing party (the PRI), who had prided themselves on professional handling of the economy, did not want negative news. They kept the peso propped up by spending foreign reserves to buy pesos. The financial community around the world knew this, and, knowing that the peso was being supported by large reserves, traders did not sell pesos (McKinnon 1996).

But about May 1994, the Mexican government stopped reporting its currency reserves on a monthly basis. At first, it claimed that the reports were to be issued, but that statistical errors and technical problems prevented reporting. By the fall of 1994, it was not clear how deep the government reserves were. About that time, Mexican bankers began selling off pesos and peso-denominated bonds in large quantities (Kessler 1997; McKinnon 1996). They obviously had a better sense of where the government stood, and they sold out as quickly as they could. This, of course, put more pressure on foreign reserves, and as time went on, it became clear that the government could not prop up the price of the peso. It continued to refuse to issue reports concerning the current account situation.

In December, after six months and continued heavy selling by Mexican banks, the peso began to drop precipitously. The Mexican government reached the point where it could no longer use current account reserves to support the peso. The U.S. bailout served two purposes. First, it gave the Mexican government more reserves to stabilize the currency. Second, it bailed out U.S. bondholders who were caught with peso-denominated bonds that now were worth less than 50% of their original value.

This case shows that, yes, world financial markets eventually punished the peso. But it also shows that the Mexican and American governments, for basically political reasons, propped it up in the first place. The Mexican people were sacrificed, while Mexican bankers were saved (U.S. bondholders were also bailed out), leading to speculation that because of their close links to the government, they had privileged information (McKinnon 1996). This is a complex story that implicates markets, governments, and economic elites. It also fails to make international currency traders the obvious scapegoats.

A similar story can be told about the financial crises in Asia in the late 1990s. Here, the main culprits were the International Monetary Fund (IMF) and the World Bank, which encouraged developing societies to liberalize their financial markets during the early 1990s. They also encouraged governments to float their currencies. The problem was that Asian governments lacked bureaucratic capacity to monitor and regulate local financial transactions (Eichengreen 1999). This meant that a large number of loans were made to firms whose accounting practices and prospects were not clear to lenders. Local banks also were not regulated and lacked the organizational capacity to monitor loans as well.

When it became obvious that too much money had come into local currency and property markets, currency runs took place. The IMF and the World Bank, who encouraged governments to pursue financial liberalization without the requisite capacity to monitor their financial sectors, then forced those governments to undertake policies that produced business recessions across Asia. Governments were forced to raise interest rates to punishing levels and cut back on expenditures. Most banks were pushed into bankruptcy as borrowers defaulted when the economy slowed. World currency markets and lenders who were not careful in their loan activities played a role in these crises. But the financial crises were caused at least as much by the policies pushed by international organizations and put into action by willing governments.

The creation of world markets for equity and debt has also served useful purposes for firms and governments. The growth of equity markets has increased the capital that firms and their owners can draw on, and the increased growth in corporate bond markets makes it easier to borrow money at lower interest rates to fund new investment. Debt markets for government bonds have also grown internationally. The size of these markets means that governments can borrow money for less interest than they might otherwise. The OECD governments have run huge deficits throughout the past 15 years, and these would have been more difficult to fund without international markets. The United States more than doubled its indebtedness in less than 10 years with very little effect on its economy. The German government was able to finance the reunification of East and West Germany by issuing massive amounts of bonds.

Governments and firms have always needed to borrow money to fund their activities. World financial markets have grown in size and complexity. But it is difficult to ascertain if government dependence on these markets has increased to the point of limiting fiscal and monetary policy. If governments want to borrow money, they can, albeit they may have to pay higher interest rates. Moreover, there is reason to believe that governments have benefited from these markets by being able to run deficits and produce some exchange rate stability.

Trade, Competition, Industrial Policy, and the Welfare State

There is a tendency to view governments as helpless in the face of global competition (Strange 1996; Cerny 1997; Frieden 1991; Castells 1996). In spite of a plethora of evidence that economies are mostly organized with firms remaining rooted to a particular system of national property rights and governance, political scientists and sociologists seem convinced that the forces of globalization are soon going to make states irrelevant to their political economies. Strange (1996), for example, argues that firms in globally integrated markets simply bypass states in their relentless search for lower-cost production and new markets. Governments are never as clever or effective as markets, so they just should give up and get out of the way.

The argument is also made that governments that try and intervene in competitive global capitalism are presented with a trade-off between efficiency (i.e., allowing capital to deploy itself so as to maximize its opportunities in global capitalist competition) and equity (i.e., the use of various kinds of state-sponsored devices to protect workers from precisely this kind of flexibility). Essentially, governments are being told by globologists that the "new global competition" leaves them very few policy options. They must get smaller, remove fetters to the actions of capital, and take rights away from workers or face the consequence that their best firms will either leave the country and invest elsewhere.

There are two problems with this argument. First, it assumes that labor costs are essentially the only variable driving international economic competition in markets where firms from different societies meet. The argument is that the only way to compete for good jobs with Third World countries, or with the United States and its unfettered labor markets, is to follow government policies that lower wages and lessen workers' protection. One can construct theoretical reasons to support such a policy, but there are good theoretical arguments and, more important, empirical evidence to show that this view is wrong.

The basic theoretical problem is that competitiveness in any given industry is a mix of factors, some having to do with costs (including labor costs), but the most important ones having to do with the competencies of firms in organizing production and creating new technologies (Piore and Sabel 1984; Porter 1991; Womack, Jones, and Roos 1991; Chandler 1990). For example, in the automobile industry, the rise of Japanese automakers had little to do with labor costs and a great deal to do with the distinctive way they organized production (Womack, Jones, and Ross 1991). Japanese workers in these firms enjoy high wages and job security that are supposed to be anathema to international competition (Dore 1997).

Second, it assumes that all government policies have negative effects on economic growth by consuming economic resources that would otherwise be put to more productive uses by the private sector. This argument is wrong both theoretically and empirically. In economics, the positive role of states derives from the problem of market failure in the context of the provision of public goods. The "new institutional economics" suggests several mechanisms by which government spending and policies might positively affect growth. Endogenous growth theory argues that spending on education, health, and communications and transportation infrastructure has positive effects on growth (Barro 1990; Romer 1990; Aschauer 1990). North (1990), Maddison (1995), and Evans and Rauch (1999) have suggested that states also provide political stability, legal institutions, stable monetary systems, and reliable governments.

The political-cultural approach outlined here agrees with this perspective. Without these social institutions, economic actors refuse to make investments in economies of scale and scope (for evidence on this point see the essays in the volume edited by Chandler, Amatori, and Hikino [1997]). Evans and Rauch (1999) have shown recently that the "competence" of bureaucratic officials has a positive effect on economic growth. Some economists are prepared to believe that different forms of industrial policies may be effective by providing investment in research and development, capital for risky ventures, and military spending (Tyson 1992). This laundry list shows that it is not so easy to discuss what is often called the "efficiency-equity trade-off" in making economic policy. At the very least, the choice is not just for or against governments, but for or against policies that may help economic growth (Evans 1995).

If this is the case, where does the negative view of intervention by states in their economies come from? There is a strand of thought in economics that assumes that governments are rent seekers (Buchanan, Tellison, and Tulloch 1980). This implies that all of their activities are illegitimate in the sense that they try to maximize their share of national income and, by doing so, take resources away from the private sector. But the idea that all states are predatory is not just a product of social choice theory. It is related to the scholarly and policy interest in the past 15 years in assessing how nations can attain competitive advantages for their firms in markets.

From the point of view of intellectual trends, many scholars became interested in Japan and the "Asian miracle" in the 1980s (Johnson 1982; Dore 1973; Hamilton and Biggart 1988). This caused them to try and decipher why Japan, Taiwan, and Korea were able to develop so quickly; and the role of governments was part of the focus of attention. Others admired the German economy for its neocorporatist political system, formal cooperation between labor and capital, and its relatively small firms that were oriented toward exporting high-quality manufactured goods (Albert 1991). Still others saw the future of manufacturing in flexible specialization, as in the small firms in the industrial districts of Italy, Silicon Valley, or Bavaria (Piore and Sabel 1984; Saxenian 1994). These highly networked firms could respond quickly to changes in market demand. Various scholars became convinced that one of these models held the key to industrial competitiveness among nations.

States played an important part in most of these stories. During the 1990s, the resurgence of the U.S. economy propelled scholars to turn back to the United States and extol the virtues of American-style corporate governance and labor relations as the key to economic success. Given the American view that states should play a minimal role, it is not surprising that governments are now out of favor.

But, these fads in intellectual thought do not do justice to the difficulty of unraveling the causes of economic growth. They tend to overstate the significance of a single cause as the way to attain competitive advantage and the road to economic growth and understate the multiplicity of factors at work. They are quick to assume that whatever factor is isolated is the main mechanism by which efficiency is attained (in the American model, reducing the size of government, reducing workers' rights, the shareholder value conception of the firm). It is useful to consider more systematically some of the surprising empirical evidence about the link between trade, economic growth, and the size of government.

Rodrik (1996) has produced data examining the relationship between the size of government and the trade dependence of OECD countries. His evidence shows that the most trade-dependent societies have the largest, not the smallest, governments. His econometric study, which included over one hundred countries from the 1960s until the 1990s, concludes that this relationship occurs because societies where trade is more important have compensated for the risks of trade by using government spending to ensure some stability. His results show that higher exports at an earlier point in time are associated with increased, not decreased, social spending. These empirical results fly in the face of neoliberal thinking about states and markets. If competitive world markets have been putting pressure on states to shrink, why has the opening up of markets for world trade caused their expansion?

Garrett (1995) has presented evidence that the main cause of this growth in government protection in OECD countries is the interaction between the presence of powerful left political parties, trade unions, and high levels of trade. The high degree of protection offered by states more susceptible to world market forces results mostly from organized politics. Garrett also has evidence that high levels of trade do dampen taxes on capital once a certain point is reached, evidence somewhat in support of the neoliberal argument.

Have the actions of states, which have grown in the past 30 years, made their economies grow slower and create fewer jobs? It may have been good politics to protect citizens and use the state as a countercyclical employer of last resort, but did it make for poor economic performance? Surprisingly, there is little econometric evidence for the negative effects of different forms of government spending, and measures of union power such as national collective bargaining on employment and growth. The empirical literature on this question either looks at highly aggregated data over time or does case studies of particular interventions in particular societies. There is good evidence that government investment in infrastructure and education has paid off for economic growth in societies (Aschauer 1990). The comparative capitalisms literature has demonstrated fairly effectively that governments have played positive roles in the development process as well (Evans 1995; Campos and Root 1996; Wade 1996). The literature comparing specific industrial policies and their effectiveness for advanced industrial societies offers both positive and negative evidence for the role of governments (Johnson 1982; Ziegler 1997; Herrigel 1996; Crouch and Streeck 1997; for a recent review see Pauly and Reich 1997). But the overall evidence does not point in the direction of big activist states having overwhelmingly negative effects on growth.

Most economic theories see distortions in labor markets caused by union power that produces labor market rigidities. Minimum wages, collective bargaining, and social policies that make it difficult or expensive for firms to hire or fire workers can be shown to theoretically reduce employment and raise unemployment. But the empirical literature on these issues turns out to be more ambiguous. For example, the recent OECD (1998) report on jobs looks at how collective bargaining has affected economic growth and job creation in OECD countries in the past 20 years. The results are worth quoting: "While higher unionization and more co-ordinated bargaining lead to less earnings inequality, it is more difficult to find consistent and clear relationships between those key characteristics of collective bargaining systems and aggregate employment, unemployment, or economic growth" (OECD 1998, 2).

This brief review pushes us to a startling conclusion. There is no evidence that trade has made states "smaller" over the past 30 years. In fact, it is quite the opposite. There is evidence that high exposure to trade combined with organized labor has produced more social protection and larger states. There are theoretical reasons to believe that states continue to matter in producing economic growth by providing public goods, the stable rule of law, and under certain conditions, good industrial policy. There is little evidence that unions or collective bargaining lessens job growth systematically or increases unemployment. There is evidence that a strong labor movement and labor party act to redistribute income and raise wages in society in general.

There is also little evidence that the competitiveness of firms in industries characterized by world trade are driven primarily by differences in wage rates. Instead, it is innovation in technology and organization that provides distinct competitive advantages (Porter 1991). This set of conclusions, based on current theorizing in economics and the current knowledge available in the empirical literature, is totally contradictory to the claims of globologists. States are not disappearing, inequality is not increasing everywhere, and low labor costs and weak protection of workers are not the main engine of economic growth in any industrial society with, perhaps, the exception of America.

TABLE 9.5
Unemployment and GDP Growth in Selected Countries, 1975–1995

Country	1975		1980		1985		1990		1995	
	(1)	(2)	(1)	(2)	(1)	(2)	(1)	(2)	(1)	(2)
U.S.	4.8	−1.7	7.0	−0.2	5.4	2.7	6.7	1.0	5.6	3.2
Japan	1.9	2.4	2.0	4.2	2.6	3.7	2.1	5.6	2.9	3.4
W. Germ.	3.6	−3.3	2.9	1.8	7.1	2.5	4.8[a]	4.6	6.5[a]	1.6
France	4.0	−1.3	6.2	1.7	10.2	1.4	8.9	2.4	12.3	1.0
Italy	5.3	−3.5	7.5	4.0	9.6	2.3	10.3	2.2	9.5	4.2
U. K.	4.3	−1.3	6.4	−1.4	11.2	3.7	6.8	1.0	9.6	2.5
Canada	6.9	0.6	7.4	3.3	10.4	4.0	8.1	0.9	9.5	4.2

Source: OECD (1996b), table 2.7.
Note: Column 1 is percentage unemployed; column 2 is GDP growth.
[a] Western half of Germany only.

It is useful to turn to the case of Europe as compared to the United States in the past 15 years. It is here that arguments about global competition and the role of the state in industrial competitiveness are getting their most serious airing (Crouch and Streeck 1997; Boyer and Drache 1996; Dore and Strange 1996). Table 9.5 presents data on unemployment and economic growth in the past 20 years. In Western Europe, unemployment rates began to grow in the early 1980s and have remained high in both recessions and periods of economic growth. American unemployment rates have gone up and down depending on economic conditions. This data has frequently been taken as evidence that European work rules prevent employers from hiring workers and that the slow economic growth of the past 15 years is due to these practices, which prevent labor markets from clearing. Because American firms can respond to opportunities by hiring workers and downturns by laying them off, they are more likely to create new jobs. Because European firms cannot take on new workers easily, they forgo opportunities, and therefore in the aggregate the effect is slow economic growth.

There are a number of counterarguments to this interpretation of the data. First, it places an enormous theoretical burden on one variable as the cause of slow European economic growth. It postulates that European firms are responding to only one factor in deciding whether or not to make decisions on new investment: labor costs. This flies in the face of most theories of markets, which usually suggest that investments are made because people believe that demand exists for products. High factor costs could affect investment, but they are only one part of the investment decision.

TABLE 9.6
Part-Time Employment among Men in Selected Advanced Industrial Countries,
1993

Country	% Employed Part-time
U.S.	11.5
Japan	11.4
W. Germany	2.9
France	4.1
United Kingdom	6.6
Canada	9.8

Source: OECD (1995), table 2.14.
Note: Figures are for men ages 20–64.

Second, the data on unemployment should not be accepted at face value.
Table 9.6 presents evidence on the prevalence of part-time employment
among prime age working males across societies. The United States has
almost 12% of its workforce employed part-time. In Germany and France,
these numbers are 2.9 and 4.1% respectively. Surveys have revealed that,
in the United States, about 5% of the 12% of part-time workers wish they
had full-time jobs (Farber 1999). Since Europeans often have the choice
about whether or not to work because of high unemployment and health
benefits, involuntary part-time employment is relatively minor. Beckett
and Western (1999) have recently considered how the high rate of incarcer-
ation of young men in the United States also underestimates the unemployment rate. They show that U.S. unemployment rates would be between 0.5% and 1.5% higher if American prison populations were at
European levels. If one adds involuntary part-time workers (5%) and people in prison (1%) to U.S. unemployment rates, then one can easily see
that European and American unemployment rates are really quite similar.
Put another way, Europe's generous level of social benefits means that
workers have the choice to be selective about work, while, in the United
States, workers have no choice but to work. In this way, the unemployment
performance in the United States looks less stunning.

European societies have chosen policies that operate with more open
economies (witness the higher level of export dependence), but also have
ones that offer more social protection. The OECD societies that have been
the most open to trade, that is, Western Europe, have the highest social
welfare benefits in the world and relatively low amounts of wage and in-

come inequality. The United States, the least dependent on trade, has the fewest benefits and tolerates the highest levels of income and wage inequality. Unemployment in Europe is very high compared to the United States. But a large part of that gap is attributable to low U.S. benefits, which force involuntary part-time employment. Europeans' social safety nets make people less poor and less likely to have to accept work that they do not want. During the economic troubles of the 1990s, there have been some revisions in European welfare states benefits, but they remain well above U.S. levels (Kitschelt et al. 1999).

Globalization and Neoliberalism as an American Project

I have hinted that the ideology of globalization can be separated from its "real" effects. I would like to briefly discuss some of the changes that have transformed the American economy and labor relations in the past 15 years. Then I would like to consider how these changes are "universalized" to all advanced economies. I believe that this intellectual process is what produces the globalization rhetoric in both its neoliberal and neo-Marxist forms.

The American economy during the 1970s was beset by high inflation, slow economic growth, and poor performance by large firms. The causes of this "malaise" are complex, but begin with the first "oil shock" in 1973. What is interesting and important is how this crisis became "defined" and "solved." When Ronald Reagan came to power in 1980, he did so with the idea that markets were a better way to organize society than governments. He proposed a deregulatory agenda whereby taxes were to be cut, government regulation was to be attacked, and government was to be shrunk.

In the core of the American economy, the idea took hold that firms were nothing more than their balance sheets and their basic function was to provide returns to owners or shareholders. Therefore, assets on balance sheets that were underperforming were to be sold off, and the profits either dispersed to shareholders or reinvested where higher rates of return might appear. This view of the firm was a response to the 1970s, when managers had decided in the face of low stock market prices, high asset inflation, and high interest rates to understate the value of their assets and finance their expansions with cash (Friedman 1985b; see chapter 7). Financial investors began to realize that because of low stock prices, firms could be bought up and broken up, with the potential for great gain. So began the merger movement of the 1980s.

As the decade evolved, the shareholder value conception of the firm emerged from financial economics (see, Jensen 1989 for a polemic on this point), and most argued that financial performance was the only criterion to invoke in making strategic decisions. It can be demonstrated that many of the tactics of firms in the 1980s, mergers, divestitures, taking on debt, buying back stock, union busting, downsizing, closing plants even if they remained profitable, and laying off workers even if the firm was profitable, are related (see chapter 7). In the 1980s, it was not only blue-collar workers who lost jobs, but middle managers as well. Managers in firms reduced costs any way they could and paid attention only to the financial valuation of the firm.

Public policy reinforced this view. The conservative rhetoric of personal responsibility and the intimation that everything governments did was bad, while everything that occurred in and around markets was good, became dominant. The increases in income, wage, and wealth inequality that resulted from these processes were first denied and then seen to be natural. Analysts of the American economy began to see this "new model" as the solution to America's competition problems from the 1970s, and to the Japanese challenge of the early 1980s (Jensen 1989). The rhetoric about global competition and the use of the shareholder value conception of the firm became allied. A focus on shareholder value would make firms "lean and mean," and this would aid them in competition, both domestically and against the Japanese.

An ideology is a set of ideas that reflect a point of view. The ideology of globalization and shareholder value have become united, so that globalization is now not just the Japanese challenge, but now the challenge of a more diffuse "other," and shareholder value means that firms should maximize profits for owners, and governments should just stay out of it. This ideology is a generalization about the American experience.

One interesting question: has this set of ideas worked? The answer, of course, depends on what you mean. While American firms have increased their exports substantially, the United States continues to run a substantial trade deficit. If lean and mean American firms are so competitive, why hasn't this advantage extended across the economy? The American economy has created a large number of jobs, but a substantial percentage of them are low wage and part-time. Income inequality continues to increase as a result. While jobs are being created and the economy grows, so does inequality, made worse by the increase in low-wage and part-time employment.

Conclusion

I have tried to provide arguments and evidence against accepting too quickly the neoliberal and neo-Marxist view that the globalization of production has produced a new stage of capitalism, one where inequality increases, governments are increasingly irrelevant, and the skilled meritocracy tyrannizes. While world trade has increased in the past 15 years, it has neither created widespread changes in the organization of production nor undermined the power of governments. There is little evidence that increases in societal inequality or decreases in the efficacy of governments to provide for their citizens have occurred as a result of globalization.

I argue that where globalization has really occurred is in the integration of some of the markets for the multinational corporations of the advanced societies. Here, there is evidence for the development of world markets, defined as small numbers of firms that take one another into account in their behavior and whose interactions are governed by a conception of control. These firms have moved beyond just selling products in different societies (i.e., trade) and undertaken a global organization of their production. Their distribution of that productive capacity is in response to the actions of their principal competitors, the largest firms from other industrialized societies. It is these firms that have pushed more international political integration to make global markets more transparent in their rules of competition and cooperation.

The political-cultural approach taken to globalization in this book concretizes the study of this process. It forces analysts to be careful in their empirical statements and precise in providing evidence for the process. It also suggests that the degree of globalization might be overstated and that its effects are more muted. This is an empirical question. The response to globalization by governments is also explicable from this perspective. They strive to protect local industries not focused on the global market under threat by non–home country firms, and they strive to open the markets of the competitors of their own global firms. They continue to play a key role in both negotiating trade agreements and protecting local elites.

World capitalism has been with us for a long time. Governments and firms have evolved more and more sophisticated ways to engage in creating new world markets and providing international governance for them. The links between these international trade "projects" and national economics are still up for exploration. This constitutes a frontier issue for economic sociology. The political-cultural approach offers some conceptual analyses about how change may be measured. It also suggests that globalization is not an impersonal force, but very much reflects the social and political construction of markets by firms and states.

10

Conclusions

Two Tales of One Industry

The explosion of information technology that occurred at the end of the twentieth century has created a whole new set of markets. Many believe that these new technologies are transforming the world we live in (Castells 1996). Moreover, these markets are supposed to be creating new kinds of firms that are flatter, more networked, and, thus, quicker to take advantage of opportunities (Castells 1996; Saxenian 1994). The new firms learn and change constantly because if they stop, they die. In doing so, they are creating wealth beyond what anyone has ever imagined. They are also transforming work for the people who run them. People leave and exit firms rapidly, and stock options are a huge part of what attracts work teams to put in extremely high hours to push a new product innovation to market.

In this new world, firms do not form monopolies because technology will not let it happen. Firms that try to create proprietary processes or products find others inventing new things in order to go around them. So Apple (with its proprietary computer operating system) and Sony (with its Beta VCR system) found themselves on the losing end of markets as consumers preferred open systems that produced more standard products that were cheaper. Intel and Microsoft with the "open" architecture of their products spawned whole industries of suppliers of hardware and software built on the openness of their systems.

The lesson of these firms was that fortunes were not to be made by trying to be proprietary, but instead by being "open." The way to win was to get there first and have your product adopted as the standard because it was the best. To prevent being blown away by the next generation of the technology, one needed to keep one's product developing, and organizational learning was the only answer. Keeping in touch with competitors and customers and using networks to evolve products were the only way to stay in the game. This closed the virtuous circle by which the best technology won out, and the firm that produced the technology only stayed in place if it continued to evolve as other technologies evolved.

In the "old" industrial economics, the bigger a firm got, the less product the market could absorb and the lower the price for the product; the marginal profit on selling an additional unit of the product would eventually drop to zero. A whole new branch of economics claims that this "law" has been repealed. Information technologies produce "increasing returns to scale" (Arthur 1994). The cost of making a product such as software is high at the beginning. But if the product becomes a standard, the market locks in around the product. This lock-in occurs because consumers get used to a particular product and because other related producers build their products around it. The marginal cost of producing additional products is very low because the cost of disks, in the case of software, is so small. If the product becomes an industry standard, the profits go up as each additional unit of output is sold because the cost of producing an additional amount of the product is near zero.

This is the main way the story of the new markets emerging in the fields of information technology and telecommunications is told. It is one that has captured the attention of journalists, policymakers, and scholars. This telling of the story suggests that the political-cultural approach is not very useful to understanding what is going on in these markets. Let me play devil's advocate and make the "new economy" argument against the political-cultural approach more explicit.

Firms that appear to pursue stability-oriented tactics, such as creating proprietary products, have been and are losers. Winners need to accept "open standards" and work constantly to hold their place in the value chain. The only way to do this is to be fast and first and recognize that "new" change can always make your products obsolete. Learning, networks, and nimbleness are the essence of the "new economy."

The political-cultural approach with its focus on governments and stability and building hierarchies within markets, from this point of view, just cannot make sense of the digital revolution with its rapid change in technologies, its constant shift of fortunes, and its nimble, networked firms. Silicon Valley and its imitators in Austin, Seattle, Washington, D.C., Boston, New York City (Silicon Alley), and Ann Arbor are living proof that the future belongs to quick, constantly learning, small firms that maintain alliances and networks to keep them alive. The big and hierarchical move too slow. Trying to control technology is like trying to hold back the ocean with your arms. So the incumbent-challenger structure of markets is irrelevant.

Moreover, all of this change in the "new economy" is being done without any input from governments. Governments are not actively regulating these markets, choosing winning and losing technologies, or making investments that promote one set of firms over another. It is the knowledge-based industries, invented in universities, driven by entrepreneurs, who learn from each other, that are creating this new community of firms. By and large, Silicon Valley has not relied on the government in any important way for its development. Indeed, the decentralized nature of the markets and the open standards of products are often characterized as antithetical to the slow-moving, unimportant bureaucracies of governments. From this perspective, the political-cultural approach with its emphasis on stability, bigness, and governments seems more suited to making sense of the nineteenth than the twenty-first century.

The political-cultural approach has answers to these objections. Most important to recognize is that these are the early days of many of these new markets. The political-cultural approach begins analyzing these markets by noting their fluidity. As I have outlined in chapter 4, at the beginning of markets, there is always a social movement–like flow of firms. New entrants proliferate, and many conceptions of control seem possible. The small, networked, constantly learning firm is a strategy for new firms to follow as these markets emerge. Firms face an uncertain market, and no one knows which products will be hits. The "networked, learning firm" is a model to deal with these problems. In essence, it makes a virtue out of a vice. If one cannot engage in controlling the competition, one can try to be connected enough to other firms to know what is happening and anticipate where the market is going.

The question is, will these markets settle on these forms because it will be impossible for bigger firms pursuing more stability-oriented tactics to emerge because of the rapid shifts in technology? Or will some grow large by stabilizing technologies and having control whereby their products lock in a particular market? The political-cultural approach does not assert that a conception of control emerges to stabilize every market. It only argues that if firms can create such a conception, they will. So, in this case, the issue is whether or not the current arrangements will permanently set the terms of these markets. From this perspective, the real issue in using the political-cultural approach is to try to understand two aspects of these markets as they are evolving: first, what role have governments played in their development and might they play in the future, and, second, what are the likely conceptions of control that will eventually produce stable market outcomes for firms?

The main technologies that are driving the digital revolution along had their origin in the early postwar era in the United States. The transistor, semiconductor, and computer industries were all underwritten by the federal government, and in particular by the Defense Department (Newman 1998). The early Silicon Valley firms, such as Hewlett Packard, Loral, and Lockheed, had the Defense Department as the main customer for their advanced electronic products. The federal government, and especially the Defense Department, funded research at Stanford and the University of California that led to many of the scientific breakthroughs. The Internet started out as the "Arpanet" funded by the Defense Department. The purpose of creating a decentralized network of communication was to ensure communication in event of a nuclear war. Scientists and university scholars were given access to the Internet first. Most of the basic innovations for these information technologies came from research done in universities with government support.

Congress has written laws that serve the interests of firms. Patent law and property rights issues have favored the holders of patents. The State of California, for example, has very well developed intellectual property rights laws that, not surprisingly, favor programmers. The Telecommunications Act of 1996 produced rules of competition that are generally favorable to the current incumbent phone and cable firms. These laws have not forced competition between telecommunications and cable companies, but have reinforced the positions of incumbents.

Silicon Valley firms have gotten the government to relax immigration laws to provide a stream of engineers, while these same firms simultaneously moved production offshore. As of 2001, commerce on the Internet is not subject to sales tax, giving electronic retailers a 5–7% price advantage over their bricks-and-mortar competitors. In sum, government is everywhere. It nurtures technologies, allows private exploitation of them, and provides legal and regulatory structures to make it easier for firms to raise and make money. It also allows firms to define the rules of competition. In the year 2000, there were serious politicians who were proposing to ban taxing sales on the Internet permanently. It is difficult to interpret this action as being about anything but an industrial policy favoring one set of industries over another.

The question of finding stable conceptions of control is complex and would require in-depth analysis that would be impossible to undertake for all information technology markets here. But I note that there are already high levels of concentration in the main products produced in the information technology revolution. Microsoft (software), Sun (workstations that power the Internet), Cisco Systems (the hardware and switches for the Internet), Intel (computer chips), AT&T (cable and long distance), and AOL-Time-Warner (Internet service provider and cable) control over 60% of their relevant markets. It is already possible to consider what a stable conception of control in high-technology markets will look like.

While some of these firms are clear technological innovators, they are also using familiar tactics to control competition. Microsoft, Intel, and Cisco have all been targets of antitrust law suits based on forms of predatory competition. The Microsoft antitrust case provided ample evidence that Microsoft behaved like a predatory competitor. As each of these new markets has emerged, a single firm has come to dominate, that is, become the incumbent.

It is useful to speculate on the conception of control that has evolved by specifying the relations between incumbents and challengers in these markets as they stabilize. The incumbent firms observe the innovators of new technologies and either buy up or incorporate the insights of those technologies in their main products. They stay in the game by aggressively buying up winners in markets connected to their main products. Microsoft, for example, is well known for approaching small software firms and offering to buy them out. If smaller firms refuse, then their products are often reengineered and made part of the next release of the Windows operating system.

If the incumbents in these industries use their market position to buy out or force out competitors, then what do the challengers do? Challenger firms have a potentially profitable niche strategy available to them. Challenger firms are the innovators who take risks. If they are successful, then they face three potential positive futures (at least from the perspective of their owners): they can go "public" and sell stock, sell the firm to one of the industry giants, or try to become one of these giants themselves.

This is a conception of control that defines the structure of incumbents and challengers. It means that investors have the ability to reap returns if their products are successful, and it provides the largest firms with new innovations to keep their large firms in the center of new technology markets. Challengers and incumbents have a symbiotic relation to one another whereby they compete but share tacit rules that allow all to survive.

The issue of "openness" in computer systems and the related problem of creating technical standards for products is complex (Edstrom 1999). The ability to attach a particular piece of hardware or software to an existing structure makes that structure more valuable. Thus, "openness" benefits the producers of new products and the owners of such standards. The large stable firms update their products, and because of the technological lock-in around their standards, they attain stability. "Openness," therefore, is one way to get a stable market. I would argue that "openness" evolved when the attempt to create proprietary systems failed. If firms could not control technology markets through patents, then the second best solution was to get their product to be an industry standard. Doing so creates stability because it allows industry leaders to form and markets to coalesce around stable standards. The core technologies that form the open standard benefit the incumbent firms that control them. Technical standards can operate in a similar way.

If I am correct, then, as the industry develops, we can expect consolidation into large firms in many of the major products. We can also expect that firms will pursue one of two tactics in the construction of new markets: either be a small, challenger firm prepared to be bought out, or try to become one of the large diversified firms that offer standards for others to build on and that buy up new technology to protect their franchise. This conception of control, if it emerges and stabilizes, is the deep structure by which firms will make money. The incumbents are the large firms. The challengers are the small firms where fortunes can still be made, but only as a means to an ends. The owners of challenger firms are in the game to cash out.

Stability and Efficiency

I want to use this example to come back to one of the most difficult problems the political-cultural approach raises: the problem of efficiency and effectiveness in analyzing the way markets work. The first story of the information technology revolution emphasizes efficiency. It suggests that the dynamics of technology have created a social structure that exploits technology in the most efficient manner. The venture capitalists, teams of engineers, and their alliances and networks operate to produce innovation and wealth. The social structure encourages entrepreneurs, rewards the successful, and does not punish the failures (since what products will win is not clear at the start of a new market). This view of market formation sees the social structures (i.e., the links among teams of engineers, their principal competitors in other teams, and venture capitalists) that underlie these new markets as producing an efficient allocation of resources.

The opposite view begins with the observation that the political institutions of American society have underwritten these innovations and provided a regulatory framework whereby property rights are enforced, governance structures favor certain incumbents, and rules of exchange have been softened to allow migration of workers and tax-free status for Internet sales. It also suggests that firms within the industry face competitive conditions and that, like all other firms who confront those conditions, they attempt to construct conceptions of control to stabilize competition. The first attempt, using proprietary systems (such as the Apple operating system), failed as a model. The compromise strategy was to become an open standard to organize the market. Intel and Microsoft pioneered this strategy. To protect their position, dominant firms would buy up new technologies to reinforce the centrality of their standards. This has resulted in a small number of large firms that control huge portions of the most important markets.

These two views seem antithetical to each other. If there is efficiency, how can there be stability that is not related to producing the "best" products at the cheapest prices? And if small firms with networks and alliances seem to be the source of innovation, how can other social structures that look like large firms come into existence and persist? My view is that the economic and the political-cultural approaches are not necessarily antithetical. Instead, they observe somewhat different sets of facts and draw conclusions consistent with their perspectives. As the defender of the political-cultural perspective, I argue that the efficiency viewpoint is not so much wrong as incomplete. It is incomplete in several ways.

First, it ignores the broader political-legal context that certainly affects the production of market institutions. Even in industries that appear to be entirely outside of the purview of governments, the history of regulation, investment, and innovation is often dependent on governments. Current property rights, governance structures, and rules of exchange are often used and modified as new industries emerge. Labor relations, education institutions, and public infrastructure all play a part in the formation of new markets. Further, in most industries, eventually governments are called upon to play some role (again witness the role of Congress in allowing immigration for engineers and preserving the tax-free status of Internet sales). The need to produce or ratify local market institutions conducive to incumbents and challengers eventually sends firms to governments.

Second, by looking only at the emergence of new markets, we fail to see how they evolve. One of the great strengths of the population ecology approach (Hannan and Freeman 1989) is that it understands that what occurs at the beginning of a market is not necessarily how a market will end up. Much market fluidity is the result of when one observes the dynamism of a particular market. By looking at markets in the cross section, one misses their underlying dynamics. What stage markets have reached in the process of forming greatly affects how one understands them.

In the case of new technology markets, the idea that the "small, networked firm" is a stable conception of control is an empirical question. To answer it would require careful consideration of the main markets and their dynamics over some period of time. We now have enough of these markets that have histories to allow us to be skeptical that the essential features of small, networked firms are in fact stable forms. We know that usually one or a few firms have come to dominate each of these markets as they have shaken out.

There are a number of problems that most analysts who focus on the network characteristics of these markets fail to consider. First, they often look only at networks as important features of the market and conclude that they must be pivotal. They fail to locate these networks in the broader role structure of firms (i.e., who the incumbents and challengers are). In any attempt to figure out what is going on in the market and what organizations and institutions are pivotal for success, network approaches rarely consider the local understandings about market processes. What do the relationships actually mean to the actors? How do they work? In essence, network approaches lack an understanding of the entire market as a field. Focusing only on social relationships that can be observed, they do not consider the broader meaning of those relationships in an incumbent-challenger structure and whether or not the market is emerging, stable, or being transformed.

Some of the network analyses of high-technology industry actually suggest a more political-cultural interpretation of network dynamics. Stuart (1998) and Stuart, Hoang, and Hybels (1999) have shown that small firms tend to survive more frequently if they manage to form alliances with more prominent firms, either other big producers or venture capitalists. Uzzi (1999) shows a similar effect for firms that have ties to important financial organizations. The political-cultural interpretation of these ties is that the owners of small firms exist in a world of uncertainty. By tying themselves to more powerful actors, they appear more legitimate to both customers and suppliers and therefore are more likely to be stable. The networks are not about learning about competitors or new products. Instead, they are about trying to control resource dependencies and attain legitimacy in order to promote the firm's survival.

The problem of competition is central to all markets. Those who run firms have to deal with the competition in order to reliably produce goods and make profits. This is true in all markets regardless of the technology involved. The search for stable social relations is often key to competitive advantage. If firms are not stable, then over time no one will make investments in them. If they are not stable, then they cannot reliably produce goods and services. The development of conceptions of control is the core question in any emerging market. Put simply, efficiency may not be possible without stability. Identifying the key dynamics that define who are incumbent and challengers, and making sense of the conception of control that allows the reproduction of that structure, is the job of the analyst.

Finally, there may be more than one way to stabilize a market to attain efficiency. The costs of getting various forms of stable structures are probably difficult to estimate. Many stable structures for markets and firms seem to exist, even within the same industry across societies. It must be the case that there are many ways to organize firms and markets. To judge the relative efficiency of one set of arrangements would require careful comparative analysis that is difficult to do and rarely done. Investments that produce economies of scale and scope depend on producing stable market situations. Firms in new, emerging markets often start out small and numerous. But over time, competition pushes firms to cooperate, buy one another out, and try to dominate. If the efforts of a small number of firms are successful, then the incumbent-challenger structure emerges. If not, small firms pursue tactics to find niche strategies to avoid competition.

Efficiency, Stability, and Equity

I have tried to show in this book that the political-cultural approach is useful to analyze particular markets, general transformations of firms within a given society, the construction of rules that underlie markets, and the structuring of general labor market principles in a given society. I have applied this approach to considerations of how the shareholder value conception of control came to dominate the core of the American economy. I have also used the political-cultural approach to think about global trade, the transformation of markets internationally, and the role of new information technology in transforming existing markets.

I want to consider the normative implications of the political-cultural approach. One of the most powerful rhetorics that economics invokes is the distinction between positive and normative implications of theory. There is a general presumption in economics that markets produce efficient allocation of resources. This assumption means that, even in the face of market failure, one is predisposed to believe that the price system is better than any administered system. The normative implication of a positive economic model is to promote the efficient market as a solution to the problems of social organization.

The question I want to pursue is the following: if one removes efficiency and concentrates on effectiveness, can one gain any normative leverage to aid policymakers who make rules? My central argument is that if stability produces the conditions for economic growth and all people in society play some role in making stable conditions, then states and citizens do have recourse to making normative claims on firms and market actors.

I want to suggest that the political-cultural approach not only provides a scientific challenge to economic rhetoric about efficiency, but a normative challenge to the "globalization" thesis and its cousin, the "shareholder rights" conception of control.[1] The main normative arguments that have been put forward against the view that firms should only operate to maximize shareholder value have come from scholars who have argued that shareholders are only one stakeholder in firms. Workers, customers, suppliers, and communities contribute to firms and therefore are stakeholders in those firms as well. These arguments are used to justify interventions in firm governance practices in the interest of all stakeholders. I think these arguments address an important issue. But they are too narrow in the sense that it is not just the people who have a direct stake in firms who are affected by the actions of those firms, but in fact the broader society.[2] The broader society provides the social, legal, and political conditions that allow firms to exist and prosper.

My basic argument is that governments and citizens in capitalist democracies are responsible for agreeing to produce stable arrangements that allow owners and managers to create corporations and markets. Market institutions, including labor markets and rules governing class struggle, are stabilizing features of society that allow firms to make profits. Governments (and more directly, their citizens) invest in infrastructure and education. The ability to stabilize a particular market through a conception of control is a historical product granted to corporations by governments (and their citizens). For all of these reasons, citizens and governments are responsible for the stable conditions that allow corporations to exist. Economic growth and wealth creation would not be possible without these rules and social relationships. For this reason, citizens and governments have the right to make claims on corporations.

Throughout this book, I have argued and provided evidence for the view that, in many of the European societies, workers and government bureaucrats play much larger roles in the institutions of capitalism than they do in the United States. These societies have produced enormous economic growth for their members after World War II, and they have done so with very different systems of political and economic governance. They have also produced societies where there is less income inequality and more social protection

But now, the power of these groups is being assaulted by academics, officials of such organizations as the OECD, and various policy communities, as being inefficient. As I have tried to demonstrate, the argument cannot be empirically supported that the market systems that grant more power to government officials or labor have failed to deliver economic growth and welfare for their citizens. What has happened is that European unemployment is being used as a wedge to undermine social benefits of citizens. The interesting question is why the power of state managers and workers' groups has diminished in Europe and the power of capital increased. I argue that there are several reasons.

First, the end of the Cold War has tarnished the power of arguments for a moral economy based on social justice. The Soviet example has failed, and, whether or not one considers existing socialism as real socialism, it left behind a dismal legacy. Social democracy in Europe flourished precisely because it was acceptable as an alternative to Communism as practiced by the Soviets. Ironically, the loss of a more radical regime and one so thoroughly discredited has made social democracy an easier target of conservative politicians. Second, the transformation of the European economy from a manufacturing-based toward a service-based economy has eroded the ranks of the traditional working-class supporters of the welfare states. As manufacturing jobs have disappeared in Western Europe, workers are less unionized and there is less organized support for the welfare state (Kitschelt 1995).

Third, job creation by the private sector across Western Europe has been very slow for the past 20 years. Most of the new jobs have been created by government. Unemployment has remained high, hovering around 10% in good and bad times. The globalization rhetoric is used to suggest that government intervention in labor markets has made European labor too expensive and that, therefore, internationalized firms will move production offshore (OECD 1996). The "shareholders rights" rhetoric suggests that European capitalists have not been able to reap high enough rates of return because of expensive labor and therefore have not invested in productive capacity to create jobs.

There are both empirical and theoretical problems with these arguments against the welfare state in Western Europe. The comparison that people make who use this globalization rhetoric is the United States, where huge numbers of jobs have been created in the private sector. What scholars who make these arguments ignore is that U.S. unemployment rates look lower precisely because U.S. unemployment benefits are very low. As I showed in the last chapter, if one adds involuntary part-time workers and prison inmates to U.S. unemployment rates, they look very similar to European unemployment rates. I also suggested that most observers of the U.S. scene do not think that trade has had much of an effect on wages in the overall economy.

The basic problem for defenders of the welfare state is a lack of theoretical arguments about how markets work that allow them to defend their social arrangements. Confronted by critics who argue that markets always deliver goods more efficiently than systems that favor workers or state managers, people are left to defend the unhappy normative position that they support inefficiency in product and labor markets. I would like to propose that the political-cultural approach offers a theoretical alternative to views that markets are the most efficient way to organize and thus provides a moral argument for more state and worker control.

My theoretical argument begins by noting that efficiency is difficult to measure and that even economists place the burden of efficient market arrangements on a great many different mechanisms (agency costs, transaction costs, economies of scale and scope, Nash equilibria). Moreover, most economic approaches assume that social relations generated within and across firms in markets exist because they are efficient and that the only puzzle is to discover the mechanism that makes it so. For example, the organizational mechanisms that support American-style shareholder rights capitalism are thought to produce the most efficient allocation of resources. But the evidence that such arrangements produce economies of scale and scope is slim.

The degree to which globalization (i.e., competition in their main markets from firms using the shareholder value conception of control) has really caused problems for the Western European economies is an empirical question. It may have mattered for employment in certain sectors of the economy, but it certainly has not affected employment across the board. The European economies appear to be healthy in the sense that they have a large share of the world's trade in manufactured goods and services. They are also running trade surpluses, suggesting that overall they are benefiting more from trade than they are losing. In 1998, for example, they were running a 2% trade surplus, while the United States was running a 3% trade deficit (WTO 2000). If the export sectors of their economies were so rigid and inefficient, one would not expect them to be so successful. The role of so-called labor market rigidities as the central cause of European economic problems is even more difficult to pin down. Again, if the export-oriented sectors of the European economies were being held back by high labor costs, they would not be so successful.

If market efficiency is difficult to measure and the degree to which markets actually select efficient forms of social organization is not clear, how should we evaluate the performance of institutions in the process of economic growth? The political-cultural approach offers a general set of insights into what does produce economic growth and wealth. I have proposed that what capitalist firms need first and foremost is stability in order to earn profit. The main source of that stability is the society in which that capitalist firm is located. I have argued that the organization of markets is somewhat arbitrary, historically determined, and dependent on the outcome of the political struggle between capitalists, workers, and actors in the state. Once in place, these stable conditions, which are remarkably varied across societies, have allowed capitalists to make profits consistently in the postwar era.

This provision of stable conditions is one of the main features that firms take for granted. From the point of view of society, capitalists are allowed to make profits, and, in turn, society provides stable political and economic conditions. Capitalists enjoy the right to buy labor power. Firms use the infrastructure of society at a cost well below its provision and often get governments to provide them with lucrative situations that insure their survival and profitability by producing property rights, governance structures, and rules of exchange that allow firms to produce conceptions of control to limit competition.

From a moral point of view, this means that people and governments have the right to make claims back on firms. Firms pay taxes, but these should be in line with what they get from society. In the United States, by means of globalization rhetoric and threatening to move their production offshore, capitalists are trying to bid down the share they pay for the stability society produces.

This is a pure power move that is possible because states and workers across national borders cannot easily cooperate to keep one another from defecting in the game by which firms try to get wages and benefits bid down across societies. Let me be clear. I think that the theory of comparative advantage in trade theory is right: more trade is better for the overall economic welfare of a society. But that benefit must be balanced by the real claims of a given society. Even in its own terms, trade theory suggests that trade generally produces more inequality within a society, even as it raises national income.

No one knows how high tax rates or wage rates have to get to destroy the productive base of a society. We have good evidence that Germany and Scandinavia, with their extensive welfare states and workers' rights, have continued to be prosperous societies and societies with high levels of high-value-added exports. There is no evidence that the current balance of power between workers and capitalists is totally unproductive or inefficient. What is now going on across Western Europe is not about efficiency in particular markets. It is a decline in the political power of workers and state actors, and an assault on the agreements forged that privileged most citizens over capitalists. Put simply, capitalist forces are organized to try to rewrite the bargain.

I suggest that the political-cultural approach recognizes how dependent firms are on society and simultaneously how difficult it is to compare the relative efficiency of societal arrangements. This implies that proponents of the welfare state should not immediately give in to the moral claims of "globalization" or "shareholder rights." Instead, they should assert that the relationship between firms and society is symbiotic and that there is little evidence that the global forces are producing convergence toward U.S.-style arrangements.

A counterargument would be that, as long as American firms enjoy lower labor costs and have more flexible labor markets because of the lack of a social safety net, European firms will lose out. There will be pressure to converge on U.S. standards. The problem with this argument is that it is too sweeping. To make it, one has to assume that there is direct competition between all of the firms in Europe and the United States. This just is not true. One has to also assume that labor costs are the decisive factor in cost structures. What we know is that the percentage of labor costs in most goods has dropped dramatically as productivity has increased. So cost advantages in labor are not necessarily decisive even in markets where there is direct competition. This argument also assumes that firms can move their plants and expertise costlessly around the world. This is not the case, particularly for goods and services that require technical expertise.

The argument also does not place much value in the view that some products are more desirable than others for consumers. People do not make all of their decisions to consume on price alone. So European automakers and machine tool makers produce high-end products that dominate their markets. Finally, this argument does not take into account other costs that firms incur. For example, since European societies with public systems of health care spend less than America's privatized system, higher labor costs in Europe are in the aggregate offset by higher health care costs in the United States.

My defense of welfare states is that the arguments of their opponents are just not empirically true. The empirical evidence does not narrowly support the "globalization" or "shareholder value" view. It is the case that societies exist with a plethora of arrangements. Therefore, the link between efficiency and institutions is severed. Citizens have a moral claim on their economies precisely because of the interdependencies between economy and society. Claims that privilege shareholders are power moves by capitalist groups to rewrite the rules of the game to benefit themselves narrowly.

Conclusion

I have tried to offer theoretical and empirical arguments about why the national organization of business persists. The formation of property rights, governance structures, conceptions of control, and rules of exchange is the outcome of political processes whereby a balance of power is established between governments, firms, and workers. This state-building process produces the institutional backdrop for subsequent economic development. The creation of new markets occurs using (and sometimes modifying) the existing rules. The interests organized by these institutions have a stake in preserving their power and the current arrangements. The overall effect is the preservation of national capitalisms.

I have tried to provide insight into the general process of market formation given a certain institutional set of arrangements. Managers seek out stable outcomes for their firms, and a stable market implies a status hierarchy of firms whereby dominant firms enforce a conception of control over the market. I have developed this model to suggest that these processes work differently as markets are constructed, as they stabilize, and as they are transformed. Many examples have been provided. I suggested how to use this model to study real market processes.

I considered how the model helps us make sense of the globalization of the world economy. I provided a working definition to that allows one to know if a market is globalized, and I argued that the dynamics of markets as specified by the political-cultural approach offer useful insight into the empirical spread of global markets. My model implies how local firms respond to invasion and how governments intervene. I have argued that states can be both protectionist and oriented toward free trade, thereby reflecting the interests of firms in different markets.

Finally, I have considered the normative basis of the political-cultural approach. I have argued that the welfare state in Western Europe is under assault by proponents of the view that globalization causes the homogenization of national practices. The political-cultural approach recognizes that firms are dependent on society for their stability. Further, there is no general evidence that one set of institutions is more efficient than any other in the industrialized world today. This implies that society can make claims on firms to respond to the economic pressures provided by globalization.

The political-cultural approach is useful theoretically and empirically, but also normatively. The future of welfare states should not depend on the overblown rhetoric of those who argue that only shareholders have rights over the courses of action that firms take. Instead, before changing labor market practices, welfare, and unemployment benefits, people and governments should make sure that this disease is indeed caused by these policies.

Governments and firms have a symbiotic relation to one another. Governments need to help advanced economies to transition away from low-value-added manufacturing to high-value-added services and manufacturing. There is little evidence that taking the social safety net away is efficient. There are lots of reasons to believe that the overall stability of firms is a result of stable institutions. Moreover, the ability of firms to find conceptions of control is one of the main ways that the people who own and run them secure their wealth. Societies should promote policies to keep markets vibrant. But the people who live in a society are part of what makes that overall stability possible.

Notes

Chapter 1
Bringing Sociology Back In

1. The recent *Handbook of Economic Sociology*, edited by Neil Smelser and Richard Swedberg (1994), gives the reader an excellent overview of the field. It shows the diversity of issues and approaches and the heterogeneous construction of constructs.

2. Harrison White's (1981) pathbreaking paper was one of the few statements that focused on theoretically demonstrating that the neoclassical market could not work on its own terms.

3. For instance, see Alfred Chandler's seminal work (1962, 1977, 1990); Nelson and Winter (1981); Williamson 1985; and Arthur 1988, 1989, 1994.

4. This distinction was formalized by Karl Polanyi (1957) and became identified in economic anthropology as the "formal-substantive" distinction concerning the meaning of the institutions we call what "economic."

5. Karl Polanyi (1957) identified two alternative mechanisms of economic organization: redistribution and reciprocity. Redistribution occurred where some group took goods from all people and gave them to others (often a state or protostate). Reciprocity was common, particularly among people who were kin or connected by ethnicity or tribe. In this situation, people would share with others, knowing that in times of need, the action would be reciprocated.

6. I would argue that much of the recent literature on the role of information technology in transforming business has a Durkheimian flavor to it. Castells's (1996) book pushes the idea that modern society is driven by the exchange of information through networks that increased and changed patterns of social interaction. Durkheim thought that the division of labor in modern society was driven by similar forces. As people were able to be in communication with people in distant places, it changed the way they thought about themselves and others.

7. Efficiency refers to the idea that the factors of production are deployed so as to maximize returns. Different versions of economic theory propose different social structures by which this happens, such as economies of scale and scope, the use of contracts, transaction costs, and agency costs.

8. For instance, one way to read population ecology is that competitive forces essentially select which firms survive (Hannan and Freeman 1977), which seems to mimic the neoclassical view. But in later work, Hannan and Freeman (1989) see the process by which niches are formed as more dynamic, social, and constructed. This view has a more ambiguous relation to economic theory, one that they do not explore.

9. Population ecology views government intervention as an exogenous shock to markets (Ranger-Moore et al. 1991). Institutional theory views governments as a force for coercion (see the papers in Scott and Meyer 1994). Scholars who focus on networks acknowledge that the existence and meaning of certain types of networks

depend on government intervention (Palmer et al. 1995; Gerlach 1992). Work on economic development sometimes puts government center stage (Evans 1995; Johnson 1982). My own work on firms takes governments explicitly into account (Fligstein 1990).

10. There is a sociological literature that argues that firms structures and markets are loosely coupled (Meyer and Rowan 1977). While there may be truth to this assertion, little of this literature can be used to directly understand how people in firms act.

11. This issue usually comes into play when scholars of organizational behavior consider whether or not actors can change their organizations to adapt to new conditions. There are two stylized positions in this debate. One emphasizes that managers can examine and understand their environments and undertake actions to improve the performance of their organizations. The other stresses that environments select firms and that managers are unable to act quickly enough to analyze problems and implement solutions.

12. Population ecology is the part of economic sociology that has considered these questions in the most explicit way.

Chapter 2
Markets as Institutions

1. Incumbent firms that capture markets will try to obtain regulatory capture of states to buttress their position in markets. In societies with more interventionist traditions, governments can try to organize the market and control competition from the outset.

2. The idea of a market as a field does not assume that all market actors are in physical proximity, only social proximity. In modern society, trade shows, stock exchanges, commodity exchanges, shopping malls, shops in general are locales for physical markets. But markets do not have to be located in physical space. Many sales are made directly between buyer and seller, often through salespeople. But in these situations, buyers often compare prices of sellers by talking to multiple suppliers.

3. This model, with a little modification, can also be applied to labor markets, where some workers are organized and others are not.

4. Sellers can greatly affect the stability of market structures. If sellers stop buying a certain good, then the social organization of the market will do the producers no good. If markets are totally dependent on a single seller, then that seller can dictate market structure as well. But generally, even in these situations, sellers will frame their actions vis-à-vis one another in order to promote the survival of their firm (White 1981).

5. Institutional economics has recognized the importance of property rights for market stability (Jensen and Meckling 1976; Fama and Jensen 1983a, 1983b; Williamson 1985; North 1990). The division of property rights makes the firm possible in the first place, allows investment to occur, and constrains and enables managers and workers. In places where firm property rights do not exist, investment is haphazard and the economy is operated at the point of the barrel of a gun.

6. The term "governance" structure has been used to refer to both property rights questions (Jensen and Meckling 1976) and issues about how to draw the boundaries of firms (Williamson 1985). I have chosen to separate the question of who owns firms from the question of how markets and firms are actually organized in terms of how firms compete, how they are to be internally organized, and if competitors can cooperate to control competition. Legitimate and illegitimate ways to compete and organize are not considered governance in economics.

7. I discuss the dynamics of particular markets and the formation of conceptions of control in chapter 14.

8. Late developers have the advantage of being able to borrow institutions from other societies. Japan, for example, self-consciously examined organizational practices of many societies to aid its late development project (Westney 1987).

9. My purpose is not to propose a theory of the state. Instead, I want to focus on how the theory of fields helps make sense of the organization of modern states and consider the links between the markets as fields and the states as fields.

10. Much of this discussion is inspired by the recent literature in political science that defines itself as historical institutionalism (March and Olsen 1989; Hall 1989; Steinmo, Thelen, and Longstreth 1992).

11. I am using *domain* in a very abstract fashion. I want to include pluralist, corporatist, and even totalitarian regimes under this rubric. I have in mind the general idea that governmental capacity includes relations that organize people who run governments, firms, and workers. But these relations can be hierarchical, voluntary, or democratic. They can be inscribed in constitutions or can evolve from pre-existing social institutions.

12. The purpose here is not to develop a theory of the forms of states, but only to note their potential influence on market formation through their power to make the rules that govern all forms of social activity in a given geographic area.

13. This perspective does not imply that the state is pivotal for every economic process. Even in societies where states have a history of intervention, state involvement is variable and its effects are variable as well. The state's role depends on which market is being discussed and the current conditions in that or related markets.

14. In practice, the distinction between intervention and mediation may be difficult to make. Johnson described MITI's actions more as direct interventions into markets, while Evans stresses the mediator role. As the Japanese economy has become more developed, firms have developed their own capacity for having policy preferences. This makes MITI more a shaper of consensus.

Chapter 3
The Politics of the Creation of Market Institutions

1. These cases are peculiar because Japan and France had strong central states previous to their entry into capitalism. Thus, there were competent state officials who had the capability to intervene into economic processes. As development proceeded, these officials training shifted toward engineering and economics. They became more adept at mediating relations between workers and capitalists and often had the power to directly intervene in firms' decision making.

2. I will explore this issue more fully in the context of deindustrialization and globalization. In essence, U.S. workers are much more vulnerable to changes in the social organization of product markets. This is not because of globalization, but because of the political and institutional history of the United States.

Chapter 4
The Theory of Fields and the Problem of Market Formation

1. Finance economics, agency theory, and transaction cost theory are all attempts to specify how profit-maximizing social relations evolve to govern firms and industries. Some proponents argue that all firms in every market (defined in product or geographic terms) ultimately converge (Jensen 1989), but others recognize that preexisting social relations may provide additional efficiencies (Williamson 1991). Evolutionary theory (Nelson and Winter 1980) and path dependence arguments (Arthur 1989) can be used in a very similar way to account for the dynamics of real markets.

2. In White's (1981) model, this is done by firms' watching one another's pricing and production behavior and then deciding to differentiate their product from their competitors. The main difference between White's argument and the argument proposed here is that I want to view this process as political rather than economic.

3. White's (1981) model is very close to what the population ecologists would call firms trying to create a "niche." The search for a niche is an attempt to avoid direct competition by differentiating your product from those of your competitors.

4. My view of markets is roughly consistent with the idea of organizational fields, in that a market consists of firms who orient their actions toward one another (Powell and DiMaggio 1983). I have elaborated this view by considering how markets are constructed and the roles that conceptions of control and politics play in this process.

5. I do not mean to imply that markets and industries are the same thing. Markets involve buyers and sellers of a commodity, whereas industries refer to producers of similar commodities. Another issue is that most large firms participate in many markets. For instance, there are a number of markets where steel is sold. The firms who produce the product often sell in different markets. Since the basic product is similar across the markets (although its end use may be different, e.g., rails, automobiles, bridges) and the participants in these markets take one another into account in their actions, it is useful to speak of the steel industry. The general abstract dynamics discussed within markets can be played out across producers of some product or set of related products.

6. Invader organizations or new actions by challenger organizations do not necessarily produce a new conception of control. Actions can be oriented toward shifting the identities of challengers and incumbents within a market, and thereby preserving the basis of the noncompetitive order. It is only when the situation is fluid (i.e., the market is in crisis) that it is possible to create a "social movement" around a new conception of control.

7. One could argue that economic theory developed its preference for price competition in the context of massive attempts to control competition. The norma-

tive side of neoclassical theory emphasized that markets were always more efficient than other forms of social organization. But it may be the case that the neoclassical fixation on direct forms of control (such as price fixing, monopoly, and cartels) caused them to miss the deeper truth here: entrepreneurs and managers in their search for stability were oriented toward discovering any means necessary. Thus, neoclassical theory could only theorize one kind of social structure oriented toward controlling competition.

8. This is not the place to develop a theory of market transition. But it is clear that the transition is going differently in the various post-Soviet societies. The transitions depended a great deal on how far market institutions existed before 1989 and how power has devolved into private hands. In Russia, for instance, it appears that the largest firms have ended up in the hands of the people who controlled them before 1989. This has created a powerful set of capitalists who are benefiting a great deal from the chaos induced by market transition.

Chapter 5
The Logic of Employment Systems

This chapter is based on a paper entitled "The Logic of Employment Systems," coauthored with Haldor Byrkjeflot (1996).

1. For some examples, see Baron and Bielby 1980; Baron 1984; Hodson 1986; Wright 1979, 1997; Hodson, Kaufman, and Fligstein 1981; Doeringer and Piore 1971; Edwards 1979; Kalleberg and Lincoln 1988.

2. As we shall see later, it is useful to distinguish between state professionalism and associational professionalism.

3. The independence of professionals in the market for business services does not necessarily mean that these groups have established a particularly powerful position vis-à-vis managers. It might be exactly because they are so firmly under management control and do not represent any challenge, that they are allowed to produce their services in the market.

Chapter 6
The Dynamics of U.S. Firms and the Issue of Ownership
and Control in the 1970s

1. This chapter is based on a paper entitled "Bank Control, Owner Control, or Organizational Dynamics," coauthored with Peter Brantley (1992).

2. It should be noted that there are a number of versions of agency theory (for instance, Ross 1977; MacNeil 1985; Holmstrom 1982). Here, I develop only enough of the general points so as to acquaint the reader with the perspective.

3. The bank versus owner versus managerial control debate is one way to frame thinking about the nature of the organizational fields of large firms, while the political-cultural approach is another. Both view the largest corporations in the United States as occupying a social space in which they take one another into account in their actions. The political-cultural approach views the basic dynamic as focused on markets and competitors, and the various control perspectives view the American corporations as a network of interlocking firms.

4. The various measures of control proposed by Herman (1981), Larner (1970), Burch (1972), and Kotz (1978) were operationalized as dummy variables in unreported analyses. These analyses provide results that are very similar to the results presented here: that is, a lack of effect for the control measures. Since each author used very different criteria, it was thought that using the actual percentages of the stock controlled by various groups was a more effective measure of the general control concept.

5. The years 1970 and 1980 were chosen because firms begin and end their fiscal years at different times. Therefore, the data may include part of the years 1969 and 1970 as well as 1970 and 1980. If 1969 were selected as the year to predict results, then some of the data would refer to 1968 and this might have created problems of time-ordering.

6. Financial reporting can be uneven. Different firms can calculate these measures in different ways, and so one must be cautious in accepting the definitions of the accounting terms across all organizations and time. Of course, one hopes that such variations are random.

Chapter 7
The Rise of the Shareholder Value Conception of the Firm and the Merger Movement in the 1980s

1. This chapter is based on a paper called "Financial Reorganization of American Corporations in the 1980s," coauthored with Linda Markowitz (1993).

2. Some of them found financial and legal mechanisms to resist hostile takeovers. Poison pills and other devices to prevent hostile takeovers were frequently used to entrench existing managers in the face of others who would displace them (Useem 1993; Davis and Stout 1992).

Chapter 8
Corporate Control in Capitalist Societies

1. This chapter is based on a paper called "Corporate Organization in Comparative Perspective," coauthored with Robert Freeland (1995).

Chapter 9
Globalization

1. I restrict my discussion to the economic uses of globalization. There has also been discussion of how world culture has changed as a result of the increase of global transactions.

2. There are, of course, economists who are skeptical of these arguments (for example, Krugman 1995a). There are also Marxist scholars who take a position closer to the one developed here (for example, Brenner 1998).

3. This does not imply that trade is a zero-sum game (i.e., that Asia has gained at the expense of the rest of the developing world). In fact, the amount of exports has increased in all societies. In Asia it has been increasing at a faster rate.

4. The trend here is misleading, as the last two data points include East Germany.

5. A similar argument pervades the popular and scholarly press concerning the Internet (Castells 1996).

6. Table 9.6 presents Gini coefficients from Smeeding, Higgins, and Rainwater (1970) that show this.

Chapter 10
Conclusions

1. For instance, the *Economist* (July 15–20, 1996) argued that if European business did not adopt the "shareholder rights" conception of control, it was certain to fall farther and farther behind the United States.

2. Recently, Joseph Stiglitz, an economist and formerly a high-ranking official in the World Bank, has made many of these same points in a speech made at the World Bank.

Bibliography

Abbott, A. 1988. *The System of Professions*. Chicago: University of Chicago Press.
———. 1989. "The New Occupational Structure: What Are the Questions?" *Work and Occupations* 16(3): 273–91.
Abegglen, J., and G. Stalk Jr. 1985. *Kaisha: The Japanese Corporation*. New York: Basic Books.
Abolafia, M. 1996. *Making Markets: Opportunism and Restraint on Wall Street*. Cambridge: Harvard University Press.
Akyuz, Y., and C. Gore. 1996. "The Investment-Profits Nexus in East Asian Development." *World Development* 24(3): 461–70.
Albert, M. 1991. *Capitalisme contre Capitalisme*. Paris: Le Seuil.
Albrow, M. 1997. *The Global Age: State and Society beyond Modernity*. Stanford, Calif.: Stanford University Press.
Alchian, A. A., and H. Demsetz. 1972. "Production, Information Costs, and Economic Organization." *American Economic Review* 62(5): 777–95.
Allen, M. 1974. "The Structure of Interorganizational Elite Co-optation: Interlocking Corporate Directorates." *American Sociological Review* 39(3): 393–406.
Allison, P. 1982. "Discrete Time Methods for the Analysis of Event Histories." *Sociological Methodology* 13:61–98.
Amit, R., and B. Wernerfelt. 1990. "Why Do Firms Reduce Business Risk?" *Academy of Management Journal* 33(3): 520–33.
Amsden, A. 1989. *Asia's Next Giant: South Korea and Late Industrialization*. New York: Oxford University Press.
Anastassopoulos, J. P., G. Blanc, and P. Dussauge. 1987. *State-Owned Multinationals*. New York: John Wiley and Sons.
Aoki, M. 1988. *Information, Incentives, and Bargaining in the Japanese Economy*. Cambridge: Cambridge University Press.
Arrighi, G. 1998. "Globalization and the Rise of East Asia." *International Sociology* 13:59–79.
Arthur, B. 1988. "Self-Reinforcing Mechanisms in Economics." In P. Anderson and D. Pines, eds., *The Economy as an Evolving Complex System*. Redwood City, Calif.: Addison-Wesley.
———. 1989. "Competing Technologies, Increasing Returns, and Lock-in by Historical Events." *Economic Journal* 99:116–31.
———. 1994. *Increasing Returns and Path Dependence in the Economy*. Ann Arbor: University of Michigan Press.
Armstrong, P. 1984. "Competition between the Organizational Professions and the Evolution of Management Control Strategies." In Kenneth Thompson, ed., *Work, Employment, and Unemployment: Perspectives on Work and Society*. Philadelphia: Open University Press.
Aschauer, D. 1990. *Public Investment and Private Sector Growth*. Washington, D.C.: Economic Policy Institute.

Averitt, R. 1968. *The Dual Economy: The Dynamics of the American Industry Structure.* New York: Norton.

Axford, B. 1995. *The Global System: Politics, Economics, and Culture.* New York: St. Martin's Press.

Bairoch, P. 1996. "Globalization, Myths and Realities: One Century of External Trade and Foreign Investment." In R. Boyer and D. Drache, eds., *States against Markets: The Limits of Globalization.* London: Routledge.

Bairoch, P., and R. Kozul-Wright. 1996. "Globalization Myths: Some Historical Reflections on Integration, Industrialization, and Growth in the World Economy." UNCTAD Discussion Paper no. 113.

Baker, W. 1984. "The Social Structure of a National Securities Market." *American Journal of Sociology* 89(4): 775–811.

———. 1990. "Market Networks and Corporate Behavior." *American Journal of Sociology* 96(3): 589–625.

Baker, W., and R. Faulkner. 1991. "Role as Resource in the Hollywood Film Industry." *American Journal of Sociology* 97:279–309.

Baker, W., R. Faulkner, and G. Fisher. 1998. "Hazards of the Market: The Continuity and Dissolution of Interorganizational Market Relationships." *American Sociological Review* 63(2): 147–77.

Barley, S., J. Freeman, and R. Hybels. 1992. "Strategic Alliances in Commercial Biotechnology." In N. Nohria and R. Eccles, eds., *Networks and Organizations: Structure, Form, and Action.* Boston: Harvard Business School Press.

Barnett, W., and G. Carroll. 1993. "How Institutional Constraints Affected the Organization of Early U.S. Telephony," *Journal of Law, Economics, and Organization* 9:98–126.

Baron, J. 1984. "Organizational Perspectives on Stratification." *Annual Review of Sociology* 10:37–69.

Baron, J., and W. T. Bielby. 1980. "Bringing the Firms Back In: Stratification, Segmentation, and the Organization of Work." *American Sociological Review* 45:737–66.

Baron, J., F. Dobbin, and P. D. Jennings. 1986. "War and Peace: The Evolution of Modern Personnel Administration in U.S. Industry." *American Journal of Sociology* 92(2): 350–83.

Baron, J., M. Hannan, and M. D. Burton. 1999. "Building the Iron Cage: Determinants of Managerial Intensity in the Early Years of Organizations." *American Sociological Review* 64(4): 527–47.

Barro, R. 1990. "Government Spending in a Simple Model of Endogenous Growth." *Journal of Political Economy* 98:103–25.

Barsoux, J-L., and P. Lawrence. 1990. *Management in France.* London: Cassell Educational.

Baumol, W. J. 1959. *Business Behavior, Value, and Growth.* New York: Macmillan.

Baums, T., R. Buxbaum, and K. Hopt, eds. 1993. *Institutional Investors and Corporate Governance.* New York: Walter de Gruyter.

Beck, E. M., P. M. Horan, and C. M. Tolbert. 1978. "Stratification in a Dual Economy: A Sectoral Model of Earnings Determination." *American Sociological Review* 43(5): 704–20.

Bendix, R. 1964. *Nation Building and Citizenship: Studies of Our Changing Social Order*. New York: Wiley.

Berger, S., and R. Dore, eds. 1996. *National Diversity and Global Capitalism*. Ithaca, N.Y.: Cornell University Press.

Berle, A. A. and G. C. Means. 1933. *The Modern Corporation and Private Property*. New York: Macmillan.

Bielby, W. T., and J. Baron. 1984. "A Women's Place Is with Other Women: Sex Segregation within Organizations." In B. Reskin, ed., *Sex Segregation in the Workplace: Trends, Explanations, Remedies*. Washington, D.C.: National Academy Press.

Biggart, N., and M. Guillén. 1999. "Developing Difference: Social Organization and the Rise of the Auto Industries of South Korea, Taiwan, Spain, and Argentina." *American Sociological Review* 64(5): 722–47.

Block, F. 1996. *The Vampire State and Other Myths and Fallacies about the U.S. Economy*. New York: New Press.

Bluestone, B. 1995. "The Inequality Express." *American Prospect* 20 (winter): 81–93.

Bluestone, B., and B. Harrison. 1982. *The Deindustrialization of America: Plant Closings, Community Abandonment, and the Dismantling of Basic Industry*. New York: Basic Books.

Boltanski, L. 1987. *The Making of a Class: Cadres in French Society*. Cambridge: Cambridge University Press.

Boltho, A. 1996. "Has France Converged on Germany? Policies and Institutions since 1958." In S. Berger and R. Dore, eds., *National Diversity and Global Capitalism*. Ithaca, N.Y.: Cornell University Press.

Bourdieu, P. 1977. *Outline of a Theory of Practice*. Cambridge: Cambridge University Press.

———. 1996. *The State Nobility: Elite Schools in the Field of Power*. Stanford, Calif.: Stanford University Press.

Bourdieu, P., and L. Wacquant. 1992. *An Invitation to Reflexive Sociology*. Chicago: University of Chicago Press.

Bowles, S., and H. Gintis. 1976. *Schooling in Capitalist America*. New York: Basic Books.

Boyer, R. 1990. *The Regulation School: A Critical Introduction*. New York: Columbia University Press.

———. 1997. "French Statism at the Crossroads." In C. Crouch and W. Streeck, eds., *Political Economy of Modern Capitalism: Mapping Convergence and Diversity*. London: Sage.

Boyer, R., and D. Drache, eds. 1996. *States against Markets: The Limits of Globalization*. London: Routledge.

Brancato, C. K., and P. A. Gaughan. 1988. "The Growth of Institutional Investors in U.S. Capital Markets." Institutional Investor Project, Columbia Center for Law and Economic Studies, Columbia University.

Braverman, H. 1974. *Labor and Monopoly Capital: The Degradation of Work in the Twentieth Century*. New York: Monthly Review Press.

Brenner, R. 1998. "The Economics of Global Turbulence." *New Left Review* 32:1–265.

Brint, S. 1994. *In an Age of Experts: The Changing Role of Professionals in Politics and Public Life*. Princeton, N.J.: Princeton University Press.

Buchanan, J., R. Tellison, and G. Tulloch. 1980. *Toward a Theory of the Rent-Seeking Society*. College Station: Texas A&M Press.

Burawoy, M. 1985. *The Politics of Production: Factory Regimes under Capitalism and Socialism*. London: Verso.

Burawoy, M. and P. Krotov. 1992. "The Soviet Transition from Socialism to Capitalism: Worker Control and Economic Bargaining in the Wood Industry." *American Sociological Review* 57(1): 16–38.

Burch, P. 1972. *The Managerial Revolution Reassessed: Family Control in America's Large Corporations*. Lexington, Mass.: Lexington.

Burrage, M. 1990. "Beyond a Sub-set: The Professional Aspirations of Manual Workers in France, the United States, and Britain." In M. Burrage and R. Torstendahl, eds., *Professions in Theory and History*. Sage: London.

Burt, R. 1983. *Corporate Profits and Cooptation: Networks of Market Constraints and Directorate Ties in the American Economy*. New York: Academic Press.

Byrkjeflot, H. 1993. "Engineering and Management in Germany and the USA: The Origins of Diversity in Organizational Forms." Dissertation prospectus, Department of Sociology, University of California, Berkeley.

Cable, J. R., J. P. R. Palfrey, and J. W. Runge. 1980. "Federal Republic of Germany, 1964–74." In D. Mueller, ed., *The Determinants and Effects of Mergers*. Cambridge, Mass.: Oelgeschlager, Gunn, and Hain.

Cable, V. 1995. "The Diminished Nation-State: A Study in the Loss of Economic Power." *Daedalus* 124:27–56.

Campbell, J., J. R. Hollingsworth, and L. Lindberg. 1991. *Governance of the American Economy*. Cambridge: Cambridge University Press.

Campbell, J., and L. Lindberg. 1990. "Property Rights and the Organization of Economic Activity by the State." *American Sociological Review* 55(5): 634–47.

Campos, J., and H. Root. 1996. *The Key to the Asian Miracle: Making Shared Growth Credible*. Washington, D.C.: Brookings.

Caplan, J. 1990. "Professions as a Vocation: The German Civil Service." In G. Cocks and K. Jarausch, eds., *German Professions, 1800–1950*. New York: Oxford University Press.

Carruthers, B. 1996. *City of Capital: Politics and Markets in the English Financial Revolution*. Princeton, N.J.: Princeton University Press.

Castells, M. 1996. *The Information Age: Economy, Society, and Culture*. Vol. 1: The Rise of the Network Society. Oxford: Blackwell.

Caves, R. 1992. *American Industry: Structure, Conduct, Performance*. 7th ed. Englewood Cliffs, N.J.: Prentice-Hall.

Cerny, P. 1997. "International Finance and the Erosion of Capitalist Diversity." In C. Crouch and W. Streeck, eds., *Political Economy of Modern Capitalism*.

Chandler, A. 1962. *Strategy and Structure: Chapters in the History of the Industrial Enterprise*. Cambridge: MIT Press.

———. 1977. *The Visible Hand*. Cambridge: Harvard University Press.

———. 1990. *Scale and Scope: The Dynamics of Industrial Capitalism*. Cambridge: Belknap Press of Harvard University Press.

Chandler, A., F. Amatori, and T. Hikino. 1997. *Big Business and the Wealth of Nations*. Cambridge: Cambridge University Press.

Coase, R. 1937. "The Nature of the Firm." *Economica* 4(16): 386–405.

Commons, J. 1934. *Institutional Economics. Its Place in Political Economy*. New York: Macmillan.

Compustat. 1989. *Manual*.

Cox, A. 1986. *State, Finance, and Industry: A Comparative Analysis of Postwar Trends in Six Advanced Industrial Economies*. Brighton: Wheatsheaf.

Crouch, C., and W. Streeck, eds. 1997. *Political Economy of Modern Capitalism: Mapping Covergence and Diversity*. London: Sage.

Crozier, M. 1973. *The Stalled Society*. New York: Viking.

Danziger, S., and P. Gottschalk. 1993. *Uneven Tides: Rising Inequality in America*. New York: Russell Sage.

Davis, G., K. Diekmann, and C. Tinsley. 1994. "The Decline and Fall of the Conglomerate Firm in the 1980s: The Deinstitutionalization of an Organizational Form." *American Sociological Review* 59(4): 547–70.

Davis, G., and S. Stout. 1992. "Organization Theory and the Market for Corporate Control: A Dynamic Analysis of the Characteristics of Large Takeover Targets, 1980–1990." *Administrative Science Quarterly* 37(4): 605–33.

Davis, G., and T. Thompson. 1994. "A Social Movement Perspective on Corporate Control." *Administrative Science Quarterly* 39(1): 141–73.

Deane, M., and R. Pringle. 1995. *The Central Banks*. New York: Viking.

DiMaggio, P. 1985. "Structural Analysis of Organizational Fields: A Blockmodel Approach." *Research in Organizational Behavior* 8:335–70.

———. 1988. "Interest and Agency in Institutional Theory." In L. Zucker, ed., *Institutional Patterns and Organizations: Culture and Environment*. Cambridge, Mass.: Ballinger.

DiMaggio, P., and W. Powell. 1983. "The Iron Cage Revisited: Institutional Isomorphism and Collective Rationality in Organizational Fields." *American Sociological Review* 48(2): 147–60.

———, eds. 1991. *The New Institutionalism in Organizational Analysis*. Chicago: University of Chicago Press.

Djelic, M-L. 1998. *Exporting the American Model: The Postwar Transformation of European Business*. Oxford: Oxford University Press.

Dobbin, F. 1994. *Forging Industrial Policy: The U.S., Britain, and France in the Railway Age*. New York: Cambridge University Press.

Dobbin, F., and J. Sutton. 1998. "The Strength of a Weak State: The Rights Revolution and the Rise of Human Resource Management Divisions." *American Journal of Sociology* 104(2): 441–76.

Dobbin, F., J. Sutton, J. Meyer, and W. R. Scott. 1993. "Equal Opportunity Law and the Construction of Internal Labor Markets." *American Journal of Sociology* 99(2): 396–427.

Doeringer, P., and M. Piore. 1971. *Internal Labor Markets and Manpower Analysis*. Lexington, Mass.: D. C. Heath.

Donaldson, L. 1995. *Contingency Theory*. Hants, Eng.: Aldershot.

Dore, R. 1973. *British Factory, Japanese Factory: The Origins of National Diversity in Industrial Relations*. Berkeley and Los Angeles: University of California Press.

Dore, R. 1997. "The Distinctiveness of Japan." In C. Crouch and W. Streeck, eds., *Political Economy of Modern Capitalism: Mapping Convergence and Diversity.* London: Sage.

Dore, R., and M. Sako. 1989. *How the Japanese Learn to Work.* London: Routledge.

Dore, R., and S. Strange. 1996. *National Diversity and Global Capitalism.* Ithaca, N.Y.: Cornell University Press.

Dow Jones. 1979–88. *Daily Stock Price Record.* New York: Dow Jones.

Dumez, H., and A. Jeunematre. 1990. "A Style of Economic Regulation: A Comparison between France and West Germany." *Government and Policy* 8(2): 139–48.

Dunlop, J. 1957. "The Task of Contemporary Wage Theory." In G. W. Taylor and F. Pierson, eds., *New Concepts in Wage Determination.* New York: McGraw-Hill.

Dunning, J. 1983. "Changes in the Level and Structure of International Production: The Last 100 Years." In M. Casson, ed., *The Growth of International Business.* London: Allen and Unwin.

Durkheim, E. 1985. *The Division of Labor in Society.* New York: Free Press.

Dyas, G. P., and H. T. Thanheiser. 1976. *The Emerging European Enterprise: Strategy and Structure and French and German Industry.* Boulder, Colo.: Westview Press.

Edstrom, M. 1999. "Controlling Markets in Silicon Valley: A Case Study of Java." M.A. thesis, Department of Sociology, University of California, Berkeley.

Edwards, R. 1979. *Contested Terrain: The Transformation of the Workplace in the Twentieth Century.* New York: Basic Books.

Eichengreen, B. 1999. *Toward a New International Financial Architecture.* Washington, D.C.: Institute for International Economics.

Eis, Carl. 1978. *The 1919–30 Merger Movement in American Industry.* New York: Arno Press.

Elias, N. 1994. *The Civilizing Process.* Oxford: Blackwell.

Emirbayer, M., and J. Goodwin. 1994. "Network Analysis, Culture, and the Problem of Agency." *American Journal of Sociology* 103:271–307.

Esping-Anderson, G. 1990. *Three Worlds of Welfare Capitalism.* Princeton, N.J.: Princeton University Press.

European Community. 1985. *Completing the Internal Market: White Paper from the Commission to the European Council.* Luxembourg: Office for Official Publications of the European Community.

Evans, P. 1979. *Dependent Development: The Alliance of Multinational, State, and Local Capital in Brazil.* Princeton, N.J.: Princeton University Press.

———. 1995. *Embedded Autonomy: States and Industrial Transformation.* Princeton, N.J.: Princeton University Press.

Evans, P. and J. Rauch. 1999. "Bureaucracy and Growth: A Cross-National Analysis of the Effects of Weberian State Structures on Economic Growth." *American Sociological Review* 64(5): 748–65.

Evans, P., T. Skocpol, and D. Rueschemeyer. 1985. "On the Road toward a More Adequate Understanding of the State." In P. Evans, T. Skocpol, and D. Rueschemeyer, eds., *Bringing the State Back In.* New York: Cambridge University Press.

Eyal, G., I. Szelenyi, E. Townsley. 1998. *Making Capitalism without Capitalists.* London: Verso.

Fama, E. 1965. "The Behavior of Stock Market Prices." *Journal of Business* 38:34–105.

———. 1980. "Agency Problems and the Theory of the Firm." *Journal of Political Economy* 88(2): 288–307.

———. 1981. "Stock Returns, Real Activity, Inflation, and Money." *American Economic Review* 71(4): 545–65.

Fama, E., and M. Jensen. 1983a. "Separation of Ownership and Control." *Journal of Law and Economics* 26(2): 301–25.

———. 1983b. "Agency Problems and Residual Claims." *Journal of Law and Economics* 26(2): 327–49.

Fama, E., and G. W. Schwert 1977. "Asset Returns and Inflation." *Journal of Financial Economics* 5(2): 115–46.

Farber, H. 1999. "Alternative and Part-Time Employment Arrangements in Response to Job Loss." *Journal of Labor Economics*. 17:5142–69.

Faulkner, R., and A. Anderson. 1987. "Short Term Projects and Emergent Careers: Evidence from Hollywood." *American Journal of Sociology* 92:879–909.

Federal Trade Commission. 1981. *Report on Mergers and Acquisitions*. Washington, D.C.: U.S. Government Printing Office.

Fligstein, N. 1985. "The Spread of the Multidivisional Form among Large Firms, 1919–1979." *American Sociological Review* 50(3): 377–91.

———. 1987. "The Intraorganizational Power Struggle: The Rise of Finance Personnel to Top Leadership in Large Corporations, 1919–1979." *American Sociological Review* 52(1): 44–58.

———. 1990. *The Transformation of Corporate Control*. Cambridge: Harvard University Press.

———. 1996. "Markets as Politics: A Political-Cultural Approach to Market Institutions." *American Sociological Review* 61(4): 656–73.

———. 1997a. "Fields, Power, and Social Skill: A Critical Analysis of the 'New Institutionalisms.' " Working paper, Center for Culture, Organizations, and Politics, University of California, Berkeley.

———. 1997b. *Markets, Politics, and Globalization*. Uppsala, Sweden: Acta Universitatis Upsaliensis.

———. 1998. "Big Business and the Wealth of Nations: Review Essay." *American Journal of Sociology* 104(3): 902–5.

———. 2000. "The Process of Europeanization." *Politique européenne* 1:25–42.

Fligstein, N., and H. Byrkjeflot. 1996. "The Logic of Employment Systems." In J. Baron, D. Grusky, and D. Treiman, eds., *Social Differentiation and Social Inequality*. New York: Westview Press.

Fligstein, N., and P. Brantley. 1992. "Bank Control, Owner Control, or Organizational Dynamics: Who Controls the Modern Corporation?" *American Journal of Sociology* 98(2): 280–307.

Fligstein, N., and K. Dauber. 1989. "Structural Changes in Corporate Organization." *Annual Review of Sociology* 15:73–96.

Fligstein, N., and R. Fernandez. 1988. "Worker Power, Firm Power, and the Structure of Labor Markets." *Sociological Quarterly* 29(1): 5–28.

Fligstein, N., and R. Freeland. 1995. "Theoretical and Comparative Perspectives on Corporate Organization." *Annual Review of Sociology* 21:21–43.

Fligstein, N., and I. Mara-Drita. 1996. "How to Make a Market: Reflections on the Attempt to Create a Single Market in the European Union." *American Journal of Sociology* 102(1): 1–33.

Fligstein, N., and L. Markowitz. 1993. "Financial Reorganization of American Corporations in the 1980s." In W. J. Wilson, ed., *Sociology and the Public Agenda*. Beverly Hills, Calif.: Sage.

Fligstein, N., and D. McAdam. 1993. "A Political-Cultural Approach to the Problem of Strategic Action." Typescript.

Fombrun, C., and M. Shanley. 1990. "What's in a Name: Reputation Building and Corporate Strategy." *Academy of Management Journal* 33:233–58.

Fortune. 1970. July.

———. 1980. July.

Foucault, M. 1977. *Discipline and Punish: The Birth of the Prison*. New York: Pantheon.

Frank, A. G. 1969. *Dependency Theory, Capitalism, and Underdevelopment*. New York: Monthly Review Press.

Frank, R., and P. Cook. 1995. *The Winner-Take-All Society*. New York: Free Press.

Franks, J., and C. Mayer. 1990. "Takeovers: Capital Markets and Corporate Control: A Study of France, Germany, and the U.K." *Economic Policy: A European Forum* 10:189–231.

Freeland, R. 1994. "The Struggle for Control of the Modern Corporation: Organizational Change at General Motors, 1924–1958." Ph.D. diss., Department of Sociology, University of California, Berkeley.

Frieden, J. 1991. "Invested Interests: The Politics of National Economic Policies in a World of Global Finance." *International Organization* 45:425–51.

Friedman, B. 1985a. "The Substitutability of Debt and Equity Securities." In B. Friedman, ed., *Corporate Capital Structures in the United States*. Chicago: University of Chicago Press.

Friedman, B., ed. 1985b. *Corporate Capital Structures in the United States*. Chicago: University of Chicago Press.

Friedman, L. 1973. *A History of American Law*. New York: Simon and Schuster.

Gamson, W. 1975. *The Strategy of Social Protest*. Homewood, Ill.: Dorsey Press.

Garrett, G. 1995. "Capital Mobility, Trade, and the Domestic Politics of Economic Policy." *International Organization* 49(4): 657–87.

Geertz, C. 1983. *Local Knowledge: Further Essays in Interpretive Sociology*. New York: Basic Books.

Gerlach, M. 1987. "Business Alliances and the Strategy of the Japanese Firm." *California Management Review* 30(1): 126–42.

———. 1992. *Alliance Capitalism: The Social Organization of Japanese Business*. Berkeley and Los Angeles: University of California Press.

Gibson, R. 1992. *Game Theory for Applied Economists*. Princeton, N.J.: Princeton University Press.

Giddens, A. 1971. *Capitalism and Modern Social Theory: An Analysis of the Writings of Marx, Durkheim, and Weber*. Cambridge: Cambridge University Press.

———. 1981. *A Contemporary Critique of Historical Materialism*. London: Macmillan.

Gottschalk, P., and M. Joyce. 1995. "The Impact of Technological Change, Deindustrialization, and Internationalization of Trade on Earnings Inequality: An International Perspective." In K. McFate, R. Lawson, and W. J. Wilson, eds., *Poverty, Inequality, and the Future of Social Policy*. New York: Russell Sage.

Gottschalk, P., and T. Smeeding. 1995. "Cross-national Comparisons of Levels and Trends in Income Inequality." Working paper no. 126, Luxembourg Income Study, Maxwell School of Public Policy, Syracuse University.

Granovetter, M. 1985. "Economic Action and Social Structure: The Problem of Embeddedness." *American Journal of Sociology* 91(3): 481–510.

———. 1994. "Business Groups." In N. Smelser and R. Swedberg, eds., *The Handbook of Economic Sociology*. New York: Russell Sage.

Graves, S. 1988. "Institutional Ownership and Corporate R & D in the Computer Industry." *Academy of Management Journal* 31(2): 417–28.

Green, D. 1986. "The State, Finance, and Industry in France." In A. Cox, ed., *State, Finance, and Industry: A Comparative Analysis of Postwar Trends in Six Advanced Industrial Economies*. Brighton: Wheatsheaf.

Greif, A. 1989. "Reputations and Coalitions in Medieval Trade: Evidence on the Magrebhi Traders." *Journal of Economic History* 49:857–82.

Gulati, R., and M. Gargiulo. 1999. "Where Do Interorganizational Networks Come From?" *American Journal of Sociology* 104(5): 1439–93.

Guthrie, D. 1997. "Between Markets and Politics: Organizational Responses to Reform in China." *American Journal of Sociology* 102(5): 1258–1304.

———. 1999. *Dragon in a Three-Piece Suit: The Emergence of Capitalism in China*. Princeton, N.J.: Princeton University Press.

Guthrie, D., and L. M. Roth. 1999. "The State, Courts, and Maternity Leave Policies in U.S. Organizations: Specifying Institutional Mechanisms." *American Sociological Review* 64(1): 41–63.

Hadley, E. 1970. *Antitrust in Japan*. Princeton, N.J.: Princeton University Press.

Hall, P., ed. 1989. *The Political Power of Economic Ideas: Keynesianism across Nations*. Princeton, N.J.: Princeton University Press.

Hamilton, G., and N. Biggart. 1988. "Market, Culture, and Authority: A Comparative Analysis of Management and Organization in the Far East." *American Journal of Sociology* 94 (supplement): S52–S94.

Hamilton, G., and C. S. Kao. 1990. "The Institutional Foundations of Chinese Business: The Family Firm in Taiwan." *Comparative Social Research* 12:135–51.

Hannan, M., and J. Freeman. 1977. "The Population Ecology of Organizations." *American Journal of Sociology* 82(5): 929–64.

———. 1984. "Structural Inertia and Organizational Change." *American Sociological Review* 49(2): 149–64.

———. 1989. *Organizational Ecology*. Cambridge: Harvard University Press.

Hansmann, H. 1996. *The Ownership of Enterprise*. Cambridge: Harvard University Press.

Harrison, B., and B. Bluestone. 1988. *The Great U-Turn: Corporate Restructuring and the Polarizing of America*. New York: Basic Books.

Hart, J. 1992. *Rival Capitalists: International Competitiveness in the United States, Japan, and Western Europe*. Ithaca, N.Y.: Cornell University Press.

Harvey, D. 1995. "Globalization in Question." *Rethinking Marxism* 8:1–17.

Haveman, H., and H. Rao. 1997. "Structuring a Theory of Moral Sentiments: Institutional and Organizational Coevolution in the Early Thrift Industry." *American Journal of Sociology* 102(6): 1606–51.

Hendershott, P. H. and R. D. Huang. 1985. "Debt and Equity Yields, 1926–1980." In B. Friedman, ed., *Corporate Capital Structures in the United States*. Chicago: University of Chicago Press.

Herman, E. 1979. "Kotz on Banker Control." *Monthly Review* 31:46–57.

———. 1980. "Reply to David Kotz." *Monthly Review* 32:61–64.

———. 1981. *Corporate Control, Corporate Power: A Twentieth-Century Fund Study*. Cambridge: Cambridge University Press.

Herrigel, G. 1996. *Industrial Constructions*. Cambridge: Cambridge University Press.

Hirsch, P. 1986. "From Ambushes to Golden Parachutes: Corporate Takeovers as an Instance of Cultural Framing and Institutional Integration." *American Journal of Sociology* 91(4): 800–837.

———. 1987. *Pack Your Own Parachute*. Reading, Mass.: Addison-Wesley.

Hodson, R. 1986. "Modeling the Effects of Industrial Structure on Wages and Benefits." *Work and Occupations* 13(4): 488–510.

Hudson, R., and R. Kaufman. 1982. "Economic Dualism: A Critical View." *American Sociological Review* 47(4): 727–39.

Hudson, R., R. Kaufman, and N. Fligstein. 1981. "Defrocking Dualism: A New Approach to Industrial Sectors." *Social Science Research* 47:727–39.

Hogan, W. T. 1971. *Economic History of the Iron and Steel Industry in the U.S.* Lexington, Mass.: Lexington.

———. 1984. *Steel in the United States: Restructuring to Compete*. Lexington, Mass.: Lexington.

Hogan, W. T., and P. Milgrom. 1994. "The Firm as an Incentive System." *American Economic Review* 84(4): 972–91.

Hollingsworth, J. R., P. Schmitter, and W. Streeck, eds. *Governing Capitalist Economies: Performance and Control of Economic Sectors*. New York: Oxford University Press.

Hollingsworth, J. R., and W. Streeck. 1994. "Countries and Sectors: Concluding Remarks on Performance, Convergence, and Competitiveness." In J. R. Hollingsworth, P. Schmitter, and W. Streeck, eds., *Governing Capitalist Economies: Performance and Control of Economic Sectors*. New York: Oxford University Press.

Holmstrom, B. 1982. "Moral Hazard in Teams." *Bell Journal of Economics* 13(2): 324–40.

Hooks, G. 1990. "The Rise of the Pentagon and U.S. State Building: The Defense Program as Industrial Policy." *American Journal of Sociology* 96(2): 358–404.

Houthakker, H., and P. Williamson. 1996. *The Economics of Financial Markets*. New York: Oxford University Press.

Jacobs, J. 1989. *Revolving Doors: Sex Segregation and Women's Careers*. Stanford, Calif. Stanford University Press.

———. 1992. "Women's Entry into Management: Trends in Earnings, Authority, and Values among Salaried Managers." *Administrative Science Quarterly* 37(2): 282–301.

Jacoby, S. 1997. *Modern Manors: Welfare Capitalism since the New Deal*. Princeton, N.J.: Princeton University Press.

Jenny, F., and A. P. Weber. 1980. "France, 1962–72." In D. Mueller, ed., *The Determinants and Effects of Mergers: An International Comparison*. Cambridge, Mass.: Oelgeschlager, Gunn, and Hain.

Jensen, M. 1989. "Eclipse of the Public Corporation." *Harvard Business Review* 67(5): 61–73.

Jensen, M. and W. Meckling. 1976. "Theory of the Firm: Managerial Behavior, Agency Costs, and Ownership Structure." *Journal of Financial Economics* 3(4): 305–60.

———. 1983. "Organization Theory and Methodology." *Accounting Review* 58(2): 319–39.

Jensen, M., and R. S. Ruback. 1983. "The Market for Corporate Control: The Scientific Evidence." *Journal of Financial Economics* 11(1–4): 5–50.

Johnson, C. 1982. *MITI and the Japanese Miracle: The Growth of Industrial Policy*. Stanford, Calif.: Stanford University Press.

Jurgens, U., T. Malsch, and K. Dohse. 1993. *Breaking from Taylorism: Changing Forms of Work in the Automobile Industry*. Cambridge: Cambridge University Press.

Kalleberg, A. 1988. "Comparative Perspectives on Work Structures and Inequality." *Annual Review of Sociology* 14:203–25.

Kalleberg, A., and J. Lincoln. 1988. "The Structure of Earnings Inequality in the United States and Japan." *American Journal of Sociology* 94 (supplement): S121–S153.

Kapstein, E. 1994. *Governing the Global Economy*. Cambridge: Harvard University Press.

Kay, N. 1997. *Pattern in Corporate Evolution*. Oxford: Oxford University Press.

Keister, L. 1998. "Engineering Growth: Business Group Structure and Firm Performance in China's Transition Economy." *American Journal of Sociology* 104(2): 404–40.

Kennan, J., and R. Wilson. 1993. "Bargaining with Private Information." *Journal of Economic Literature* 31(1): 45–104.

Kenwood, A. G., and A. L. Lougheed. 1992. *The Growth of the International Economy, 1820–1990*. London: Routledge.

Kerr, C. 1954. "The Balkanization of Labor Markets." In E. W. Bakke et al., *Labor Mobility and Economic Opportunity*. Cambridge: MIT Press.

Kessler, R., and D. Greenberg. 1981. *Linear Panel Analysis*. New York: Academic Press.

Kessler, T. 1997. "Political Capital: The State and Mexican Finance Reform." Ph.D. diss., Department of Political Science, University of California, Berkeley.

Kester, W. C. 1991. *Japanese Takeovers: The Global Contest for Corporate Control*. Cambridge: Harvard Business School Press.

———. 1992. "Governance, Contracting, and Investment Time Horizons: A Look at Japan and Germany." *Continental Bank Journal of Applied Corporate Finance* 5(2): 83–98.

Kester, W. C. 1996. "American and Japanese Corporate Governance: Convergence to Best Practice?" In R. Dore and S. Strange, eds., *National Diversity and Global Capitalism*. Ithaca, N.Y.: Cornell University Press.

Kitschelt, H. 1995. *The Transformation of European Social Democracy*. New York: Cambridge University Press.

Kitschelt, H., P. Lange, G. Marks, and J. Stephens. 1999. *Continuity and Change in Contemporary Capitalism*. New York: Cambridge University Press.

Kluegel, J., D. Mason, and B. Wegener. 1995. *Social Justice and Political Change: Public Opinion in Capitalist and Post-Communist States*. New York: Aldine de Gruyter.

Kocka, J. 1980. "The Rise of the Modern Industrial Enterprise in Germany." In A. Chandler and H. Daems, eds., *Managerial Hierarchies*. Cambridge: Harvard University Press.

Kogut, B., W. Shan, and G. Walker. 1992. "Competitive Cooperation in Networks in Biotechnology," In N. Nohria and R. Eccles, eds., *Networks and Organizations*. Boston: Harvard Business School Press.

Koike, K., and T. Inoki. 1990. *Skill Formation in Japan and Southeast Asia*. Tokyo: University of Tokyo Press.

Kolko, G. 1963. *The Triumph of Conservatism: A Reinterpretation of American History*. New York: Free Press.

Komiya, R. 1990. *The Japanese Economy: Trade, Industry, and Government*. Tokyo: University of Tokyo Press.

Kono, T. 1984. *Strategy and Structure of Japanese Enterprises*. London: Macmillan.

Kotz, D. 1978. *Bank Control of Large Corporations in the United States*. Berkeley and Los Angeles: University of California Press.

———. 1980. "Reply to Edward Herman." *Monthly Review* 32:57–60.

Krasner, S. 1988. "Sovereignty: An Institutional Perspective." *Comparative Political Studies* 21(1): 66–94.

Kreps, D., and R. Wilson. 1982. "Sequential Equilibria." *Econometrica* 50(4): 863–94.

Krugman, P. 1994a. *Peddling Prosperity: Economic Sense and Nonsense in the Age of Diminished Expectations*. New York: Norton.

Krugman, P. 1994b. "Technology's Revenge." *Wilson Quarterly*, autumn: 56–64.

———. 1995. "Growing World Trade: Causes and Consequences." *Brookings Papers on Economic Activity* 1:327–62.

Kuwahara, Y. 1989. *Managerial Staffing in Large Japanese Companies*. Honolulu: Industrial Relations Center, University of Hawaii.

Lamoreaux, N. 1985. *The Great Merger Movement in American Business, 1895–1904*. New York: Cambridge University Press.

Lane, C. 1989. *Management and Labour in Europe: The Industrial Enterprise in Germany, Britain, and France*. Aldershot, Eng.: Edward Elgar.

Larner, R. J. 1970. *Management Control and the Large Corporation*. New York: Dunellen.

Larson, M. S. 1977. *The Rise of Professionalism: A Sociological Analysis*. Berkeley and Los Angeles: University of California Press.

Lash, S., and R. Urry. 1987. *The End of Organized Capitalism*. Cambridge: Polity Press.

Laumann, E., and D. Knoke. 1987. *The Organizational State: Social Change in National Policy Domains*. Madison: University of Wisconsin Press.

Lawrence, P., and J. Lorsch. 1967. *Organization and Environment: Managing Differentiation and Integration*. Boston: Harvard Business School Press.

Lawrence, P., and T. Spybey. 1986. *Management and Society in Sweden*. London: Routledge and Kegan Paul.

Lazerson, M. 1988. "Organizational Growth of Small Firms: An Outcome of Markets and Hierarchies?" *American Sociological Review* 53(3): 330–42.

Leff, N. 1978. "Industrial Organization and Entrepreneurship in the Developing Countries: The Economic Groups." *Economic Development and Cultural Change* 26(4): 661–75.

Leifer, E., and H. White. 1987. "A Structural Approach to Markets." In M. Mizruchi and M. Schwartz, eds., *Intercorporate Relations: The Structural Analysis of Business*. New York: Cambridge University Press.

Li, K. T. 1988. *The Evolution of Policy behind Taiwan's Development Success*. New Haven: Yale University Press.

Lincoln, J., M. Gerlach, and P. Takahashi. 1992. "Keiretsu Networks in the Japanese Economy: A Dyad Analysis of Intercorporate Ties." *American Sociological Review* 57(5): 561–85.

Lincoln, J., and A. Kalleberg. 1990. *Culture, Control, and Commitment: A Study of Work Organizations and Work Attitudes in the United States and Japan*. Cambridge: Cambridge University Press.

Liu, A. 1987. *Phoenix and the Lame Lion: Modernization in Taiwan and Mainland China, 1950–80*. Stanford, Calif.: Hoover Institution Press.

Lorie, J. H., P. Dodd, and M. H. Kimpton. 1985. *The Stock Market: Theories and Evidence*. Homewood, Ill.: Dow Jones–Irwin Press.

MacNeil, L. 1985. "Relational Contracts." *Wisconsin Law Review* 483–525.

Maddison, A. 1995. *Explaining the Economic Performance of Nations*. Hants, Eng.: Edgar Elgar.

Manne, H. 1965. "Mergers and the Market for Corporate Control." *Journal of Political Economy* 73(1): 110–20.

March, J. 1962. "The Business Firm as a Political Coalition." *Journal of Politics* 24(4): 662–78.

March, J., and J. Olsen. 1989. *Rediscovering Institutions: The Organizational Basis of Politics*. New York: Free Press.

March, J., and H. Simon. 1958. *Organizations*. New York: Wiley.

Marris, R. 1964. *The Economic Theory of Managerial Capitalism*. Glencoe, Ill.: Free Press.

Marsh, P. 1982. "The Choice between Equity and Debt: An Empirical Study." *Journal of Finance* 37(1): 121–44.

Marx, K. 1975. *Capital* Vol. 1. New York: Vintage Press.

Maurice, M., F. Sellior, and J. J. Silveste. 1984. "Rules, Contexts, and Actors: Observations Based on a Comparison between France and Germany." *British Journal of Industrial Relations* 22(3): 346–63.

McAdam, D. 1982. *Political Process and the Development of Black Insurgency, 1930–1970*. Chicago: University of Chicago Press.

McKinnon, R. 1996. "The Mexican Financial Crisis of 1994." Working paper, Center for Economic Policy Research, Stanford University.

McNamara, K. 1998. *The Currency of Ideas: Monetary Policy in the European Union*. Ithaca, N.Y.: Cornell University Press.

Meyer, J., J. Boli, G. Thomas, and F. Ramirez. 1997. "World Society and the Nation State." *American Journal of Sociology* 103:144–81.

Meyer, J., and B. Rowan. 1977 . "Institutionalized Organizations: Formal Structure as Myth and Ceremony." *American Journal of Sociology* 83(2): 340–63.

Milgrom, P., and J. Roberts. 1982. "Limit Pricing and Entry under Incomplete Information: An Equilibrium Analysis." *Econometrica* 50(2): 443–59.

Miliband, R. 1969. *The State in Capitalist Society*. London: Weidenfeld and Nicolson.

Miller, M. 1977. "Debt and Taxes." *Journal of Finance* 32(2): 261–75.

Mintz, B., and M. Schwartz. 1985. *Power Structure of American Business*. Chicago: University of Chicago Press.

Mizruchi, M. 1982. *The American Corporate Network, 1904–1974*. Beverly Hills, Calif.: Sage.

————. 1989. "Similarity of Political Behavior among Large American Corporations." *American Journal of Sociology* 95(2): 401–24.

Mizruchi, M., and M. Schwartz. 1987. *Intercorporate Relations: The Structural Analysis of Business*. Cambridge: Cambridge University Press.

Mizruchi, M., and L. Stearns. 1988. "A Longitudinal Study of the Formation of Interlocking Directorates." *Administrative Science Quarterly* 33(2): 194–210.

Modigliani, F., and M. Miller. 1958. "The Cost of Capital, Corporation Finance, and the Theory of Investment." *American Economic Review* 48(3): 261–97.

Moody's. 1980–88. *Moody's Manual of Industrials*. Selected years.

Mueller, D. 1980. *The Determinants and Effects of Mergers*. Cambridge, Mass.: Oelgeschlager, Gunn, and Hain.

Muller, D., F. Ringer, and B. Simon. 1987. *The Rise of the Modern Educational System: Structural Change and Social Reproduction, 1870–1920*. Cambridge: Cambridge University Press.

Muller, D., and N. Majluf. 1984. "Corporate Financing and Investment Decisions When Firms Have Information That Investors Do Not Have." *Journal of Financial Economics* 13(2): 187–221.

Myers, S. 1984. "The Capital Structure Puzzle." *Journal of Finance* 39(3): 575–92.

Nelson, R., and S. Winter. 1982. *An Evolutionary Theory of Economic Change*. Cambridge: Harvard University Press.

Nee, V. 1996. "The Emergence of a Market Society: Changing Mechanisms of Stratification in China." *American Journal of Sociology* 101:908–49.

Newman, N. 1998. "Net Loss: Government, Technology, and the Political Economy of Community in the Age of the Internet." Ph.D. diss., Department of Sociology, University of California, Berkeley.

Nohria, A., and R. Eccles. 1992. *Networks and Organizations*. Boston: Harvard Business School Press.

North, D. 1990. *Institutions, Institutional Change, and Economic Performance*. Cambridge: Cambridge University Press.

North, D., and R. Thomas. 1973. *The Rise of the Western World: A New Economic History*. Cambridge: Cambridge University Press.

Ocasio, W., and H. Kim. 1999. "The Circulation of Corporate Control: Selection of Functional Backgrounds of New CEOs in Large Manufacturing Firms, 1981–1992." *Administrative Science Quarterly* 44(3): 532–62.

Organisation for Economic Cooperation and Development (OECD). 1994. *Foreign Trade by Commodities*. Paris: OECD.

———. 1995. *Economic Outlook*. Paris: OECD.

———. 1996a. *Economic Survey*. Paris: OECD.

———. 1996b. *Main Economic Indicators*. Paris: OECD

———. 1996c. *Statistics for Industrial Societies*. Paris: OECD.

Orru, M., N. Biggart, and G. Hamilton. 1991. "Organizational Isomorphism in East Asia." In W. Powell and P. DiMaggio, eds., *The New Institutionalism in Organizational Analysis*. Chicago: University of Chicago Press.

———. 1998. *Local Management for More Effective Employment Policies*. Paris: OECD

Padgett, J., and C. Ansell. 1993. "Robust Action and the Rise of the Medici, 1400–1434." *American Journal of Sociology* 98(6): 1259–1319.

Palmer, D. 1983. "Broken Ties: Interlocking Directorates and Intercorporate Coordination." *Administrative Science Quarterly* 28(1): 40–55.

Palmer, D., B. Barber, X. Zhou, and Y. Soysal. 1995. "The Other Contested Terrain: The Friendly and Predatory Acquisition of Large U.S. Corporations in the 1960s." *American Sociological Review* 60(4): 469–99.

Palmer, D., R. Friedland, P. D. Jennings, and M. Powers. 1987. "The Economics and Politics of Structure: The Multidivisional Form and the Large U.S. Corporation." *Administrative Science Quarterly* 32(1): 25–48.

Pauly, L., and S. Reich. 1997. "National Structures and Multinational Corporation Behavior." *International Organization* 51:1–31.

Pennings, J. 1980. *Interlocking Directorates: Origins and Consequences of Connections among Organizations' Board of Directors*. San Francisco: Jossey-Bass.

Penrose, E. 1959. *The Theory of the Growth of the Firm*. New York: John Wiley and Sons.

Perrow, C. 1970. "Departmental Power and Perspective in Industrial Firms." In M. Zald, ed., *Power in Organizations*. Nashville, Tenn.: Vanderbilt University Press.

Pfeffer, J. 1981. *Power in Organizations*. Marshfield, Mass.: Pittman Press.

Pfeffer, J., and H. Salancik. 1978. *The External Control of Organizations: A Resource-Dependence Perspective*. New York: Harper and Row.

Pierson, P. 1994. *Dismantling the Welfare State? Reagan, Thatcher, and the Politics of Rentrenchment*. New York: Cambridge University Press.

Piore, M., and C. Sabel. 1984. *The Second Industrial Divide: Possibilities for Prosperity*. New York: Basic Books.

Podolny, J. 1993. "A Status-Based Model of Market Competition." *American Journal of Sociology* 98(4): 829–72.

Polanyi, K. 1957. *The Great Transformation*. Boston: Beacon Press.

Polanyi, K. 1977. *The Livelihood of Man*. New York: Academic Press.

Porter, M. 1990. *The Competitive Advantage of Nations*. New York: Free Press.

Powell, W. 1990. "Neither Market Nor Nierarchy: Network Forms of Organization." In L. L. Cummings and B. Staw, eds., *Research in Organizational Behavior*.
Greenwich, Conn.: JAI Press.

Powell, W., and P. Brantley. 1992. "Competitive Cooperation in Biotechnology:
Learning through Networks?" In N. Nohria and R. Eccles, eds., *Networks and
Organizations: Structure, Form, and Action*. Boston: Harvard Business School
Press.

Powell, W., and P. DiMaggio. 1991. *The New Institutionalism in Organizational Analysis*. Chicago: University of Chicago Press.

Powell, W., and L. Smith-Doerr. 1994. "Networks and Economic Life." In
N. Smelser and R. Swedberg eds., *The Handbook of Economic Sociology*. New York:
Russell Sage.

Prechel, H. 1994. "Economic Crisis and the Centralization of Control over the
Managerial Process: Corporate Restructuring and Neo-Fordist Decision-Making." *American Sociological Review* 59(5): 723–45.

Ranger-Moore, J., J. Banaszak-Holl, and M. Hannan. 1991. "Density Dependence
in Regulated Industries: Founding Rates of Banks and Life Insurance Companies." *Administrative Science Quarterly* 36:36–55.

Reich, R. 1991. *The Work of Nations: Preparing Ourselves for Twenty-First-Century
Capitalism*. New York: Knopf.

Reskin, B., and P. Roos. 1990. *Job Queues, Gender Queues: Explaining Women's Inroads
into Male Occupations*. Philadelphia: Temple University Press.

Rodrik, D. 1996. "Why Do More Open Economies Have Bigger Governments?"
Working Paper No. 5537. Cambridge, Mass.: NBER.

Roe, M. 1994. *Strong Managers, Weak Owners: The Political Roots of American Corporate Finance*. Princeton: Princeton University Press.

Rohlen, T. P. 1983. *Japan's High Schools*. Berkeley and Los Angeles: University of
California Press.

Romer, P. 1990. "Endogenous Technological Change." *Journal of Political Economy*
98:79–102.

Ross, S. 1973. "The Economic Theory of Agency: The Principal's Problem."
American Economic Review 63(2): 134–39.

———. 1977. "The Determination of Financial Structure: The Incentive Signal-
ling Approach." *Bell Journal of Economics* 8(1): 23–40.

Roy, W. 1997. *Socializing Capital*. Princeton: Princeton University Press.

Rude, G. 1988. *The French Revolution*. London: Weidenfeld and Nicolson.

Rumelt, R. 1974. *Strategy, Structure, and Economic Performance*. Boston: Harvard
Graduate School of Business Administration.

Sachs, J., and A. Warner. 1995. "Economic Reform and the Process of Global Integration." *Brookings Papers on Economic Activity* 1:1–95.

Sassen, S. 1996. *Losing Control? Sovereignty in an Age of Globalization*. New York:
Columbia University Press.

Saxenian, A. 1994. *Regional Advantage: Culture and Competition in Silicon Valley and
Route 128*. Cambridge: Harvard University Press.

Scharpf, F. 1996. "Negative and Positive Integration in the Political Economy of European Welfare States." In G. Marx, F. Scharpf, P. Schmitter, and W. Streeck, eds., *Governance in the European Union*. London: Sage.

Scherer, F. 1980. *Industrial Market Structure and Economic Performance*. Chicago: Rand-McNally.

Schneider-Lenne, E. 1992. "Corporate Control in Germany." *Oxford Review of Economic Policy* 8(3): 11–23.

Schor, J. 1991. *The Overworked American: The Unexpected Decline of Leisure*. New York: Basic Books.

Scott, W. R. 1995. *Institutions and Organizations*. Beverly Hills, Calif: Sage.

Scott, W. R., and J. Meyer. 1994. *Institutional Environments and Organizations: Structural Complexity and Individualism*. Thousand Oaks, Calif.: Sage.

Shaiken, H. 1993. "Beyond Lean Production." *Stanford Law and Policy Review* 5:41–52.

Shapiro, M. 1980. *Courts: A Comparative and Political Analysis*. Chicago: University of Chicago Press.

Sharpe, W. F. 1964. "Capital Asset Prices: A Theory of Market Equilibrium under Conditions of Risk." *Journal of Finance* 19(3): 425–42.

Simon, H. 1957. *Administrative Behavior: A Study of Decision-Making Processes in Administrative Organization*. New York: Macmillan.

———. 1962. "On the Concept of Organizational Goals." *Administrative Science Quarterly* 1:1–22.

Skocpol, T. 1992. *Protecting Soldiers and Mothers: The Political Origins of Social Policy in the United States*. Cambridge: Belknap Press of Harvard University Press.

Skocpol, T., and E. Amenta. 1986. "States and Social Policies." *Annual Review of Sociology* 12:131–57.

Smeeding, T., M. Higgins, and L. Rainwater. 1990. *Poverty, Inequality, and Income Distribution in Comparative Perspective: The Luxembourg Income Study*. Washington, D.C.: Urban Institute Press.

Smeeding, T., B. Torrey, and M. Rein. 1988. "Patterns of Income and Poverty: The Economic Status of Children and the Elderly in Eight Countries." In J. Palmer, B. Torrey, and T. Smeeding, eds., *The Vulnerable*. Washington, D.C.: Urban Institute Press.

Smelser, N., and R. Swedberg, eds. 1994. *The Handbook of Economic Sociology*. New York: Russell Sage.

Snow, D., E. B. Rochford, S. Worden, and R. Benford. 1986. "Frame Alignment Processes, Micromobilizations, and Movement Participation." *American Sociological Review* 51(4): 464–81.

Snow, D., L. Zurcher, and S. Ekland-Olson. 1980. "Social Networks and Social Movements: A Micro-Structural Approach to Differential Recruitment." *American Sociological Review* 45(5): 787–801.

Spruyt, H. 1994. *The Sovereign State and Its Competitors: An Analysis of Systems Change*. Princeton, N.J.: Princeton University Press.

Standard and Poor's. 1979, 1986. *Register of Corporations, Directors, and Executives*. New York: Standard and Poor's.

———. 1985, 1987. *The Corporate 1000*. New York: Standard and Poor's.

Stark, D. 1992. "Path Dependence and Privatization Strategies in East Central Europe." *Eastern European Politics and Societies* 6(1): 17–54.

———. 1996. "Recombinant Property in East European Capitalism." *American Journal of Sociology* 101(4): 993–1027.

Starr, P. 1982. *The Social Transformation of American Medicine*. New York: Basic Books.

Stearns, L., and K. Allan. 1996. "Economic Behavior in Institutional Environments: The Corporate Merger Wave of the 1980s." *American Sociological Review* 61(4): 699–718.

Steinmo, S., K. Thelen, and F. Longstreth. 1992. *Structuring Politics: Historical Institutionalism in Comparative Analysis*. Cambridge: Cambridge University Press.

Stigler, G. 1968. *The Organization of Industry*. Homewood, Ill: R. D. Irwin.

Stinchcombe, A. 1959. "Bureaucratic and Craft Administration of Production: A Comparative Study." *Administrative Science Quarterly* 4(2): 168–87.

———. 1965. "Social Structure and Organizations" In J. March, ed., *Handbook of Organizations*. Chicago: Rand-McNally.

Stinchcombe, A. 1990. "Weak Structural Data." *Contemporary Sociology* 19:380–82.

Stokman, F., R. Ziegler, and J. Scott. 1985. *Networks of Corporate Power: A Comparative Analysis of Ten Countries*. Cambridge: Polity Press.

Stone Sweet, A. 2000. *Governing with Judges: Constitutional Politics in Europe*. Oxford: Oxford University Press.

Stopford, J. and S. Strange. 1991. *Rival States, Rival Firms*. Cambridge: Cambridge University Press.

Stopford, J., and L. Wells. 1972. *Managing the Multinational Enterprise: Organization of the Firm and Ownership of the Subsidiaries*. New York: Basic Books.

Strange, S. 1986. *Casino Capitalism*. Oxford: Blackwell.

———. 1996. *The Retreat of the State*. Cambridge: Cambridge University Press.

Streeck, W. 1984. *Industrial Relations in West Germany: A Case Study of the Car Industry*. New York: St. Martin's Press.

———. 1995. "A German Capitalism: Does It Exist? Can It Survive?" In C. Crouch and W. Streeck, eds., *Modern Capitalism or Modern Capitalisms?* London: Frances Pinter.

———. 1996. "Lean Production in the German Automobile Industry: A Test Case for Convergence Theory." In R. Dore and S. Strange, eds. *National Diversity and Global Capitalism*. Ithaca, N.Y.: Cornell University Press.

Streeck, W., J. Hilbert, K. H. van Kevelaer, F. Maier, and H. Weber. 1987. *The Role of the Social Partners in Vocational Training and Further Training in the Federal Republic of Germany*. Berlin: CEDEFOP.

Stuart, T. 1998. "Network Positions and the Propensities to Collaborate: An Investigation of Strategic Alliance Formation in a High Technology Industry." *Administrative Science Quarterly* 43(3): 668–98.

Stuart, T., H. Hoang, and R. Hybels. 1999. "Interorganizational Endorsements and the Performance of Entrepreneurial Ventures." *Administrative Science Quarterly* 44(2): 315–49.

Sutton, J., F. Dobbin, J. Meyer, and W. R. Scott. 1994. "The Legalization of the Workplace." *American Journal of Sociology* 99(4): 944–71.

Swidler, A. 1986. "Culture in Action: Symbols and Strategies." *American Sociological Review* 51(2): 273–86.

Taggart, R. A. 1985. "Secular Patterns in the Financing of U.S. Corporations." In B. Friedman, ed., *Corporate Capital Structures in the United States*. Chicago: University of Chicago Press.

Tarrow, S. 1994. *Power in Movement: Social Movements, Collective Action, and Politics*. Cambridge: Cambridge University Press.

Thelen, K. 1991. *Union of Parts: Labor Politics in Postwar Germany*. Ithaca, N.Y.: Cornell University Press.

Thompson, J. D. 1967. *Organizations in Action: Social Science Bases of Administrative Theory*. New York: McGraw-Hill.

Thorelli, H. 1955. *The Federal Antitrust Policy: Origination of an American Tradition*. Baltimore: Johns Hopkins University Press.

Thornton, P., and W. Ocasio. 1999. "Executive Succession in the Higher Education Publishing Industry, 1958–90," *American Journal of Sociology* 105:801–43.

Tilly, C., ed. 1975. *The Formation of National States in Western Europe*. Princeton, N.J.: Princeton University Press.

Tirole, J. 1988. *The Theory of Industrial Organization*. Cambridge: MIT Press.

Tyson, L. 1992. *Who's Bashing Whom?* Washington, D.C.: Institute for International Economics.

Useem, M. 1984. *The Inner Circle: Large Corporations and the Rise of Business Political Activity in the U.S. and U.K.* New York: Oxford University Press.

———. 1993. *Executive Defense: Shareholder Power and Corporate Reorganization*. Cambridge: Harvard University Press.

U.S. House of Representatives. House Banking and Currency Committee. 1969. *Commercial Banks and Their Trust Activities*. 91st Cong., 2d sess.

———. House Committee on Interstate and Foreign Commerce. 1971. Institutional Investor Study Report. 92nd Cong., 2d sess.

U.S. Senate. Senate Committee on Government Operations. 1973. "Disclosure of Corporate Ownership." 93rd Cong., 2d sess.

Uusitallo, H. "Comparative Research on Welfare States: The State of the Art." *European Journal of Social Research* 12:403–22.

Uzzi, B. 1996. "The Sources and Consequences of Embeddedness for the Economic Performance of Organizations: The Network Effect." *American Sociological Review* 61(4): 674–98.

———. 1997. "Social Structure and Competition in Interfirm Networks: The Paradox of Embeddedness." *Administrative Science Quarterly* 42(1): 35–67.

———. 1999. "Embeddedness in the Making of Financial Capital: How Social Relations and Networks Benefit Firms Seeking Financing." *American Sociological Review* 64(4): 481–505.

Veblen, T. 1932. *The Theory of Business Enterprise*. New York: Scribner's.

———. 1939. *Imperial Germany and the Industrial Revolution*. New York: Viking.

Vernon, R. 1971. *Sovereignty at Bay: The Multinational Spread of U.S. Enterprises*. New York: Basic Books.

Voss, K. 1993. *The Making of American Exceptionalism: The Knights of Labor and Class Formation in the Nineteenth Century*. Ithaca, N.Y.: Cornell University Press.

Wade, R. 1990. *Governing the Market: Economic Theory and the Role of Government in East Asian Industrialization*. Princeton, N.J.: Princeton University Press.

———. 1996. "Globalization and Its Limits: Reports of the Death of the National Economy Are Greatly Exaggerated." In S. Berger and R. Dore, eds., *National Diversity and Global Capitalism*. Ithaca, N.Y.: Cornell University Press.

Wall Street Journal, 1980–88. *Index*. New York: Dow Jones.

Wank, D. 1999. *Commodifying Communism: Business, Trust, and Politics in a Chinese City*. Cambridge: Cambridge University Press.

Weber, M. 1978. *Economy and Society*. Berkeley and Los Angeles: University of California Press.

Weingast, B., and W. Marshall. 1988. "The Industrial Organization of Congress, or Why Legislatures, Like Firms, Are Not Organized as Markets." *Journal of Political Economy* 96(1): 132–63.

Western B., and K. Beckett. 1999. "How Unregulated Is the U.S. Labor Market? The Penal System as Labor Market Institution." *American Journal of Sociology* 104:1030–60.

Westney, E. 1987. *Imitation and Innovation: The Transfer of Western Organizational Patterns to Meiji Japan*. Cambridge: Harvard University Press.

White, H. 1981. "Where Do Markets Come From?" *American Journal of Sociology*. 87(3): 517–47.

———. 1992. *Identity and Control: A Structural Theory of Social Action*. Princeton, N.J.: Princeton University Press.

Whitehill, A. M. 1991. *Japanese Management: Tradition and Transition*. London: Routledge.

Whitley, R. 1990. "Eastern Asian Enterprise Structures and the Comparative Analysis of Forms of Business Organization." *Organization Studies* 11(1): 47–74.

———. 1992. *European Business Systems: Firms and Markets in Their National Contexts*. London: Sage.

Wilkins, M. 1970. *The Emergence of Multinational Enterprise: American Business Abroad from the Colonial Era until 1914*. Cambridge: Harvard University Press.

———. 1974. *The Maturing of Multinational Enterprise: American Business Abroad, 1914–1970*. Cambridge: Harvard University Press.

Williamson, O. 1964. *The Economics of Discretionary Behavior: Managerial Objectives in a Theory of the Firm*. Englewood Cliffs, N.J.: Prentice-Hall.

———. 1975. *Markets and Hierarchies. Analysis and Antitrust Implications: A Study in the Economics of Internal Organization*. New York: Free Press.

———. 1981. "The Modern Corporation: Origins, Evolution, Attributes." *Journal of Economic Literature* 19(4): 1537–68.

———. 1985. *The Economic Institutions of Capitalism: Firms, Markets, Relational Contracting*. New York: Free Press.

———. 1988. "Corporate Finance and Corporate Governance." *Journal of Finance* 43(3): 567–91.

———. 1991. "Comparative Economic Organization: The Analysis of Discrete Structural Alternatives." *Administrative Science Quarterly* 36(2): 269–96.

Williamson, O., and W. Ouchi. 1981. "The Markets and Hierarchies Program of Research: Origins, Implications, Prospects." In A. H. Van de Ven and W. F. Joyce, eds., *Perspectives on Organization Design and Behavior*. New York: Wiley.

Womack, J., D. Jones, and D. Roos. 1991. *The Machine That Changed the World*. New York: Rawson Associates.

Woolcock, S. 1996. "Competition among Forms of Corporate Governance in the European Community: The Case of Britain." In R. Dore and S. Berger, eds., *National Diversity and Global Capitalism*, Ithaca, N.Y.: Cornell University Press.

World Bank. 1993. *The East Asian Miracle*. New York: Oxford University Press.

World Trade Organization. (WTO) 1997. *Annual Report*. Geneva: World Trade Organization.

———. *Annual Report*. Geneva: World Trade Organization.

———. 2000. *Annual Report*. Geneva: World Trade Organization.

Wright, E. O. 1979. *Class Structure and Income Determination*. New York: Academic Press.

———. 1997. *Class Counts*. New York: Cambridge University Press.

Wright, R., and J. Jacobs. 1994. "Male Flight from Computer Work: A New Look at Occupational Resegregation and Ghettoization." *American Sociological Review* 59(4): 511–36.

Yates, J. 1989. *Control through Communication*. Baltimore: Johns Hopkins University Press.

Yoshino, M. 1968. *Japan's Managerial System: Tradition and Innovation*. Cambridge: MIT Press.

Zeitlin, M. 1974. "Corporate Ownership and Control: The Large Corporation and the Capitalist Class." *American Journal of Sociology* 79(5): 1073–119.

Zelizar, V. 1983. *Markets and Morals*. Princeton, N.J.: Princeton University Press.

Ziegler, N. 1997. *Governing Ideas: Strategies for Innovation in France and Germany*. Ithaca, N.Y.: Cornell University Press.

Zucker, L. 1977. "The Role of Institutionalization in Cultural Persistence." *American Sociological Review* 42(5): 726–43.

———. 1987. "Institutional Theories of Organization." *Annual Review of Sociology* 13:443–64.

———. 1988. *Institutional Patterns and Organizations: Culture and Environment*. Cambridge, Mass.: Ballinger.

Index